CONAN DOYLE
DETECTIVE

CONAN DOYLE
DETECTIVE

True crimes investigated by the creator of
SHERLOCK HOLMES

PETER COSTELLO

ROBINSON
London

Constable & Robinson Ltd
3 The Lanchesters
162 Fulham Palace Road
London W6 9ER
www.constablerobinson.com

First published by Robinson,
an imprint of Constable & Robinson Ltd, 1991
as *The Real World of Sherlock Holmes*;
this revised and enlarged edition published, 2006

A copy of the British Library Cataloguing in
Publication Data is available from the British Library.

ISBN-13: 978-1-84529-412-0
ISBN-10: 1-84529-412-2

Printed and bound in the EU

1 3 5 7 9 10 8 6 4 2

à
BERNARD HEUVELMANS
('Sherlock au Zoo')
1916–2001

cher maître, cher ami

CONTENTS

FOREWORD

Sir Arthur Conan Doyle had a lifelong interest in crime and detection. Yet despite the immense popularity of his own detective stories, it is all too often overlooked that the creator of Sherlock Holmes was himself a criminologist of distinction, and that he often acted as a 'consulting' detective, that unique vocation he gave his own immortal character.

Conan Doyle could easily have applied to himself Holmes' own words in *The Sign of Four*: 'I am the last and highest court of appeal in detection. When Gregson, or Lestrade, or Athelney Jones are out of their depths – which, by the way, is their normal state – the matter is laid before me. I examine the data, as an expert, and pronounce a specialist's opinion. I claim no credit in such cases. My name figures in no newspapers.'

When he introduced Holmes to Watson in the laboratory of Bart's Hospital, young Stamford remarked of Holmes, 'You seem to be a walking calendar of crime'. Later in Baker Street, Watson discovered that Holmes appeared 'to know every detail of every horror perpetrated in the century'. Holmes borrows this knowledge from his creator, for Conan Doyle owned a criminological library and was widely read in the criminal history of several countries: 'You will find a parallel case in Riga in '54,' as Holmes says.

This book relates some of the cases from Conan Doyle's private calendar of crime, including some of the greatest sensations of the period, from Jack the Ripper to Sacco and Vanzetti, from Dr Crippen to the mysterious disappearance of Agatha Christie.

This is not another book about Sherlock Holmes, nor is it a straightforward biography of Conan Doyle. Perhaps it should really be called 'a study in scarlet'. It tries to put old facts in a new light by going back to the beginning of Conan Doyle's life, and picking up the scarlet thread of murder and crime which runs through it to the end. Many will perhaps be surprised, thinking of Conan Doyle as the author of anodyne tales, to find him in 1929, only a few months before his death, visiting the scene of a brutal sex-murder in South Africa and taking up his inquiry into the case with the same relish for crime that he had as a fifteen-year-old schoolboy brought to the denizens of the 'Chamber of Horrors' in Madame Tussaud's famous waxworks on a holiday visit to London in 1874.

His biographers in the past paid little attention to this aspect of Conan Doyle's rich and well-filled life, although his heroic efforts to vindicate the innocence of George Edalji and Oscar Slater are always spoken of.

Here I have tried to collect accounts, many by Conan Doyle himself, others based on his documentation, of all the crimes that interested him, and to cast new light on those with which he was directly involved. They are told largely from his point of view, which means that they do not always coincide with other versions, but the documentation will allow interested readers to pursue them in greater detail. Even to the most enthusiastic admirers of Sherlock Holmes, I think much of the material in these chapters will be either new or unfamiliar.

Peter Costello
Dublin

CHAPTER ONE

A DETECTIVE CALLS

In March 1885, Arthur Conan Doyle was in practice as a doctor in Southsea, a suburb of Portsmouth, the great naval base on the south coast of England.

He was twenty-five years old, nearly four years graduated from Edinburgh University, a poor professional man with few patients. At this date he had little to show either for his long-held literary ambitions.

About 10 o'clock in the evening of Friday, 27 March, on what had already proved to be a most difficult day, he and an elderly ex-naval friend he calls 'Captain Whitehall' returned to Conan Doyle's house, 1 Bush Villas, Elm Grove, near the town centre.

A burly man with heavy whiskers stood waiting on the step inside the railing on which Conan Doyle's brass plate was displayed under the red lamp which marked a doctor's surgery.

'Are you Dr Doyle, Sir?' the man asked.

Conan Doyle admitted that he was.

'I am a detective from the local police station. I was ordered to enquire into the death of a young man in your house lately.'

In every writer's life there is one incident which suddenly crystallizes what had been until then incoherent feelings and ambitions.

Though his biographers have made nothing of it before now,

this sinister visit by a police detective to the young Conan Doyle resulted, in my opinion, in the creation of Sherlock Holmes, and in the fixing of Conan Doyle's lifelong fascination with the mysteries of crime and detection.

Recalling this incident a few years later in the course of writing his now almost forgotten autobiographical novel *The Stark Munro Letters* (published in September 1895), Conan Doyle confessed that this visit came 'like a thunderbolt out of the blue sky': police inquiries are always disturbing, especially for the innocent.

He invited the detective into the house. Had the officer any objections to the presence of his friend and colleague Captain Whitehall? – a query later to be echoed again and again in the stories of Sherlock Holmes and Dr Watson.

Conan Doyle found when they were seated in the front room, overlooking the street, which he used as his consulting office – much of the house was still unfurnished – that the policeman was a person of tact, with a pleasant manner. The police station he worked out of was nearby in Albert Road, just at the east end of Elm Grove. He began to put his questions. (The dialogue quoted here is not my invention, but is taken directly from Conan Doyle's text, with the real names restored where possible.*)

'Of course, Dr Doyle,' the officer began, 'you are much too well known in the town for anyone to take this matter seriously.'

He paused.

'But the fact is that we have had an anonymous letter this morning saying that the young man died yesterday and was to be buried at an unusual hour today, and that the circumstances were suspicious.'

Anonymous letters to the police, as they both knew well, are all

* Though fiction of a kind, *The Stark Munro Letters* largely follows the events of Conan Doyle's early life with fidelity, and may well have been drawn from an actual series of letters Doyle wrote at the time to a friend living abroad.

too often the quiet start of the most sensational of criminal investigations.

'He died the day before yesterday,' Conan Doyle explained. 'He was buried at eight today.'

Then he told the detective the story from the beginning.

Conan Doyle had come to Southsea only in the summer of 1882, towards the end of June, and he was still facing the usual difficulties of a young doctor in a new town of getting his practice off the ground. His neighbour, a well-established doctor named William Royston Pike, a decade older than Doyle and who lived at the top of Yarborough Road, a mere hundred yards away, was very kind to him. A few days before, Pike had called him into consultation about a difficult case. He wanted Conan Doyle to give his opinion on a patient, a young man named Jack Hawkins, the son of a widow who had arrived in Southsea the previous October.

The doctors called on the family, who were in lodgings at 2 Queen's Gate, down on the Osborne Road, overlooking the common facing the sea. Aside from the mother and twenty-five-year-old son, there was a pretty daughter, slightly older, named Louise.

Doyle realized when he saw the family that he had already encountered them. Sometime before, while on a railway journey, he had shared a compartment with them. The son had thrown an epileptic fit and Conan Doyle had helped the ladies attend to him. The young man was dosed with the bromide his mother carried with her and soon recovered. Mrs Hawkins explained that they were on their way from Gloucester to Southsea. She gave him her card and suggested he call on them if ever he was in Southsea. (This at least is the account given in *The Stark Munro Letters*.) But now, in their present distress about Jack's developing illness, they did not recognize him: only later did Louise realize why the young doctor's face had seemed familiar.

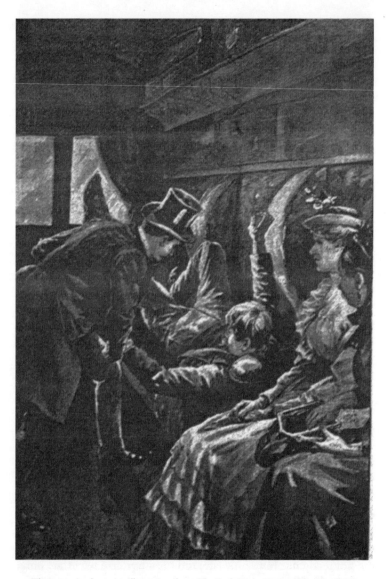

The scene in the train, illustration from *The Stark Munro Letters* (*The Idler* 1894)

There was no doubt about the case. Jack had meningitis – the fit in the train would have been an early sign, a premonitory symptom. Death – in those days before antibiotics – was certain, only a matter of time. Indeed at this date meningitis was a mysterious illness – the active agent would not be isolated until 1887. A few days later the mother and daughter called on Conan Doyle. They were distraught. Jack's illness was upsetting their host and he could not continue to be nursed where he was.

Conan Doyle's house was empty (except for his younger brother Innes and a housekeeper who occupied the basement). He offered to take the boy into his own home as a 'resident patient' – much like Mr Blessington in the Sherlock Holmes story of that title.

Once in bed at 1 Bush Villas the boy's condition worsened. As his sister would later die from tuberculosis, it is more than likely that this ran in the family, and that Jack was suffering from the tubercular form of the illness. He had been taking bromide of potassium, which relieved his symptoms, such as those spasms which had been so distressing in the train. Conan Doyle was following a typical treatment of the period and was giving him a medicine in which a little chloral was mixed.

Conan Doyle was well aware of the limits of medication. He owned two books on *materia medica*, which he kept to the end of his life. One, by Alexander Milne, he had had at medical school and it was interleaved with a handwritten list of medicines and their doses. The other was by Alfred Garrod. Both were standard textbooks of the day.

However, with chloral care was needed. Though frequently used then as a substitute for morphia in treating *delirium tremens*, St Vitus' Dance, tetanus and whooping cough, it was a drug which had to be used with great caution. A contemporary medical text book says of chloral that 'the depressing action . . . upon the heart renders it dangerous' (Pepper, 1886, I, 834). An over-large dose in some individuals could kill rather than cure. Dixon Mann, that much-used authority in the field of medical jurisprudence, states clearly that 'The toxic action of choral· hydrate is extremely irregular' (Mann, 1898, 542). A dose as small as three grains was reported to have killed a child.

Dr Pike called on the evening of Tuesday, 24 March, and Conan Doyle asked him to come upstairs and have a look at the patient. In retrospect, Conan Doyle realized this small incident may have been one of the most momentous in his life. It had been a trivial request, but as Dr Joseph Bell his old teacher at Edinburgh University had always insisted, such trivialities were of the greatest importance. It was the merest chance that Dr Pike had called and had seen the boy: if he had not, the history of detective fiction might well have been different.

Jack's temperature had come down to 101.5°F and that night he slept. This was not in fact a reassuring sign but a dangerous one. At eight in the morning (Wednesday, 25 March) the housekeeper brought up the arrowroot ordered the night before, as part of the liquid diet indicated in the illness. Conan Doyle was roused from sleep by her hoarse scream. The young man was dead.

Jack's face was relaxed now, free from pain, so peacefully smiling that Conan Doyle could hardly recognize the fevered features of the previous day. Anatomists he had heard lecture at university had said this was merely a post-mortem relaxation of the facial muscles. But Conan Doyle thought they might be wrong: there was great promise in the faces of the dead. The first note of the great theme of his last years, which were to be devoted to spiritualism and communication with the dead, had been struck.

After he had broken the news to the family, the arrangements for registering the death, obtaining a burial order, hiring an undertaker, purchasing a plot, and arranging for the funeral had to be seen to. Even after the funeral that morning, which Conan Doyle had attended with Captain Whitehall, there had been official formalities to be dealt with. It was these tedious chores which had taken some time, even with help from his friend.

The detective listened attentively to all of this, and took a note or two of the pertinent facts.

'Who signed the certificate?' he asked.

'I did,' Conan Doyle replied.

This was correct procedure, yet the detective raised his eyebrows slightly. 'There is really no-one to check your statements then?' he asked.

'Oh yes, Dr Pike saw him the night before he died. He knew all about the case.'

The detective shut his notebook with a snap. Dr Pike had been the Medical Officer of Health in Southsea and was well known to the police as the Honorary Physician to the Royal Hospital in the town.

'That is final, Dr Doyle. Of course, I must see Dr Pike as a matter of form, but if his opinion agrees with yours I can only apologize to you for this intrusion.'

The detective left, followed by the salty imprecations of Conan Doyle's naval friend against the rascal who had written the anonymous letter. If he caught up with them . . . 'By God sir, you'd have a real case to look after then.' In fact no light was ever cast on the local enemy who had anonymously denounced Dr Doyle to the police.

This account is taken, as I say, directly from Conan Doyle's novel, *The Stark Munro Letters*. He had signed the certificate, which was quite regular – but he had failed to indicate, as he should have done, how long the condition had existed. A technical error perhaps, but Conan Doyle realized, of course, that such a police interview could have had serious consequences for a young doctor. He had an estranged friend in Plymouth, Dr George Turnavine Budd – one of the models, many think, for Professor George Challenger – whose professional decline followed on the heels of the unfavourable comments of the local coroner after one of his patients had died.

Post mortems and inquests had serious implications for a doctor's reputation; families never like them. But this case would have involved an exhumation, which could have been done only by special order of the Home Office. That would have meant ruin. A tragic death might well have become a matter of murder overnight. In the classic British legal expression, Conan Doyle would have become 'the man now helping the police with their inquiries'.

Conan Doyle now found himself emotionally attracted, perhaps out of a sense of pity, to Jack's sister Louise, 'a very gentle and amiable girl'. Some financial interests depended on the young man's death – £100 a year for Louise, her now enlarged share of their late father's estate. Such a sum would have a significant value to a poor doctor, whose own annual income was about £270 a year.

If Dr Pike had not arrived that night, it was more than likely there would have been an exhumation. And then – well, there was the chloral in the body. A sharp lawyer or local gossip could have made much of the point. And besides, the first breath of suspicion would have blown away his modest, but rising, practice. 'What awful things lurk at the corners of life's highway, ready to pounce upon us as we pass,' he has the hero of his novel, Dr Stark Munro, reflect.

Conan Doyle had not committed a crime. At worst a professional error could be imputed to him, if even that. The fact that he himself had been the victim of an anonymous letter, that the innocent circumstances of an ordinary yet tragic death could so easily have been distorted by the mere presence of a drug and the matter of an inheritance, that what he had done in all innocence could be made to seem highly suspicious, all these facts made a deep impression on Conan Doyle.

He wrote about the incident with great feeling in his novel, and, guided by his own emotions, we should not overlook its deep significance: Conan Doyle knew now how guilty the innocent might seem.

This, moreover, was his first encounter with a detective. It changed his life.

Haunted, I suspect, by a nagging doubt that he might actually have precipitated Jack Hawkins' death by careless medication, Conan Doyle's sense of chivalry prompted his protection of the girl. He became engaged to Louise, or Touie as he now called her, less out of love than of a sense of duty. He was not, he knew, in love with her. When in later years he did fall in love, he knew it for a very different feeling. Touie was dear to him, he later told his brother Innes. Yet there was a large part of his intimate life that was not filled by Louise. This emotional emptiness was filled after he met Jean Leckie, his second wife, with whom he conducted a long relationship until they were able to marry after Louise died. But that was all in the distant future when Arthur and Louise became engaged.

Some months later, on 6 August 1885, at Thornton-in-Lonsdale parish church, then in Yorkshire (but now in Cumbria), Dr Arthur Conan Doyle Esq. MD married Miss Louise Hawkins, 'youngest daughter of the late Jeremiah Hawkins, Esq. of Minsterworth, in the country of Gloucester' according to the notice that the family inserted rather grandly in *The Times* of London.

Louise Hawkins had been born on 10 September 1857, 20 months before Conan Doyle's own birth, the daughter of Jeremiah and his wife Emily, née Butts, at Prasebrook Cottage, Dixton, in Monmouthshire. The Hawkins family had been established in Minsterworth since the mid-eighteenth century, where they had been gentry of some standing, but later seem to have declined in wealth. Hence the retirement, after her father's death, to more economic lodgings on the south coast.

It was now little more than four months since Jack's death – mourning seems not to have lasted long in either the Doyle or the Hawkins family.

And only eight months later, in March 1886, the first anniversary of Jack Hawkins' death and the detective's sinister visit, in the same house in Southsea, in the very same consulting room where he himself had been questioned about a suspected murder, Conan Doyle began to write *A Study in Scarlet*, his first detective story (see his handwritten notes, opposite). He was beginning to exorcize the fears that haunted him.

In that short novel the consulting room, the police detective on a false trail, the blustering friend, the frightened young woman, even death by poison, were to find a strange new fictional form.

Sherlock Holmes had arrived.

Study in Scarlet

Ormond Sacker - ~~from Sudan~~ from Afghanistan
      Lived at 221 B Upper Baker Street
with
    J Sherrinford Holmes -.
        The Laws of Evidence

    Reserved -
Sleepy eyed young man - philosopher - Collector of rare Violins.
An Amati -   Chemical laboratory

      I have four hundred a year -

I am a Consulting detective -

What rot this is " I cried - throwing the volume
   petulantly aside " I must say that I have no
patience with people who build up fine theories in their
own armchairs which can never be reduced to
practice -   Lecoq was a bungler —
Dupin was better. Dupin was decidedly smart —
His trick of following a train of thought was more
sensational than clever   but still he had analytical genius.

CHAPTER TWO

DR DOYLE AND MR HOLMES

The original notes which Conan Doyle made in March 1886 when he sat down to write his detective story still survive. It is astonishing to find that, despite some initial fumbling for plot and title, the essential concept of Dr Watson and Sherlock Holmes was there from the beginning.

These two immortals of literature – does anyone anywhere need to be told who they are? – arose from a deep, creative need in Conan Doyle himself, reflecting contrasting aspects of his own nature. They were not worked for; they were inspired. And for that we have to thank the anonymous detective of the Southsea police.

Suspicion of murder, the fear we all feel faced with official inquiries, began the creative process that led to *A Study in Scarlet*. I will have more to say later about the biographical and literary background to the writing of the book, but for the moment we will concentrate on the psychology of the affair.

All his life Conan Doyle was conscious of the narrow margin of fate that protects the innocent, the minor twist of evidence that could acquit or hang an accused. This is reflected in his fiction, and finds expression in an interest in crime and detection, and in a deep, lifelong concern for the victims of injustice.

That Dr Doyle and Dr Watson were strikingly similar has long been obvious. 'I am the man in the street,' claimed Conan Doyle, and that is Watson's role in the Holmes stories. Doyle's honest simplicity, his ordinariness, his complete Watson-ness, have been taken by some of his biographers as the key to his life story.

Clearly Dr Watson, whatever other models he may have had in real life, such as Conan Doyle's own secretary Major Herbert Wood, is largely drawn from Doyle himself.

For a start both are medical men of much the same age with sporting interests. Both have a bluff, hearty appearance. Both seem conventional, imperialist in politics, non-intellectual men of action. Dr Watson even shares Conan Doyle's love for Southsea, and his literary tastes, such as a liking for the sea-stories of William Clark Russell. Compared with his anti-social friend, Dr Watson (an author after all!) is a public figure. And he marries conventionally, like Dr Doyle, a girl he meets in the course of a professional case. As mentioned earlier, even in appearance Dr Watson must have resembled Conan Doyle. They were both men in their late twenties, Watson being only a few years older than Conan Doyle.

In contrast to this is Conan Doyle as Sherlock Holmes.* In Southsea, Doyle often refers in his letters to his 'Bohemian' way of life, which ended naturally enough with his marriage to Louise Hawkins. Doyle owned the chemical apparatus on which Holmes' malodorous experiments were conducted. His were the untidy lodgings, shared with a congenial companion (his brother Innes), crowded with memorabilia, books of cuttings, criminal records. Mrs Hudson of Baker Street had her real life model in the Scottish housekeeper (an old family servant of the Doyles) who cared for Conan and Innes Doyle in Southsea. The purple dressing-gown,

---

* There is no mystery about his name. The Doyles had spent their honeymoon in Ireland, where his uncle Henry was director of the National Gallery in Dublin. Henry Doyle's wife's mother was a daughter of Thomas Sherlock of Butlerstown Castle, Co. Waterford. Holmes, like Conan Doyle, was of Irish descent.

the shag-filled pipe, the long hours of lonely introspection on the meaning of life were all part of Conan Doyle's life before they were bestowed upon Holmes.

Doyle, too, took drugs; not the morphine or cocaine of Sherlock Holmes, but others, in a simple spirit of experiment. 'I have to be careful for I dabble with poisons a good deal,' says Holmes: one of Conan Doyle's first publications was a note, 'Gelseminum as a Poison', in the *British Medical Journal* (20 September 1879), relating the effects of the drug on his own system, a dangerous procedure indeed.

Doyle, like Holmes, valued his privacy, but was always available for consultation. He gave Holmes his talent for boxing, but the great detective's violin playing came from elsewhere.

Conan Doyle recommended William Winwood Reade's book *The Martyrdom of Man* (1872) to his friends as 'one of the most remarkable ever penned' before Sherlock Holmes did. 'Daring speculations', Watson thought, though Holmes drew a lesson from Winwood Reade as they pursued the mysterious fugitives in *The Sign of Four*. Doyle's own private broodings over his lapse from the Catholic faith of his youth, in which Reade played a part, left their mark on his fiction.

In the early 1880s, before the creation of *A Study in Scarlet*, Conan Doyle in Southsea was indolent, inquisitive, cerebral, complex, and often unconventional. And unmarried.

Sherlock Holmes, then, represents another, less familiar, side of Conan Doyle's character, and in the Holmes stories written at speed with little time for thought, he often expresses feelings more deeply hidden in his more studied writings. Samuel Rosenberg in his amusing inquiry *Naked Is the Best Disguise* discusses some of these hidden aspects of the tales, largely from a literary point of view. But there is more than a literary point of view to Conan Doyle and Sherlock Holmes.

Conan Doyle as Dr Watson was an establishment figure,

accepting a knighthood, standing for Parliament, and defending British policy over Ireland, the Boers and the Great War.

Conan Doyle as Sherlock Holmes was a closet radical, refusing a title, defending victims of injustice and political persecution at home and abroad. While writing his officially favoured history of the campaigns on the Western Front in 1916, Conan Doyle also lobbied to save the life of Sir Roger Casement from a traitor's death.*

For his biographer John Dickson Carr, Conan Doyle's identification with Holmes was the great hidden joke of the writer's life. For Adrian Conan Doyle it was something more; he had no doubts that his father was essentially 'the real Sherlock Holmes', and would respond with anger to all attempts to see Sherlock Holmes as based on any other real-life figure; indeed he had a long-standing feud with the American novelist Irving Wallace on this score.

Adrian Conan Doyle was born in 1910, well past what is usually thought of as the heyday of Sherlock Holmes, even though his father went on publishing the stories until 1927. He recalls some vividly Sherlockian scenes from the family's private life in the 1920s.

My memories as a youth are mottled with sudden, silent periods when, following upon some agitated stranger or missive, my father would disappear into his study for two or three days on end. It was not a question of affectation but complete mental absorption that checked and counter-checked, pondered,

* Casement, as we shall see in Chapter Seventeen, was an Irish patriot who had been in the British consular service in Africa and South America, before travelling to Germany during the First World War. Here he tried to assemble a 'Brigade' of Irish prisoners of war with the purpose of returning to Ireland and overthrowing British rule. Casement was arrested as he landed surreptitiously in Ireland in 1916, was convicted of treason and hanged. Conan Doyle displayed an unconventional disregard for the homosexual passages in Sir Roger's notorious *Black Diaries*.

dissected and sought the clue to some mystery that had been hurried to him as the last court of appeal. The hushed footfalls of the whole household, the tray of untasted food standing on the threshold, the subconscious feeling of tension that would settle on family and staff alike, were not less than the reflected essence of the brain, the lamp, and the letter that wrought their unpublicized drama on the inner side of the curtained door.

This is pure Baker Street. But the key word, I think, is *unpublicized*, for I suspect that many of the cases on which Conan Doyle gave his advice, sometimes even his direct assistance, as a consulting detective, have gone unrecorded. Adrian Conan Doyle was always impressed by his father's skill, in the style of Sherlock Holmes, in deducing facts about complete strangers.

In power of deductive observation I have never known his equal. These strange gifts played their part in Conan Doyle's private life. In travelling through the capital cities of the world, it was one of my keenest enjoyments to accompany my father to any principal restaurant, and there listen to his quiet speculations as to the characteristics, professions and other idiosyncrasies, all quite hidden from my eyes, of our fellow diners. Sometimes we could not prove the correctness or otherwise of his findings as the particular subject might be unknown to the head-waiter; but whenever those concerned were known to the maître d'hotel, the accuracy of my father's deduction was positively startling.

These remarks were confirmed by Lady Doyle herself, writing in 1934, four years after Conan Doyle's death. 'The public does not realize that my husband had the Sherlock Holmes brain, and sometimes he privately solved mysteries that had non-plussed the police. He was able, through his remarkable powers of deduction and inference, to locate missing people whose relatives had given them up as lost or murdered.'

None of this should surprise us. Conan Doyle himself once observed that 'a man cannot spin a character out of his own inner consciousness and make it really lifelike unless he has the possibilities of that character within himself.'

In one of his early stories, 'The Recollections of Captain Wilkie' (published in 1895), Conan Doyle describes a character doing just what Adrian describes, observing people in the train with him, practising a skill he had learnt from 'an Edinburgh professor,' a clue the relevance of which will emerge in the next chapter. But to practise the skill well there must have been an innate talent for it already there, the talent of the natural detective.

Previous biographers have written largely of Conan Doyle as Watson: the public figure, the Boer War doctor, the historian, the religious controversialist, and so on.

This book, by contrast, is about Conan Doyle as Sherlock Holmes; about the inner, secret Conan Doyle, rather than the bluff exterior; about the writer as detective, the artist as criminologist.

CHAPTER THREE

THE CHAMBER OF HORRORS

Conan Doyle's ambition to write a detective story may have seemed a new impulse to him in March 1886, but his interest in crime and detection reached back a long way before that, though in his early years it was not as central to his life as it later was.

He was born in Edinburgh on 22 May 1859, the son of genteelly impoverished Irish, Catholic, and artistic parents. From childhood he belonged to these three excluded communities on the edge of British society. He knew from an early age what it was to face prejudice and unpopularity, and he learnt also to stand his ground and fight back. Sympathy for the oppressed came easily to him.

The young Arthur could happily identify with one of those chivalrous knights errant that crowded the pages of his favourite novelist, Sir Walter Scott. If he owed his imagination to his dreamy father, his mother's high regard for the medieval values of chivalry influenced his whole life.

The romance of crime came later. Crime, in those early days in Edinburgh, was remote but not unfamiliar. It is said that his father, Charles Altamont Doyle, sketched the personalities involved in celebrated criminal trials in the Edinburgh Courts for the *Illustrated Times* – perhaps even those of the notorious poisoners Madeleine Smith (1857) and Dr Pritchard (1865). He also illustrated books, for instance providing two dozen illustrations for *Queens of Society* in 1860.

The happiest years of Conan Doyle's childhood were spent in a cottage called Liberton Bank, owned by Miss Mary Burton. Her nephew, William Burton, was Arthur's best friend then, and *The Firm of Girdlestone* was dedicated to him. William's father, John Hill Burton, worked in the Scottish prison service. Although he is now best remembered for *The Book-Hunter*, John Burton also published, in 1852, a more pertinent volume entitled *Narratives from Criminal Trials in Scotland*, among other writings on law and penology. His name may have suggested the Dr Hill Barton on Dr Watson's calling-card in 'The Illustrious Client'; and his book may have sown the seed of the urge to collect crime books that Conan Doyle developed later in life.

Though literature and crime may have been topics of conversation in the Burton household, it was not until Conan Doyle was older, and already at boarding school with the Jesuit fathers at Stonyhurst, that we can pick up the trail that leads to Sherlock Holmes.

One Christmas – it seems to have been 1872 – his holidays had to be spent at the school because of difficulties at home. It was a memorable festivity with concerts, feasts and plays. On successive nights the boarders saw *The Road to Ruin*, a comedy in five acts, and *The Courier of Lyons, or The Attack on the Mail*, 'a jolly play (5 murders)', as young Arthur reported gleefully in a letter home.

The Courier of Lyons was to become a famous stage vehicle for the Irvings, father and son, in the doubled role of Lesurques-Dubosq, and had been adapted by the novelist Charles Reade from a French play which was the sensation of Paris in 1850. The first London production had been in 1854, but it was very popular and often revived.

The play deals with the robbery of the Lyons stagecoach on Floreal 8 of An IV (27 April 1796), in which four highwaymen stole over £3,000 in money and coin, killing the coachman and the courier. For this crime Joseph Lesurques, a rentier, was guillotined. Later, 'the real culprit' Jean-Guillaume Dubosq, who was a striking double of Lesurques, was arrested, convicted and executed. Had Lesurques also been involved in the robbery – or was he innocent, as his family contended as recently as 1868?

The play had been produced in Paris while the Chamber of Deputies was debating the case, and though it tampered with the facts a little, it created such a theatrical sensation as to keep the story of the crime alive in the public imagination. The play accepted that Lesurques and Dubosq were doubles and that the innocent man suffered for the crimes of his look-alike. It was an exciting melodrama which enthralled audiences till the end of the century – even schoolboy groups such as the one at Stonyhurst.

The historian Sir Charles Oman remarks, in his account of the case, *The Lyons Mail*, that playgoers 'took away the impression that, granted bad luck, the forms of justice might lead an honest man to death. The law is sometimes a fool – and may commit a murder in strict adherence to legal form.'

This was one lesson the schoolboy Conan Doyle did not forget. The theme of the persecuted innocent runs throughout his career as writer, detective and criminologist. It is astonishing to see it planted in his imagination so early by both life and literature.

Sir Charles Oman, incidentally, in his brief but acute study of the evidence, is by no means convinced of Lesurques' innocence, or that he even looked like Dubosq. Trust the historian to spoil a good story!

The young Conan Doyle was easily impressed through his vivid imagination. At Christmas time 1874 – he was then fifteen – he spent the three-week holiday in London with his Doyle relatives. Sallying out from his Uncle Richard's studio in Finborough Road, Brompton, he saw all the sights: Henry Irving in *Hamlet* at the Lyceum (another murder mystery!); St Paul's Cathedral; Westminster Abbey; the Tower of London, with its arrays of weapons, 'racks, thumb-screws, and other instruments of torture'.

And Madame Tussaud's . . .

The celebrated waxworks was then in the Baker Street Bazaar premises on the west side of Baker Street. Naturally the imaginative youth plumped for the 'Chamber of Horrors', before even the Napoleonic relics and the studied seriousness of the silent celebrities who crowded the other rooms.

'I was delighted with the room of Horrors,' he wrote to his mother in 1874, 'and with the images of the murderers.' At a Centenary dinner in 1902 for Madame Tussaud's, Conan Doyle recalled the tingling frisson with which he encountered these monsters of infamy — 'I was alternately thrilled and horrified.'

The taste for crime arises in adolescence, more often than not in those incapable of committing any crime. It is a matter of imagination, a taste for the dangerous edge of human existence, rather than any sadistic pleasure derived from pain and fear.

We know from the contemporary catalogue of Madame Tussaud's just what Conan Doyle saw in the Chamber of Horrors. There were the body-snatchers Burke and Hare — 'the model of Burke, taken within three hours after his execution; and that of Hare from life, in the prison of Edinburgh.' Other Scottish criminals in effigy were the notorious Dr Edward Pritchard who poisoned his wife in 1865, and became the last person publicly hanged in Scotland — before an audience of 100,000. Less well known perhaps were John Stewart and his wife Catherine Wright who were hanged at Edinburgh in 1829 for poisoning and robbing a passenger named John Lamond on the vessel *Toward Castle* between Tarbert and Glasgow.

There were real relics, such as the blade and lunette from the original guillotine that decapitated 22,000 people during the French Revolution, including King Louis XVI, Marie Antoinette and Robespierre. There was an intricate model of Stanfield Hall, where James Blomfield Rush, 'The Killer in the Fog', murdered the distinguished lawyer Mr Isaac Jermy, the Recorder of Norwich, and his son in November 1848; and Rush himself, clothed in the suit he wore at his trial.

Then there was the very knife used by James Greenacre to cut up the body of Hannah Brown, on Christmas Eve, 1836: 'the remains of which he disposed of in various parts of the metropolis'. It has been recorded that when asked in an omnibus what was in the cardboard box on his knees, Greenacre answered brightly, 'a nice red cabbage'. It was the unfortunate Hannah's head.

Here they were, in all their quiet horror: cut-throats, child killers, assassins, regicides, lunatics and murderous medical men. Plus the very latest sensation.

Her name was Mary Ann Cotton. 'The series of cold-blooded murders for which this wretch was hanged on the morning of Monday, 24 March 1873, are crimes against which no punishment in history can atone for. The child she rocked on her knees today was poisoned tomorrow. Most of her murders were committed for petty gain; and she killed off husbands and children with the unconcern of a farm-girl killing poultry. The story of her crimes is still fresh in the public mind,' the guide concluded.

The Chamber of Horrors was strong stuff in those days. The heads of the executed which Madame Tussaud herself had modelled during the French Revolution were too real for comfort. Yet perhaps the dead, fixed expressions of the figures made the whole thing bearable. Artifice distanced the reality of it all.

There is no doubt that this criminous museum on Baker Street excited the imagination of Conan Doyle. About the turn of the century he was to write long accounts of no fewer than three of those he had seen there: the pirates of the *Flowery Land* in 1899, and in 1901, William Godfrey Youngman, and George Mullins who was said to have killed Mrs Emsley in 1860 – a model of her house was also on display. But this was crime, the mere pathology of death. There was little here to do with detection. That was still to come.*

After Stonyhurst, young Arthur was sent for his final year to the Jesuit College at Feldkirch in the Austrian Tyrol above Lake Constance before going on to the medical school at Edinburgh University. A medical career had already been settled on for him, by his family at least. He was now seventeen. In Austria he was working at the chemistry and mathematics he would need at university from books sent out from home by Dr Bryan Charles Waller, a family friend who was taking a fatherly interest in him.

Among the books which Waller sent was some light reading as well, including a volume of the tales of Edgar Allan Poe – most probably from the collected edition, the first in Britain, published in four volumes that very year by A. & C. Black of Edinburgh, edited by J. H. Ingram.

The admirer of Scott and Macaulay was electrified. Here was a new literary revelation. It was not only the bizarre and the grotesque, the all too believable make-believe of Poe that enchanted him, for it appeals to all adolescents. There was the ratiocination as well. The logic in *The Gold Bug* that deciphered the treasure chart of Captain Kidd – here is the ancestor of those cryptograms that litter the Holmes stories, such as the one that opens *The Valley of Fear*.

But the aspect which concerns us here was the instant appeal of Poe's tales of detection, the first of their kind, featuring the Chevalier Auguste C. Dupin: *The Murders in the Rue Morgue*, *The Mystery of Marie Roget*, *The Purloined Letter*. But many of the stories combined mystery, violence and crime. No other author, Conan Doyle later confessed, so shaped his tastes or literary bent. He felt, as did Bauledaire, that Poe was one of the world's great writers. And, indeed, Edgar Allan Poe is probably the most

* The fourth case about which he wrote in 1901, that of George Victor Townley, was not represented at Madame Tussaud's waxworks in 1874.

important literary influence on Conan Doyle. Poe remained one of his great literary heroes to the end of his life.

The significance of the Poe stories, aside from their use of language and their wonderful evocation of atmosphere, was in the application of logic to minute observation. To the Chevalier Dupin, no detail was too trivial to be without significance.

Even as a medical student at Edinburgh University in 1876 Conan Doyle was interested in contemporary detective fiction – it is all too often overlooked that detective fiction, of a kind, had many practitioners between Poe and Conan Doyle. He also planned to write it.

A piece of testimony about this point has been passed over by his biographers, but is of special relevance here. A fellow Edinburgh medical student, Dr George Hamilton, later a surgeon in Liverpool, recalled that at that time 'Conan Doyle, though deeply interested in Poe's detective stories but recognizing that they were caviare to the general,' told Hamilton 'that he had the idea of writing detective fiction according to the system of Poe, but greatly simplified and brought down to the level of ordinary people.'

What was contemporary detective fiction like and how did it differ from 'the system of Poe'?

Edinburgh had the distinction, known to all literary people in the city, of having produced some of the earliest police novels. In the early 1860s James McLevy, an Edinburgh police detective of Irish origin, published two books drawing on his own experiences, *Curiosities of Crime in Edinburgh* and *The Sliding Scale of Life*. These had a brief vogue before being forgotten, but their author was little more than a very talented thief-taker. The actual detective element is non-existent, as it is in so much of the sensational literature of the period. The mere appearance of a detective in a story does not make it a detective story.

In 1878, while Conan Doyle was still a student, there was

published in Edinburgh a novel entitled *Brought to Bay; or, Experiences of a City Detective* by a writer who called himself James McGovan. There followed *Strange Clues; or, Chronicles of a City Detective* (1881), *Traced and Tracked; or, Memoirs of a City Detective* (1884), and *Solved Mysteries; or, Revelations of a City Detective* (1888). *Traced and Tracked* alone sold 25,000 copies and was translated into German and French.

James McGovan was the pen-name of William Crawford Honeyman, who died in 1919.* He was given to wearing velvet jackets and a black artistic beard. Honeyman was a noted authority on the violin and violin-playing – shades indeed of Sherlock Holmes. Honeyman called his house 'Cremona' after the city where Stradivari and Amati worked: Holmes, it will be recalled, owned a Stradivarius (though according to those original notes of 1886 Conan Doyle intended this to be an Amati). And Holmes too was a 'honeyman,' for did he not retire to keep bees on the South Downs? This smacks of an obscure Conan Doyle joke on a well-known Edinburgh character.

As these books began to appear while Conan Doyle was an Edinburgh medical student, there is a not too remote chance that he read them then, and that they influenced his later writings. Both Conan Doyle and Robert Louis Stevenson, though inspired by Edinburgh, relocated their stories in London to appeal to a wider audience. And yet . . . 3 Lauriston Gardens, where the body of the poisoned Enoch J. Drebber is found in *A Study in Scarlet*, does not exist in London. But in Edinburgh Lauriston Place, across the park from his home, was where the young Conan Doyle went to Mass.

These are suggestive elements in Conan Doyle's background. What is certain is that in Edinburgh he came into contact with the university professor who is acknowledged to have been 'the model of Sherlock Holmes': Dr Joseph Bell. For the character of his new

* The American detective story writer Ellery Queen owned a McGovan novel signed by Honeyman, who admitted his authorship in the dedication.

detective he relied upon on some aspects of his own character, and on his memories of Bell.

When Sherlock Holmes became popular in the 1890s, Dr Bell used to express his dislike of being 'the original Holmes'. But as he dined out often on the strength of it, and wrote articles and even a preface to *A Study in Scarlet* (thus making more out of the book than Conan Doyle ever did), this claim must be taken sceptically.

Bell's feats of deductive, or rather inductive, reasoning are well known, examples appearing in all books about Holmes. Mrs Jessie Saxby in an appreciation of Dr Bell published in 1913, said he was in character nothing like she imagined Holmes to be: a ruthless, reasoning, heartless man-hunter. But Holmes (whom she must never have read) was not like that.

She tells us that Bell helped many an erring soul back onto the right road. But so, it will be recalled, did Sherlock Holmes. She passes over in silence Dr Bell's role as a medical examiner to the Edinburgh police. It seems her book is little known in the circles of Holmes enthusiasts, and many of Conan Doyle's admirers have not appreciated that Dr Bell was himself something of a detective.

The case with which he is most clearly linked was the mysterious affair at Ardlamont, when young Cecil Hambrough was shot by his tutor Alfred Monson, who had insured his life. A Scottish verdict of 'Not Proven' was returned at the trial, but Dr Bell gave evidence concerning the nature of the shotgun wounds in the skull. For his tests he had fired the gun into a series of pigs' heads!

That was in 1893, by which time Holmes was already in great vogue. But much earlier Dr Bell's forensic reputation had been made in Edinburgh by his investigation of the Chantrelle affair in 1877, while Conan Doyle was still a student at the medical school.

Eugene Marie Chantrelle had himself been a medical student in Paris, and had come to live in Edinburgh a decade before, where he established a considerable reputation as a teacher. He had seduced and, just two months before the birth of their first child, married Elizabeth Dyer, one of his pupils. The girl was only fifteen. Very soon his growing addiction to drink eroded the stability of his family, and Chantrelle began to beat his wife, threaten to poison her, and to spend much of his dissolute life in the city brothels.

In October 1877 he insured his frail wife's life for £500. On New Year's Day, 1878, Elizabeth Chantrelle became ill and took to her bed. Early the following morning, the maid heard Madame Chantrelle moaning in her room. Beside her bed was half a glass of lemonade, some slices of orange and a few grapes.

The maid called Chantrelle, and herself went for a doctor. When they returned the lemonade glass was empty, and the fruit had gone. Chantrelle told the doctor that his wife had been overcome by a gas leak, and the doctor forthwith sent a note to Henry Littlejohn, the medical officer for Edinburgh: 'If you would like to see a case of coal-gas poisoning come here at once.'

Littlejohn arrived at the house with his friend Dr Bell for company. The patient was removed to the Royal Infirmary and they set about examining the sick-room. On the pillowcase and the night dress were greenish-brown spots of vomit. This aroused their suspicions, and when Elizabeth died a few hours later, tests were made which showed the vomit contained solid opium mixed with grape seeds, matching smaller quantities left in the stomach. Chantrelle was taken into custody, but protested: 'We have had an escape of gas.' Dr Bell made further inquiries and found that Chantrelle had recently bought 30 doses of opium. The case was complete.

Still Chantrelle insisted upon the gas leak. The gas company inspectors found that the pipe was broken behind the window shutter, and the maid confirmed that there had been a smell of gas when she had come back with the doctor, but there had been none before. The jury took just over one hour to decide that he was guilty, and Eugene Chantrelle became the first prisoner to be hanged at Edinburgh since the passing of the Act making capital punishment within the prison mandatory.

On the gallows Chantrelle is said to have taken one last puff of his cigar. 'Bye-bye, Littlejohn. Don't forget to give my compliments to Joe Bell. You both did a good job of bringing me to the scaffold.' Though apocryphal, his remark soon became part of Edinburgh medical folklore.

In the autumn of 1877, before the university re-opened and before this case came to trial, Conan Doyle had been surprised to meet Dr Bell on the isle of Arran, later the scene of the notorious murder in 1889 of Edwin Robert Rose by John Watson Laurie (a case in which Dr Littlejohn was also to be involved). Dr Bell had soon picked Doyle out from the rush of medical students to act as his assistant, or dresser; and it was as his assistant that Conan Doyle was able to observe the great man in action. Already he would have been aware of his professor's 'criminal activities', so to speak. Bell himself admitted later that Conan Doyle even then had exceptional talents as an observer.

During and after his years as a medical student, Conan Doyle worked with a succession of local doctors in various parts of England. He signed on as ship's doctor for a voyage to the Arctic on a whaler, and later on a cargo ship trading on the coast of West Africa. Then for a period he joined his college friend George Budd in Plymouth. They parted with some ill-feeling, and Doyle set himself up in Southsea. And it was there, as I have related, that Sherlock Holmes was created.

The genesis of *A Study in Scarlet* can be traced through his surviving notebooks.

'I have read Gaboriau's *Lecoq the Detective*, *The Gilded Clique*, and a story concerning the murder of an old woman, the name of which I forget.' Later he looked it up and added *The Lerouge Case* above the line. 'All very good. Wilkie Collins but more so.' These titles were published by Henry Vizetelly, who made something of a reputation by publishing spicy Continental literature, not all of it of literary merit, but also detection of a racy and sensational kind. The novels of Emile Gaboriau and Fortuné Du Boisgobey were leading examples.

Vizetelly's catalogue of September 1887 offered them in double volumes bound in scarlet cloth at 2/6d each. Gaboriau's sensational novels were also available in a cheaper edition at 9d, in ornamental scarlet covers – and these were the ones Conan Doyle would have read. *The Hampshire Advertiser*, which may have come under Conan Doyle's eye in Southsea, said of *The Lerouge Case*: 'M. Gaboriau is a skillful and brilliant writer, capable of diverting the attention and interest of his readers that not one word or line of his book will be skipped or read carelessly.' Vizetelly also published *My First Crime* by Gustave Macé, 'former *Chef de la Sûreté* of the Paris police'. One reviewer said that 'an account by a real Lecoq of a real crime is a novelty among the mass of criminal novels with which the world has been favoured since the great originator Gaboriau . . . a really interesting addition to a species of literature which has of late begun to pall' (*Saturday Review*). Du Boisgobey's novels, such as *The Crime at the Opera House*, were more turgid than the others owing to the newspaper serial form in which they first appeared, but they still enjoyed an enormous vogue.

Conan Doyle's little novel was not then a new kind of thing to his first readers, but one small booklet floating in a sea of sensational literature. Much of this was French in origin. In *The Wrong Box*, where one of the characters is the author of a detective story called *Who Put Back the Clock?*, R. L. Stevenson evokes 'the Muse of the Police Romance . . . a lady presumably of French extraction'. What made Conan Doyle's own stories so very different from their contemporaries was the brilliantly realized character of Sherlock Holmes. They would not grow dusty on the railway bookstalls.

Gaboriau's novels were very distinctive in their structure. They all fall into two parts. In the first the police investigate the crime down to the arrest. The second part then moves back in time to narrate from the point of view of the characters what led up to the crime. This two-part structure was adopted by Conan Doyle, though at much shorter length, for *A Study in Scarlet*, the London murders being followed by the account of what happened among the Mormons in America that led up to the crime. All his long Sherlock Holmes novels maintain this form, even *The Hound of the Baskervilles*. He took this structure directly from Gaboriau.

Lecoq was a real stimulus in other ways too. Conan Doyle scribbled inside the cover of one of his notebooks: 'The coat-sleeve, the trouser-knee, the callosities of the forefinger and thumb, the boot – any one of these might tell us, but that all united should fail to enlighten the trained observation is incredible.' This was the sentiment of Gaboriau's great detective, but the words were those of Joe Bell. Bell's deductive skill, Bell's role as a consulting detective to the Edinburgh police, even his personal appearance, all rose up in Conan Doyle's memory.

His detective would make an exact science of detection. This was the new point, but one which was already at large in such centres of forensic science as Edinburgh. Yet the seminal work by the Austrian Dr Hans Gross, *Handbuch für Untersuchungsricher als System der Kriminalistik* (*Handbook for Examining Magistrates and System of Criminalistics*), was not to appear until 1893 in German. The first English edition to be available in London (though translated and printed in Madras, India, in 1906) came out in 1907. Conan Doyle, trained in a good school, was well ahead of the police in his appreciation of minute details.

But there was also the influence of English detective fiction as it then existed, especially the works of Stevenson and Wilkie Collins. He had been reading other early detective works. He had already worked out for a Southsea audience his own solution to Charles Dickens' unfinished last novel, *The Mystery of Edwin Drood* (1870), an exercise in literary detection unravelling the clues that the author had planted in the early chapters – or had seemed to plant.

There was also that current success, Fergus Hume's Australian novel *The Mystery of a Hansom Cab*. He did not think much of this bestseller (the largest selling detective story ever written, it was later claimed), as he told his mother in March 1888. 'What a swindle *The Mystery of a Hansom Cab* is! One of the weakest tales I have read, and simply sold by puffing.'

By then, of course, *A Study in Scarlet* had appeared. It was received with good notices from the reviewers, but sales were meagre. The publisher's own advertisements were of course enthusiastic. In any case he had sold the copyright outright for £25 in November 1886. Mr Fergus Hume, meanwhile, was selling in thousands, which must have been sickening.

In 1889 Conan Doyle was commissioned to write *The Sign of Four*, which appeared in *Lippincott's Magazine* in February 1890. His mind was already turning to other things, to the Middle Ages and the writing of *The White Company*. However, his move to London as an eye-specialist with rooms in Devonshire Place, a step over from Baker Street, left Doyle with time on his hands; few patients troubled him. He wrote a story which his agent sent to the editor of a new magazine called *The Strand*. It was accepted. Conan Doyle now struck on a new formula by writing a series of short stories around Sherlock Holmes. The character was well enough established for him to need little introduction in the opening story, 'A Scandal in Bohemia'. He sent the story to his agent on 3 April 1891. Unlike a serialized novel in the magazines and newspapers, it did not matter if the reader missed an episode; each story was self-contained. This formula was to prove a key factor in the great success of *The Strand*. Naturally the editor of the magazine, H. Greenhough-Smith, was delighted. Here was exactly what he needed.

More stories were commissioned, and by the autumn of 1891 Sherlock Holmes and Conan Doyle were household names. Obscurity no longer surrounded Dr Doyle, and he gave up his medical practice to write full time. A further series of Holmes stories followed in 1892, but again Conan Doyle became restless. Other writers imitating him had begun to appear, with the 'rivals' of Sherlock Holmes. It was time for the great original to plunge to his death over the Reichenbach Falls. Sherlock Holmes 'died' in the issue of *The Strand* for December 1893.

However, to his readers he was an immortal figure, one of great influence. When Conan Doyle and his wife arrived in Egypt at the end of 1895 he was surprised to discover that the Holmes stories had already been translated into Arabic by the Khedive's government and had been issued to the police as textbooks in detective work. Conan Doyle was surprised, but not so amused, when a young Egyptian police officer, having examined his face with great care in the manner of Sherlock Holmes, according to his textbook, said Conan Doyle showed 'criminal tendencies'.

Later still, the stories were used in Hong Kong for training Chinese police as well.* Even private persons were influenced: in December a young man called Rea, who had been reading *The Adventures of Sherlock Holmes*, thought he would do 'a little of the Sherlock Holmes business' and had a card printed describing himself as a detective officer. He was fined £10. Nine years later this sort of thing was still going on, for a fixation with Holmes was said to have led to the suicide of another youth in 1914.

The Holmes stories were not without their influence on the police. Sherlock Holmes was the father as well as one of the prophets of scientific criminal detection. As detective fiction

---

* At least according to Adrian Conan Doyle. In the Doyle archive there survives a printed book in Chinese, with no date or place, Xiao Quing's *An Account Between Two Cunning Rivals*, a version of a Sherlock Holmes/Arsène Lupin novel by Maurice Leblanc, probably *Arsène Lupin contre Herlock Sholmes* (1908).

created the idea of the scientific detective, as Macdonald Hastings observes, senior detectives began to 'play the part'. Yet officialdom was slow. It was not until 1901 that Scotland Yard established a fingerprint department, some 30 years after the idea of using them for personal identification had been mooted. It was not until 1912 that an official police photographer was appointed, though in many forces photos had been attached to dossiers, at least in Ireland, since the 1860s. And it was not until 1924 that Britain followed Austria, Germany and France into scientific criminalistics, and set up a forensic laboratory and a police college. So it was that 'detective consultants' outside Scotland Yard, like Bernard Spilsbury the pathologist, Sir William Wilcox, the toxicologist, Dr Roche Lynch, the analyst and Churchill the gun expert, began to transform the fictional concepts of Doyle into a daily reality.

But the Reichenbach Falls was not to be the end of the great detective as Conan Doyle had hoped. The short novel *The Hound of the Baskervilles*, set in the past, on which he received much assistance from Bertram Fletcher Robinson, was serialized in *The Strand* from August 1901. Soon followed further short stories, from September 1903, gathered as *The Return of Sherlock Holmes* (1905), the third collection of stories, in which Holmes was truly resurrected from the dead. Another novel, *The Valley of Fear*, set largely in America, appeared in 1915. In later years there was a gradually decreasing output of Holmes stories until the series concluded in 1927 with the publication of 'Shoscombe Old Place'. These later stories were collected into *His Last Bow* (1917) and *The Case-Book of Sherlock Holmes* (1927).

It is significant, however, that Holmes himself retired in 1903 to keep bees on the South Downs, making a final investigation on the eve of the Great War only because his aid was requested by the state. All the other stories in the saga are set before 1903. This has led Trevor Hall, the critic of psychical research and acute student of Sherlock Holmes and his creator, to argue that some of the later, admittedly second-rate, stories were ideas or manuscripts which had been laid aside as unusable in earlier years. Conan Doyle, he thinks, was too deeply immersed in spiritualism in the 1920s to have any real leisure to devote to the creation of 'new' Sherlock Holmes stories – especially as the rational-minded Holmes discounted the occult in which his creator was now so engaged. Conan Doyle met the demands of editors and readers largely with old material from his files.

Whatever the original inspiration of Sherlock Holmes may have been, it lay largely in the criminal tastes of Conan Doyle himself. By 1903 his interest in crime had asserted itself in another form. Sherlock Holmes may have retired from his detective practice; Conan Doyle was only beginning his.

CHAPTER FOUR

BY EVERY POST A CALL FOR HELP

The universal fame of Sherlock Holmes in the decades after 1890 had one consequence for which Conan Doyle was unprepared: it brought him fan mail.

He did not mind the letters of admiration, but he did not care too greatly for letters from total strangers with the queerest of tales – 'lunatic letters' as he called them.

Often these letters were not addressed to Dr Conan Doyle at all, but directly to Mr Sherlock Holmes at 221B Baker Street. The London Post Office, in its ever-obliging way, forwarded them to Conan Doyle, then living in Upper Norwood.

He described some examples of his correspondents to Dr Bell in 1892. There was a young man in Glasgow who would write the exact minute of composition – say 7.14 p.m. – on his letter; a letter all the way from the south of Portugal; an American lady with curvature of the spine; a Liverpool merchant who 'burns to know who Jack the Ripper is'; and others 'who believe their neighbours are starving maiden aunts to death in hermetically sealed attics' (doubtless inspired by Louis Staunton, who was convicted with his mistress, brother, and sister-in-law of starving his wife Harriet to death).

Earlier, in February 1892, Harry How had published one of the first major interviews with Conan Doyle, in which he admitted he received many suggestions for new stories in his letters from the public.

'On the morning of my visit the particulars of a poisoning case had been sent to him from New Zealand, and the previous day a great packet of documents relating to a disputed will had been received from Bristol. But the suggestions are seldom practicable.'

We will come in due course to the New Zealand case, when describing Conan Doyle's adventures down under. The Bristol affair has yet to be traced, but may well have found its way, much altered, into one of the Sherlock Holmes stories. I suspect the papers may have related to the attempted fraud on the Smyth estate by Tom Provis, which ended in a sensational trial of 1853, that rivals in interest the Tichborne Claimant affair. But Conan Doyle rarely drew in any really direct way from life. He was too good a writer to crudely rewrite the sensations of the daily papers.

Many of the letters which he received must have been quite pathetic. A year later, Conan Doyle admitted that both he and Dr Bell 'are constantly receiving letters from persons in distress, inviting us to unravel some mystery or other in connection with the family, to use our best endeavours to trace some missing relative, or to bring to justice some delinquent whom the police have failed to capture. These letters are very amusing at times, and often contain particulars and details so elaborate as to be astonishing.'

As Holmes himself observed to Dr Watson, great crimes are often commonplace, while minor mysteries are surrounded with bizarre details. But all too often the element of madness dominated, as in the letters from one William Sharp who claimed he was not only an ill-used inventor, but also the 'real Sherlock Holmes', and that he would soon astonish the world with his feats.

At this date Conan Doyle could choose to be merely amused at his mail, and he retained few of the letters, a mistake he later regretted.

His readers, he found, had identified him with his creation. From San Francisco to Moscow he continued to hear of mysteries which only he could solve. 'I had no idea before that there were so many mysteries in existence.'

At this time he always refused to take any of them in hand, believing that their solution was 'not seriously delayed on that account'. That there were in fact so many unsolved problems, so many disappearances, so many queer turns of life, he believed was really a reflection on the inadequacy of the police.

During the years after the supposed death of Holmes and all through the Boer War Conan Doyle still continued to get such letters. But on his return from South Africa in 1901, when his interest in crime seems to have quickened, he began to take the authors of the letters a little more seriously. In 1904, when the 'final' retirement of Sherlock Holmes was announced, Conan Doyle was delighted to get letters offering the services of a housekeeper and an expert in bee-keeping.

A curious case arose at this time, which may stand as a typical example of the mysteries with which he was presented. It was a tantalizing one, he told an interviewer, 'but its development is more likely to be treated at Scotland Yard than in the pages of *The Strand* magazine'.

The case concerned a letter from Western Canada, postmarked 23 May 1901, which arrived at Whitaker's, the publishers of the famous *Almanack*, addressed to one of the staff, a Mr Rome, who had died two years before. When the letter was opened it was found to contain 3 sheets of blank paper. On the outside of the envelope was written 'Confl films' and 'Report Sy'.

Puzzled by this mysterious missive, Cuthbert W. Whitaker turned the matter over to Conan Doyle to see what he could make of it. Failing to extract anything from the letter as it stood, Conan Doyle sent the papers down to Scotland Yard in September, but the experts there could discover nothing either. There was no secret writing, and they could make nothing of the bizarre inscriptions. Conan Doyle had to admit defeat.

As Whitaker's firm published a wide range of books, including books on mining, it strikes me that the letter could have had something to do with explorations in the Canadian Rockies. The inscriptions certainly mean respectively 'Confidential Films' and 'Report of Survey' (meaning photographic negatives) – both of which suggest mining or land speculation to me. But perhaps this is too Watsonian a notion to be really true!

Such letters continued to come to Conan Doyle throughout his life. Even today some fifty letters a week arrive for Sherlock Holmes at 221B Baker Street, an address now absorbed into the head offices of the Abbey National Building Society. With such a volume of correspondence a series of staff members have been appointed by the company to act as Secretary to Sherlock Holmes since 1951. In that year an exhibition mounted in the offices for the Festival of Britain by Marylebone Library, showing the sitting-room of the Baker Street lodgings, provided the London Post Office with a convenient address to which to direct the great detective's mail.

A selection of these letters, edited by Richard Lancelyn Green, has even been published. Many are jokes, of course. Others come from children, for whom Sherlock Holmes makes an attractive alternative to Santa Claus. But many are still cries from the hearts of the lonely, the sick, and the distressed, for whom an appeal to Sherlock Holmes is a last resort. Now, as in 1892, their pathetic letters are a sad comment on the official aid available to them.

Conan Doyle's ready sympathy was always with the oppressed. In 1896 he was moved to exercise that unique privilege of the outraged Briton and write to *The Times*, making a public plea for mercy in the case of an American lady who had fallen foul of British law.

Towards the end of September a leading San Francisco businessman, Walter Michael Castle, his wife Ella and their son arrived in London. They booked into the Hotel Cecil in the Strand, and planned to return by sea to America on 7 October. Mrs Castle began a round of visits to the leading shops. She was especially interested in furriers. Her behaviour eventually aroused suspicion and one shop called in the police.

When the police arrived at the hotel on 5 October, they found in the Castles' suite, not only furs galore, but also eighteen tortoiseshell combs, seven hand muffs, two sables, nine small combs, seventeen fans, sixteen brooches, five eyeglasses, two plated toast racks and a cream jug. Many items still had their price tags attached. When the police entered, Mrs Castle made haste to lock a wardrobe in which she had hidden some of her other acquisitions. A key was procured and after the wardrobe was opened, the Castles were arrested on charges of shop-lifting, and of stealing from the Hotel Cecil.

They were charged and released on bail of £40,000. At the trial at Clerkenwell on 7 November Mr Castle pleaded not guilty and was acquitted; it was quite clear he knew nothing about his wife's kleptomania.

Mrs Castle, who had spent a week in prison, was hysterical and unable to speak. Her lawyer, Sir Edward Clarke, entered pleas of guilty to the seven counts. He called medical evidence to show she had been seriously affected by her brief imprisonment. She had gone through a nervous breakdown at the age of fifteen, and since a cold earlier in the year had suffered a return of her old nervous symptoms, and 'at certain periods' (in the quaint language of the day) she was quite unaccountable for her actions.

She was convicted, and despite the expressed sympathy of the judge, was sentenced to three months without hard labour.

The next day Conan Doyle, then living at Greyswood Beeches near Haslemere, put his Parker pen to paper:

Dear Sir,

Might I implore your powerful intercession on behalf of the unfortunate American lady, Mrs Castle, who was condemned yesterday to three months imprisonment upon a charge of theft? Apart from the evidence of the medical experts, it is inconceivable that any woman in her position in her sane senses would steal duplicates and triplicates – four toast racks, if I remember right. Small articles of silver with the hotel mark upon them, so they could not be sold or used, were among the objects which she had packed away in her trunk. It can surely not be denied that there is at least a doubt as to her moral responsibility, and if there is a doubt, then the benefit of it should be given to one whose sex and position as a visitor amongst us give her a double claim upon our consideration. It is to a consulting room and not a cell that she should be sent.

The following day the Home Secretary acted. He was aware of the social position in America of the Castles, and that the case had been followed in great detail by many papers in the United States. The American Embassy was also interested in the case, as were many influential business people in the City. Having consulted the police and the prison doctors who had dealt with Mrs Castle, he released her into the custody of her husband, who promised to take her back to America without delay. On her return to San Francisco Mrs Castle underwent an operation which it was hoped would help her sad condition.

Mrs Castle's lawyer admitted that once he would have had her plead insanity, but since the 1883 Act this was no longer possible. He had advised her to plead guilty and hope for kind treatment.

But her hysterical condition – now clearly recognizable as a form of pre-menstrual tension – would be hard to plead even today. Dr Doyle was well ahead of his time in his understanding of these peculiar periodic afflictions of women. Already he was prepared to use the influence his literary fame had won him to campaign for the innocent and misunderstood. The Castles were prominent people in the social life of San Francisco. It is unlikely they ever forgot Conan Doyle's chivalrous intervention on behalf of a couple of 'American cousins'.

It was his action in taking up the case of Mrs Castle that led to Conan Doyle's aid being sought out by many. During the late 1890s Conan Doyle was often called upon to lend his support to various causes. One of these was the Dreyfus affair.

Conan Doyle's friend the novelist David Christie Murray had become convinced the French army captain had been falsely convicted at his trial in 1895. Handwriting had been a hobby of Murray's for forty years, and he was convinced that Dreyfus, then in the penal colony in Devil's Island, was innocent. He tried to raise support for Dreyfus among leading public figures in England and wrote to Conan Doyle, among others, towards the end of 1897. Doyle replied:

> My dear Murray,
> Its being a week-end will prevent my coming up for I have always several visitors. I hope when you can come down you will let me know. Very much interested in your views upon the Dreyfus case. I fancy that the Government may know upon evidence which they dare not disclose (spy or traitor evidence) that he is guilty and have convicted him on a bogus document,
>
> > Yours very truly,
> > A. Conan Doyle.

On 30 January 1898 Murray gave a well-attended lecture at the Egyptian Hall, projecting huge enlargements of Dreyfus' own handwriting and the handwriting of the notorious *bordereau* onto the screen. He brought many who thought Dreyfus guilty round to his view. This was months before Zola's famous open letter to the President of the Republic, 'J'Accuse' carried by *L'Aurore*, which at last began the slow movement towards exonerating the captain.

Years later Doyle would not be quite so sanguine about the good faith of the British authorities when he found what they were capable of in the Edalji and Slater cases.

Papers in the Doyle Collection also show him in correspondence about 1895 with Major Arthur Griffiths, the well-known writer on crimes, criminals and prisons, on the subject of a burglar. In 1903 he was corresponding with Francis Galton, who had been involved in the introduction of fingerprinting.

We get hints of other cases, too, such as the eminently Sherlockian 'The Case of the Marquess's Jewels' about this period. This tale comes from Charles Higham, a not always reliable biographer of Conan Doyle, but a writer who was also well connected with the upper circles of London High Society. The case belongs to September 1901 and the first night of Conan Doyle's great stage success with William Gillette's adaptation of the Holmes stories on the evening of the 9th.

The first night in London was attended by Edward VII. At the final curtain, the audience gave the play a rare and prolonged standing ovation. The play, which had been a great success in New York, was also a huge hit in London, running for 216 performances.

The opening night coincided, according to Higham, with a real-life Sherlock Holmes story. Henry Paget, the 5th Marquess of Anglesey, was among the many fashionable folk who crowded the stalls. The Marquess, then in his mid-twenties, was certainly one of the noted characters of the day. His tastes, in contrast to his ancestors', were not military but artistic. He was well known for neglecting his estate, for the size of his debts since he inherited in

1898, and for the amazing hoard of jewellery he owned, the famous Anglesey Collection, valued at £150,000. He had what *The Times* obliquely referred to as 'theatrical interests' of an unconventional kind which luckily never brought him, as they did Oscar Wilde, to the attention of the unsympathetic police.

While the Marquess sat enthralled by the play at the Lyceum Theatre, his valet, a young Frenchman named Julian Gault, was helping a prostitute steal the jewels from his hotel bedroom. Gault had gone out from a walk while his master was at the theatre. He had met a girl from France, her card identifying her only as 'Mathilde'. Hearing of his fortunate placement, she persuaded him to steal the Marquess's jewels so that they could return to France and get married.

He went back to the hotel, looted some of the jewels, and decamped to her flat in Halsey Street, in Belgravia. She brought a fence to the flat – who may well have been another lover – who paid Mathilde £100 for them. When the hue and cry arose Gault tried to escape to France but was arrested on the quay at Dover. Miss Mathilde vanished into the London fog. Gault came to trial, confessed and was sentenced to five years in gaol. The jewels were still missing. The desolate Marquess, according to Higham, contacted Conan Doyle for help.

As a real-life Sherlock Holmes, Conan Doyle helped him to trace some of the jewels, which had been disposed of in London. Working in close consultation with Detective Inspector Dew of Scotland Yard, Conan Doyle deduced the identity of the fence. The woman was never found. Gault was released and went back to France. In 1911, he committed murder during a burglary, and was then guillotined. The Marquess died in 1905, soon after the bailiffs had moved into his country house, Beaudesert Hall, and sold off its treasures. His passing came as an immense relief to his more sober and upright relatives.

The present Marquess of Anglesey, himself a distinguished

historian, told me in 1985 that he knew nothing about this, and did not even know there had been a robbery. Nor was he aware of any connection with Conan Doyle. However, he has no way of confirming it either, for his grandmother Lady Hester Paget (who died in 1930) deliberately destroyed every document she could find relating to the 5th Marquess, whose lifestyle she loathed. Other family documents were later lost in a fire. In the years since then, he now tells me, nothing new has come to hand.

That many of Doyle's cases were never reported in the papers, and have left only tantalizing traces among surviving documents, can be shown by the 'Case of the Fugitive Fraudster'. On 16 January 1905, Conan Doyle was reading one of his daily papers, when he came upon a paragraph on the fifth page headlined 'A Besieged Debtor'. This dealt with a man in Bristol who had been obtaining goods on false pretences.

His interest was aroused at once. The next morning he wrote a letter to the editor of the periodical, marked 'Private'. He explained that the account of the man 'exactly corresponds to the tactics of a fellow I am following up'. He asked the journalist if he could tell him where the information had come from, or from whom he might obtain further details.

'A fellow I am following up': this is so like the daily routine of a practising private detective as to be astonishing. This is one of the many letters that Adrian Conan Doyle bought back for the Doyle archive from the owner, rather than a copy retained by Conan Doyle or his secretary. But it carries no note about its source, or any other information. This must be the sort of case which he and his mother were thinking of when they spoke of Conan Doyle's private detective work.

Alas, I have been unable to track down any more details about the case or the outcome of Conan Doyle's private inquires. It may seem a small matter beside some of the famous affairs he was involved in, and yet on such small issues a great deal might ride, matters perhaps of life or death, if we could only know.

There are some who have doubts that Conan Doyle was in fact the ever-active investigator I have suggested in this book. But here, surely, is evidence, indeed actual proof, of his continuing interest and his vigilance. The slightest clue as to his detective work, even from an unlikely source, as is the case with some of the crimes discussed in this book, should not be overlooked.

Here we might conveniently deal with some cases alluded to in passing by some of Conan Doyle's biographers, but which they left unexplained for lack of research, cases that Conan Doyle was alerted to, but which he declined to become involved in.

One of these was brought to his attention by no less a person than Rudyard Kipling, who came over to Windlesham to discuss it with Conan Doyle in the comfort of his billiard room, where many other crimes were discussed with friends and visitors.

This involved a curious death in Mussoorie, the northern Indian hill station, in the summer of 1911. Miss Garnett-Orme, a well-connected Englishwoman, was found dead in her bed, behind a locked door, at the Savoy Hotel. The chief suspect, her friend and companion Miss Eva Mountstephen, at the time of the death was in fact in another town. But it was seriously suggested by the prosecution that Miss Mountstephen had used something like auto-suggestion or hypnotism to make her friend take pre-poisoned medicine at a specific time. They shared an interest in spiritualism and crystal-gazing. There was also a claim that Miss Mountstephen, having persuaded her friend that her life was coming to an end, exerted undue pressure on Miss Garnett-Orme to make out a will in her favour. Miss Mountstephen was acquitted of murder, but the Garnett-Orme family in England challenged her right to inherit. This case was decided against her, but the Indian High Court judge remarked that the mystery of

Miss Garnett-Orme's death would never be solved. Just how she had been murdered, if murdered she was, has never been solved to this day, and the case remains a classic real-life 'locked-door mystery'.

Rudyard Kipling thought the whole affair was a most extraordinary tale, and offered Conan Doyle the name of one of the Allen family, owners and editors of the Indian papers in which some of his earliest writings appeared, as a well-informed source for detailed information. But the risk of libel would have made this a very sensitive matter for Conan Doyle to have written up in any way, especially after the acquittal of Miss Mountstephen.

India interested Conan Doyle as an Imperialist, and he often heard about it from his oldest and closest friend Dr James Ryan, who lived for many years in Ceylon, where among other duties he was the 'Inquirer into Sudden Deaths'. But though Sherlock Holmes was concerned with Indian crimes from *The Sign of Four* to 'The Singular Adventure of the Atkinson Brothers at Trincomalee', a city in Ceylon – a case which was never recorded, alas – Conan Doyle himself chose to back away from them.

Another of the appeals by post offered Conan Doyle whatever fee he asked to travel to Poland to look into the murder of an aristocrat, Prince Wladyslaw Drucki-Lubecki, on his estate near Warsaw. The letter in October 1913 was from a Felix de Halpert, who wished Doyle to work for the accused man, Baron Jan de Bisping, a wealthy landowner and the prince's business partner. Conan Doyle did not take up the challenge; and in any case the de Bisping affair involved not an ordinary murder, so to speak, but machinations by agents of the Russian Empire. Poland was then a province of Russia. The Prince and de Bisping were thought by the Russians to have secret knowledge of the strategic fortress of Grodno, and they wanted to eliminate them. The case dragged on for years, until in 1926 in a now-independent Poland, de Bisping was completely exonerated. It remains to this day one of the most mysterious crimes in Polish history, with still unresolved issues according to some recent writers.

But foreign adventures were not yet for Conan Doyle. At home in England there were enough crimes, present and past, to absorb his interest.

CHAPTER FIVE

STRANGE STUDIES FROM LIFE

His hands were clenched and his arms thrown abroad, while his lower limbs were interlocked, as though his death struggle had been a grievous one. On his rigid face there stood an expression of horror, and it seemed to me, of hatred, such as I have never seen upon human features . . . I have seen death in many forms, but never has it appeared to me in a more fearsome aspect than in that dark, grimy apartment, which looked out upon one of the main arteries of suburban London.

A Study in Scarlet (1887)

The words are, however, those of another doctor, Dr Arthur Conan Doyle, sitting in that ill-omened room, his unfrequented surgery in Southsea.* And unlike so many other crime writers – who are on the whole a bookish lot – he really had seen 'death in many forms'. Whatever the clever deductions of Sherlock Holmes might show in the end, murder was essentially a matter of a twisted corpse, one human being done to death by another human being.

---

* As mentioned earlier, Conan Doyle's income in the Southsea years never rose above £300 a year, a state of affairs which he and the tax authorities both found 'unsatisfactory'. As his fees varied, quite how many patients this sum represented is unclear, but it could have been as few as three or four a day.

But among the many forms of death which Doyle had seen, on the medical wards or in private practice, there was no murder victim, so far as we know.

Yet all through his life, like a scarlet thread, there runs a fascination with murder, with mysterious crime, with the warped minds of murderers. It is this thread which we will follow through this book.

Conan Doyle tried to dispose of Holmes in December 1893. But that was not to dispose of an interest in crime. Once having started writing detective stories, his early clinical training came to the fore and he now moved on to criminal psychology. He turned back to the history of crime, and to three cases in particular from the 1860s of which he wrote detailed accounts.

These he called 'Strange Studies from Life' and they were published in *The Strand* between March and May 1901. He originally planned to write a series of twelve, which would have been enough material for a book; but he soon gave them up, discouraged by the nature of the material. 'I don't think I ever felt more uncertain about anything,' he told Greenhough–Smith, the magazine's editor, and refused to continue.

It is by no means clear just why these particular cases attracted him initially. He was only an infant when they took place and, though notorious enough, they are not among the most celebrated of Victorian crimes. The details would not have been difficult to come by; all three had received wide press coverage and had been reported at length in the *Annual Register*; though his details do not always agree with these sources. Later writers, too, such as Joseph Forster, had recounted the same crimes. Forster in his own series, entitled *Studies in Black and Red* (1896), called them 'studies of criminal psychology in which the moral is more full of meaning than that of many sermons'.

The Holocaust of Manor Place

For his first case Conan Doyle went back to 1860 – the year in which Wilkie Collins published *The Woman in White*. The vanity of Count Fosco, the villain of that novel, finds an echo in Conan Doyle's opening remarks.

> In the study of criminal psychology one is forced to the conclusion that the most dangerous of all types of mind is that of the inordinately selfish man. He is a man who has lost all sense of proportion. His own will and his own interest have blotted out for him the duty which he owes the community. Impulsiveness, jealousy, vindictiveness are the fruitful parents of crime, but the insanity of selfishness is the most dangerous and also the most unlovely of all.

The vain man will not be thwarted, and therein lies the danger, to others as much as to himself.

At that date there lived in Wadhurst, on the Sussex and Kent border, a prosperous farmer named Samuel Streeter. He had a daughter called Mary. Being near enough to London, she had friends in the city, and it was there that she first met twenty-five-year-old William Godfrey Youngman, a tailor. He was so infatuated with her that he came down to stay at Wadhurst for an evening, and though vague about what he did for a living, he was found acceptable by Mary's father. Eventually they became engaged.

The affair started on July 28, when Youngman wrote inviting Mary to come up to London to stay with his people. The letter contained the odd instruction to 'Bring or burn all your letters, my dear girl. Do not forget . . .' There were fifteen letters, with scattered allusions to business. In particular the odd business of her insurance. She was constantly urged by Youngman to insure her life. He also promised marriage, but her friends were not permitted to know.

50

Mary may have been a simple soul, but she neglected to burn the letters. On Monday morning, 30 July, she arrived at a quarter to ten at London Bridge Station. William Youngman was there to meet her and take her to his parents' home at 16 Manor Place, in Walworth.

The household arrangements at Manor House were peculiar. The architect having not yet evolved the flat in England, the people had attained the same result in another fashion. The tenant of a two-storied house resided upon the ground-floor, and then sub-let his first and second floors to other families. Thus, in the present instance, Mr James Bevan occupied the ground, Mr and Mrs Beard the first, and the Youngman family the second, of the various floors of No. 16, Manor Place. The ceilings were thin and the stairs were in common, so it may be imagined that each family took a lively interest in the doings of its neighbour. Thus Mr and Mrs Beard of the first-floor were well aware that young Youngman had brought his sweetheart home, and were even able through half-closed doors to catch a glimpse of her, and to report that his manner towards her was affectionate.

In the Youngman family there were the father, John, two young boys, Thomas, aged eleven, and Charles, aged seven, and the mother Elizabeth, who was alone at home to welcome their visitor from the country. They dined together at midday, and afterwards the young couple set out to see the town.

From that day two incidents are recorded. Mary called in on a friend of her father's, one Edward Spicer,* who kept the Green Dragon in Bermondsey Street. She introduced her lover. Later Spicer drew her aside and whispered that it was better for her to

---

* 'Spice' in the *Annual Register* report; Conan Doyle has Spicer.

take a rope and hang herself than marry a man like that. Spicer had seen something in Youngman he did not care for, but Mary brushed off his advice.

That night the couple went to see the celebrated tragedian William Macready in a play. It was eleven o'clock before they were back in Manor Place. By now the elder Mr Youngman and the boys were home and the family had supper together. As there were only two bedrooms, Mary, Mrs Youngman and the younger boy slept in the back, and the father, William and the eleven-year-old occupied the other. The elder Mr Youngman woke early to find William by his bed. To the sleepy observation that he was up early, the young man returned to bed. At five Youngman senior got up and went off to work as a tailor. What happened next is all conjecture.

> The motives and mind of the murderer are of perennial interest to every student of human nature, but the vile record of his actual brutality may be allowed to pass away when the ends of justice have once been served by their recital.

Soon after half-past-five, Mrs Susannah Beard on the floor below was awoken by what sounded like the children running up and down. This seemed odd, so she roused her husband; they both heard a cry and a thud. Beard ran up the stairs, and was soon shrieking down, 'For God's sake, come here! There is murder!'

James Bevan, the landlord, now joined Philip Beard on the stairs, and from the landing they could see a confusion of white clad bodies on the passage floor; three dead at least. And someone moving about in the bedroom. Suddenly, William appeared in the doorway, his white night-shirt brilliant with blood and the sleeve torn away.

'Mr Beard, for God's sake fetch a surgeon. I believe there are some alive yet.' As they retreated, he called after them, 'My mother has done all this. She murdered my two brothers and my sweetheart, and I in self-defence believe that I have murdered her.'

Bevan and Beard returned with a surgeon and a doctor after collecting P.C. John Varney, of P Division who had been passing the street corner.

'Oh, policeman, here is a sight! What shall I do?' asked the youth when he saw the uniform.

'Go and dress yourself.'

'I struck my mother, but it was in self-defence. Would you not have done the same?'

Constable Varney took Youngman into custody. He admitted striking his mother. The knife found on the scene was his, he confessed. The ferocious strength needed to inflict the blows on the victims suggested that someone other than the mother had done the deed.

William Godfrey Youngman was tried for the murders. The only motive seemed to be the pathetic sum of money for which the life of the unfortunate Mary had been insured. It emerged that there was insanity on both sides of the family, and Conan Doyle observed: 'In these more scientific and more humanitarian days it is perhaps doubtful whether Youngman would have been hanged, but there was never any doubt as to his fate in 1860.'

At the trial more evidence came out about the knife having been in his hands for some time, and about the remarks of inn-keeper Edward Spicer. These slights annoyed Youngman, who threatened that if he could get hold of him he would have his head off. The prisoner stuck to his story to the very end, even to his father and to the prison chaplain, going so far in his insolence to unjustly berate his father for ill-treating the family.

On Tuesday, 4 September 1860, William Youngman was publicly hanged at Horsemonger Lane Gaol, before a concourse of 30,000 people. Conan Doyle himself did not support capital punishment, but he notes that on this occasion not a single voice was raised against it.

And so, with the snick of a bolt and the jar of a rope, ended one of the most sanguinary, and also one of the most unaccountable, incidents in English criminal annals. That the man was guilty seems to admit no doubt, and yet it must be confessed that circumstantial evidence can never be absolutely convincing, and that it is only the critical student of such cases who realizes how often a damning chain of evidence may, by some slight change, be made to bear an entirely different interpretation.

And there speaks the true voice of Sherlock Holmes.

The Love Affair of George Vincent Parker

The Student of Criminal annals will find upon classifying his cases that two causes which are the most likely to incite a human being to the crime of murder are the lust of money and the black resentment of disappointed love. Of these the latter are both rarer and more interesting, for they are subtler in their inception and deeper in their psychology. The mind can find no possible sympathy with the brutal greed and selfishness which weighs a purse with a life; but there is something more spiritual in the case of the man who is driven by jealousy and misery to a temporary madness of violence. To use the language of science it is the passionate as distinguished from the instinctive criminal type. The two classes of crime may be punished by the same severity, but we feel that they are not equally sordid, and that none of us is capable of saying how he might act if his affections and his self-respect were suddenly and cruelly outraged. Even when we endorse the verdict it is still possible to feel some shred of pity for the criminal. His offence has not been the result of self-interest and cold-blooded plotting, but it has been the consequence – however monstrous and disproportionate – of a cause for which others were responsible.

54

In the case of William Godfrey Youngman, Doyle had dealt with murder for selfish greed. In his second case he turned to a *crime passionnel*, of about the same date. In this case, lest he 'cause pain to surviving relatives', Conan Doyle changed the names of George Victor Townley to George Vincent Parker. (A park being, of course, a 'town lea', or field.)

When he refers in passing to 'the language of science', Doyle means the work of the Italian criminologist Cesare Lombroso, whose work on the psychology and physiology of 'Criminal Man' was then enormously influential. Lombroso believed that there was a definite criminal type, who could be identified and so secluded from society.

George Victor Townley was the only son of a well-known commission agent of Manchester. He had well-developed musical gifts, refined literary tastes, some skill in languages and an interest in painting: 'In a word, he was a man of artistic temperament, with all the failings of nerve and character which that temperament implies', in short, his commercial prospects were slender. In London he would have found congenial company and an opening in journalism or criticism, but among the businessmen of the Midlands he was an outsider.

He was not, though, entirely out of sympathy among women. George met Elizabeth Goodwin at a musical evening organized by her doctor uncle. The friendship developed and they shortly became engaged, though with the active disapproval of both families it degenerated into a very clandestine affair. Matters went on in this desultory fashion until the summer of 1863 when Bessie, now lodging with her grandfather at Wigwell Grange, near Wirksworth, fell in love with, and promised her hand in marriage to, a young clergyman. On 14 August Bessie Goodwin wrote to George Townley asking him to release her from their engagement.

Townley was beside himself with distress and wrote begging to see her and talk the matter over:

My dear Bessie, I will only say here that I will arrive by the train you mention (11.37am, Friday morning) and I hope, dear Bessie you will not bother yourself unnecessarily about all this as far as I am concerned. For my own peace of mind I wish to see you, which I hope you won't think selfish. *Du reste*, I only repeat what I have already said. I have but to hear from you what your wishes are and they shall be complied with, and that I have sufficient *savoir faire* not to make a bother about what cannot be helped. Don't let me be the cause of any row between you and your G. P. [Grand Parent].

Ever yours affectionately,
G.V.T.

Doyle thought this letter was very revealing. 'As professor Owen would reconstruct an entire animal out of a single bone, so from this one letter the man stands flagrantly revealed. The scraps of French, the self-conscious allusion to his own *savoir faire*, the florid assurances which mean nothing, they are all so many strokes in a subtle self-portrait.'

Elizabeth changed her mind about seeing him, but her letter crossed his, and he arrived at Wigwell Grange at twenty minutes to six on 21 August. To avoid the embarrassment of an encounter with the old man, the couple went for a walk through the lanes away from the house.

Shortly after 8.30 a workman heard a low moaning; through the dusk came a girl whom he recognized as Captain Goodwin's granddaughter: 'Take me home. Take me home. The gentleman down there has been murdering me'.

At that point Townley came up to them, admitted he had stabbed the girl, and together they raised the now unconscious Bessie and carried her back to the Grange. At the gate the workman left them and ran on to summon old Goodwin. When he returned, Townley was attempting to staunch the flow of blood from Bessie's throat with her own shawl. But with a whispered 'I am dying!' she died in their hands.

Captain Goodwin came up demanding: 'Who would murder my grand-daughter?'

'I did it.' Quite calmly, Townley explained: 'She has deceived me, and the woman who deceives me must die, I told her I would kill her. She knew my temper.'

It was amazing in hindsight that the girl lived as long as she did, for her carotid artery had been severed.

At his trial, there was no doubt about George Townley's guilt; after all, he freely admitted his crime. Everything hinged on the question of Townley's sanity. Evidence given by the prison chaplain and two specialists (one of whom was the celebrated alienist Dr Forbes Winslow) suggested that Townley's moral sense was warped, but the judge, Mr Baron Martin, ruled that at the time of the crime he had known what he was doing to be wrong, and sentenced him to hang.

Nevertheless, Baron Martin was a man of scruple, and on the morning after the trial he wrote to the then Home Secretary, Sir George Grey, that he shrank from such a decision. Grey passed the responsibility on to the Commissioners in Lunacy, and on the eve of the execution he received another report from the prison officers at Derby that Townley showed distinct signs of insanity. Townley was reprieved, and a second commission appointed to inquire into his mental state. They reported that: 'George Victor Townley is of sound mind'. But once reprieved a convict is never hanged, and Townley's sentence was commuted to life imprisonment, 'a decision,' Doyle thought, 'which satisfied, upon the whole, the conscience of the public.' Be that as it may, a year after his incarceration in Pentonville Prison, George Victor Townley left the Sunday chapel service and took a dive over the railings of the gallery and plunged head foremost on to the stone floor twenty-three feet below.

As in the case of William Godfrey Youngman, Doyle was making a subtle attack upon the very idea of capital punishment. The matter of 'reasonable doubt' about either the crime or the state of mind of the prisoner should be quite enough to bar executions. This point was even more forcefully made in his third case.

The Debatable Case of Mrs Emsley

In the fierce popular indignation which is excited by a sanguinary crime there is a tendency, in which judges and juries share, to brush aside or treat as irrelevant those doubts the benefit of which is supposed to be one of the privileges of the accused. Lord Tenterden has whittled down the theory of doubt by declaring that a jury is justified in giving its verdict upon such evidence as it would accept to be final in any of the issues of life. But when one looks back and remembers how often one has been very sure and yet has erred in the issues of life, how often what has seemed certain has failed us, and that which appeared impossible come to pass, we feel that if the criminal law has been conducted upon such principles it is probably the giant murderer of England.

Far wiser is the contention that it is better that ninety-nine guilty should escape than that one innocent man should suffer, and that therefore, if it can be claimed that there is one chance in a hundred in favour of the prisoner he is entitled to his acquittal. It cannot be doubted that if the Scotch verdict of 'Not proven', which neither condemns nor acquits, had been permissible in England it would have been the outcome of many a case which, under our sterner law, has ended upon the scaffold.

Cases in doubt are the very meat of the matter for the amateur criminologist. The haste of which Doyle speaks here has since hurried many a man to the gibbet or to gaol: Timothy Evans (posthumously pardoned in 1966 for the murder of his wife, subsequently confessed to by John Christie) and James Hanratty (the victim of circumstantial evidence and faulty identification, still awaiting posthumous pardon) are examples that come immediately to mind. The case which Doyle used in illustration of this theme was the mysterious death of Mrs Mary Emsley, murdered in August 1860.

Mrs Emsley's husband had been a builder, responsible for constructing a great deal of working-class housing. It was from these projects that he drew his wealth, and which he eventually left to support his widow. Though she was well off, Mrs Emsley continued to live in an economical fashion in her house at 9 Grove Road, Stepney, set among her inherited properties.

In looking after the houses she preferred to employ occasional labour rather than a full-time workman. Among her odd-job men were Walter Thomas Emms, a cobbler, and George Mullins, a plasterer. Mrs Emsley lived alone, suspicious of every caller, wary of opening the door to those she did not know. The house itself was small, two stories with a basement and a tiny, neglected garden. 'It was,' observes Doyle, 'a singular and most unnatural old age.'

Mrs Emsley was last seen on the evening of Monday 13 August 1860. At about seven o'clock two of her neighbours opposite saw her sitting at her bedroom window. The next morning a boy from the local drapers called, but got no answer. At about ten o'clock one of her men knocked and again there was no answer. As the day passed other callers were similarly unable to raise Mrs Emsley. Wednesday and Thursday passed. The neighbours, used to her odd ways, were not alarmed. On Friday morning, Emms, who acted as an assistant rent collector, called. Getting no reply he went around to her solicitor, Mr Rose, and a relative, Mr Faith. On their way back the trio collected PC Dillon from the police station.

The front door was locked, but the men got in through the

back. The ground floor was deserted. They went upstairs. Perhaps Mrs Emsley was merely away. But then, on the landing Emms saw the bloody outline of a boot in front of the lumber-room door.

Mrs Emsley was dead, lying huddled behind the door, preventing it from opening. On the floor were rolls of wallpaper, under her arms two other pieces. She had been killed by a sudden severe blow to the back of her head, apparently while busy choosing patterns. Whoever had killed the widow Emsley had been let in by her, presumably on a matter of business connected with the doing-up of her houses.

The murder caused as sensation. A government reward of £100 was posted, which was soon raised to £300; but to no avail. The police investigations dragged on, getting nowhere. Then on Saturday, 8 September they had a break.

Sergeant Richard Tanner was approached by George Mullins, who had been a policeman in Ireland and then in Stepney, before retiring and setting up as a plasterer. He was fifty-eight years old and of good reputation.

'You know,' Mullins explained, 'I have been for some time looking after the murderer of Mrs Emsley. I have had my suspicions, and now I know the man.'

'Who was it?' asked Tanner.

'A man called Emms.'

Mullins, it transpired, had been keeping a watch on Emms, and Tanner agreed that the house he lived in would be searched, and that Mullins could go with them. The sergeant had taken down his statement, and if any advantage derived from it the reward would be his.

'Oh, I will make it alright with you,' Mullins replied, meaning he would share the money.

Off they went then to Emms's cottage, which was beside a brickfield. Mullins claimed he had seen the cobbler take a strange package down to a ruined shed on the edge of the field. This was searched, though nothing was found. Then Mullins directed the officer to a stone slab, and behind it, sure enough, they found the parcel. Back then to the police station, Emms in confusion, 'while Mullins swelled with all the pride of the successful amateur detective'.

But at the police station George Mullins found himself charged alongside Emms with being concerned in the death of Mrs Emsley. He protested, but to no avail. Emms, however, was able to prove a complete alibi for the time of the murder, and Mullins alone was committed for trial at the Central Criminal Court on October 25.

The case against him was a strong one. In his rooms had been found tape similar to that around the parcel. Also cobbler's wax, which was an odd thing for a plasterer to have. He owned a plasterer's hammer, thought by Dr Gill to be such as would have been used to kill the old lady. Mrs Mullins had sold, only days before her husband approached the police, a gold pencil case which was shown to have belonged to Mrs Emsley. It was stained with blood. There was human hair on the plasterer's boots, one of which matched that found in the blood stain on the landing at Grove Road.

The court heard that Mullins was doing up one of Mrs Emsley's houses, and had already called upon her with wallpapers, and the key she had given him was found in her bedroom.

The police next produced a witness to say they had seen Mullins going in the direction of Grove Road, and later acting oddly with bulging pockets.

What could the defence set against this? Mullins' children said he had been home that fatal night – though it was suggested they had confused the days. As for the human hair, that was used by plasterers in their trade, and the police had failed to show there was blood on the boot that was supposed to have made the mark outside Mrs Emsley's lumber-room door.

Then Mr Best, on behalf of the prisoner, produced his own surprise witness, a Mrs Barnes who lived opposite in Grove Road, who swore that at twenty minutes to ten on Tuesday morning she had seen someone moving round the bedroom. Was it Mrs Emsley, which changed the time of the murder? Or was it the murderer, who had spent the night in the house? Either way it seemed to exclude Mullins.

Another witness testified he had seen a builder named Rowland coming away from what he thought was Mrs Emsley's house on that Tuesday morning. Rowland recalled the meeting, he had been working in the house next door, but it had been on a different day.

The Lord Chief Baron then summed up. Many of the points relied upon by the police were brushed aside lightly. He was not impressed, for example, with the tape, or the wax, or the hammer, or even the boot. No, the only damning evidence was the certainty that it was Mullins who had hidden the parcel, containing *inter alia* items of Mrs Emsley's silver, in the shed. Everything else might be got round, but not that parcel.

After three hours the jury found the prisoner guilty. But even as he passed sentence, the judge advised Mullins that if he could bring forward more evidence it would be considered.

To allude to the possibility of a man's innocence and at the same time to condemn him to be hanged strikes the lay mind as being a rather barbarous and illogical proceeding. It is true that the cumulative force of the evidence against Mullins was very strong, and the investigation proved the man's antecedents to have been of the worst. But still, circumstantial evidence, even when it all points one way and there is nothing to be urged on the other side, cannot be received with too great caution, for it is nearly always possible to twist it to some other meaning.

If Mrs Barnes the neighbour was to be believed, the police account of what had happened was wrong. Doyle stresses the question of doubt. Joseph Forster, the historical writer, in his account of the case in *Studies in Black and Red* has no doubts at all that George Mullins, policeman and plasterer, was guilty of murder. Conan Doyle, who deals with the evidence in far greater detail, was not convinced.

> After reading the evidence one is left with an irresistible impression that, though Mullins was very likely guilty, the police were never able to establish the details of the crime, and there was a risk of a miscarriage of justice when the death sentence was carried out.

Mullins was hanged on 19 November 1860. In a statement he reaffirmed his own innocence, and his belief that Emms too was innocent. This seems to suggest that he was admitting he put the package by the shed. But the items found might easily have been pilfered in a quite separate crime from the murder. There was, as Doyle underlined, no firm case against George Mullins. The Scottish verdict of 'Not proven' would have been a safer option. Here, in 1901, Doyle speaks well of Scottish justice. But this was long before he had had a chance to see it in operation.

This last article in the series appeared in *The Strand* in May 1901 – by which time Conan Doyle was already deep into a new Sherlock Holmes novel, *The Hound of the Baskervilles*.

In South Africa, during the Boer War, he became friendly with the journalist Bertram Fletcher Robinson (later the editor of *Vanity Fair*). On his return to England he and Robinson had gone on a four-day golfing holiday to Cromer in Norfolk. There, in March 1901, with the North Sea wind blowing about the hotel, Robinson had begun talking of Dartmoor, of its brooding sense of mystery and of its strange legends, in particular a tale of a spectral hound.

Doyle had to return to London. He was giving a dinner party for Major Arthur Griffiths – one-time Inspector of HM Prisons and author of many books on crime and penology, who had published the year before his own volume of detective yarns, *Tight Places: Some Experiences of an Amateur Detective* – and some other friends. But within a month he and Robinson were at Rowe's Duchy Hotel in Princeton in the heart of Dartmoor on the trail of the Hellhound.

'Here I am in the highest town in England [he wrote home]. Robinson and I are exploring the Moor over the Sherlock Holmes book. I think it will work out splendidly; indeed I have already done nearly half of it. Holmes is at his very best, and it is a highly dramatic idea – which I owe to Robinson.'

Robinson, as the dedication made clear, provided the germ of the novel in the shape of the demon hound – Baskerville was the name of Robinson's coachman who drove them about Dartmoor. There are some who think Robinson actually wrote part of the novel, into which Conan Doyle manfully forced Sherlock Holmes.

Doyle had previously visited the moor in August 1881, so his imagination had already created an idea of the place before he arrived there with Robinson. The reality of the moor was as grim as anything he could have recalled: the weird landscape, the thousand acres of heather, the stark rocks, and the creeping mists. Above all there was the prison, where there were then 1,000 convicts. The guards were armed with carbines, and had orders to shoot any prisoner attempting to escape. The death of Selden in the novel was drawn directly from Conan Doyle's observations of the prison regime.

He and Robinson tramped over the moor, often up to fourteen miles a day. They saw the Grimspound Bog, which was to be transformed in his imagination into the Great Grimpen Mire. Out on the moor they examined the prehistoric huts; and while in one of them, they heard approaching footsteps and their sudden appearance scared another tourist. This was an incident that would also be embroidered into the evolving story.

The novel was completed on an extended journey home through Sherborne, Bath, and Cheltenham, to watch the cricket. There was rejoicing at *The Strand*, yet some dismay that this was a tale from the past of Holmes and Watson. Could Conan Doyle not bring Holmes back to renew his career?

The moment was ripe. In September 1901, as mentioned earlier, the American actor William Gillette opened in his freely dramatized, but highly successful, version of Holmes at the Lyceum Theatre in London. In the current issue of *The Strand*, the second episode of the serial version of the new novel was running. Could Conan Doyle himself be persuaded to write more original stories, his readers asked? Other affairs intervened, however, and it was not until the spring of 1903 that an offer he could not refuse came from *Collier's* in America. *The Strand* added a further financial incentive, and Conan Doyle was once again at work on Sherlock Holmes. The first story of the new series was to be 'The Empty House', in which the death and resurrection of Holmes was related. This was published in America in *Collier's Weekly* in September 1903, and in Great Britain in *The Strand* the following month. Sherlock Holmes was truly back!

His readers were delighted. And even while the new stories were in preparation, perhaps as a result of this revival of interest in things criminal on Conan Doyle's part, he took an important step in his criminological studies: he became involved in a current murder sensation.

CHAPTER SIX

THE MYSTERY AT
MOAT HOUSE FARM

With the return of Sherlock Holmes the year before in *The Hound of the Baskervilles*, and the new series of stories for *Collier's Weekly* and *The Strand* in the making, it was almost inevitable that in April 1903 London journalists should seek out Conan Doyle to get his opinion on the latest sensational mystery.

In the calm security of his Hindhead home it was almost a pleasure for Doyle to give his imagination over to speculations about murder as a rest from the difficulties he was having finishing 'The Adventure of the Three Students'.

On 18 March a man had been arrested in the Bank of England in Threadneedle Street. He gave a false name and address, and on the way to the police station attempted to escape. The officers, however, had no doubt that he was a wanted man, Samuel Herbert Dougal. He was charged with uttering forged cheques in Essex, although it was known that a more serious charge might follow upon further investigations.

The journalists (who included a gentleman from *The Times*, it seems) were privy to much of what lay behind the case, but which could not yet be printed as the matter was now *sub judice*.

The police were concerned that a Miss Camille Cecile Holland who had lived with Dougal as his wife some years before had disappeared, yet her cheques were still being presented for payment. Her shares were being sold off – among them, ironically, £400 worth in George Newnes, the publishers of *The Strand* – and although the money had been lodged in her current account, it was soon withdrawn by cheques in favour of Dougal. At the time of his apprehension, he was trying to change some of the bank notes he had got for his last forged cheque for gold.

A nephew of Miss Holland had been traced by the police who was prepared to swear to the forgeries, which was enough for a holding charge. But Camille Cecile Holland would still have to be found, alive or dead.

The neighbourhood around the remote farmhouse near Clavering where Dougal lived was buzzing with rumours. Some said Miss Holland was shut up in the rambling Elizabethan house; others that she had already been killed and her body hidden in one of the numerous cupboards.

A second Mrs Dougal had succeeded Miss Holland – this one was Dougal's legal wife, who later divorced him. She was followed in turn by a series of young servant girls, all of whom Dougal seduced. He was said to entertain himself in the sunny summertime by teaching his girls to ride a bicycle in the nude.

Spurred on by this gossip, and by what had been revealed in the divorce proceedings and at the hearing of an affiliation order against Dougal by one of the servants, Superintendent Edwin Pryke called at Moat House Farm and inquired officially about Miss Holland. He learnt nothing definite; simply that she was 'travelling'.

The next day Dougal packed his bags and fled to London with his current mistress. This flight was to be financed by the forged cheque which led to his arrest. With a little more care and a small ration of luck he might have escaped to the Continent.

Now that Samuel Dougal was under arrest, more details began to emerge about the disappearance of Miss Holland.

She and Dougal, seemingly a devoted couple, had moved to the farm, which she insisted must be in her name, at the end of April 1899. They engaged a servant girl named Florence Havies, who arrived on 13 May. Three days later Dougal made sexual advances towards the girl, resulting in a row with Miss Holland, who protected her. She was last seen on Friday 19 May as she drove away with Dougal in the trap – on the way, it seems, to consult her solicitor. Dougal returned later and told the maid some story about Mrs Dougal coming back on a later train, and then that she had gone to London and planned to travel, and that, by the way, another lady was coming to stay. Miss Holland was never seen again. Alive.

Conan Doyle agreed with the police theory that she was dead, murdered by Dougal. Money, as is so often the case, seemed to lie at the root of the matter, money and Dougal's immense sexual appetite. (In one instance he had sexual relations with three sisters and their mother, though not, as far as we know, all at the same time.)

Since his arrest the local police assisted by an officer from Scotland Yard had been searching the house at Moat Farm from top to bottom. No trace of Camille Holland could be found. Days passed into weeks, still nothing was found. It was this impasse that had brought the Fleet Street journalists to sit at the feet of Conan Doyle.

Puffing at his pipe he considered the problem.

The premises had been searched?

Everywhere: cellars, barn, outhouses.

And what about the moat? asked Conan Doyle.

The moat? The journalists were puzzled.

Had they not told him that the place where Dougal lived was called Moat House Farm. Surely the name . . .

But that was lead enough. Thinking the moat was too shallow

to hide a body, the officer from Scotland Yard had neglected it in favour of other possible hiding places.

According to Edgar Wallace, at the time a Fleet Street crime reporter covering the story, the police were giving up the search in despair when one of the journalists (seemingly following up what Conan Doyle had suggested) asked why they did not explore further the moat and the channels that had once led into it.

So now the local police traced a labourer named Henry Pilgrim who had worked on the farm in 1899. The moat, which was a real one, went all the way round the house, making it into an island. A lateral trench had been dug to drain off part of it. This cut, Pilgrim recalled, had been filled up at about the time of Miss Holland's disappearance.

The course of the trench was now traced and excavated, and the old level reached. There a woman's boot was uncovered, followed by the severely decomposed remains of the whole body, its face unrecognizable after three years in damp soil.

Despite this there was little trouble about identification at the inquest, which was held in the old beamed barn of the farm. The dress on the body was identified as her own work by a local dressmaker who had made it for Miss Holland, and the boots were a special pair made for her small feet by George Lee Mold of the Edgware Road, London.

Evidence given by Henry John Churchill, the celebrated gunsmith, suggested that Miss Holland had been shot at a range of 6 inches with a pistol; evidence of Dougal owning a pistol was given. But exactly how she died Dougal never disclosed. It is thought that he shot her through the head having stopped the trap on the way to the station to plead with her not to proceed with plans for a separation which would have left him without financial support.

The two-day trial ran its course, with revelations about Dougal's insalubrious past, dead wives, deserted women and stolen money. As Captain Dougal, he had enjoyed a long army career; but his customary bravado deserted him when convicted and sentenced, and Samuel Dougal the murderer had to be fortified with brandy to face the gallows. To the persistent questions of the prison chaplain he finally gave a muffled answer from beneath the black hood, 'Guilty,' as James Billington the executioner pulled the lever.

The moat of Moat House Farm, as Conan Doyle had foreseen, had given up its dark secret. When the couple had taken the house it was called Coldhams Farm. It was Dougal himself, 'being of a romantic nature', who had changed the name of the place to Moat House Farm, thus unknowingly providing the clue that suggested to Conan Doyle the solution to the mystery of Miss Holland's disappearance.

CHAPTER SEVEN

THE CLUB OF STRANGE CRIMES

'But who are they, Raffles, and where's their house? There's no such club on the list in *Whitaker's*.'

'The Criminologists, my dear Bunny, are too few for a local habitation and too select to tell their name in Gath. They are merely so many students of contemporary crime, who meet and dine at each other's clubs or houses.'

E.W. Hornung, A *Thief in the Night* (1905)

It was not surprising that as the creator of the greatest detective in literature, and as a well-known student of criminology, Conan Doyle should have been invited to become one of the first twelve members of a very exclusive dining club called with affected simplicity 'Our Society'. This title was more than a little anodyne, for it soon became known to the world at large as the 'Crimes Club'. The year was 1904.

The members were, as Raffles suggested to Bunny, so many students of contemporary crime. But they kept their affairs secret, so that even today, a century later, little has been divulged about them. The club still exists and remains, as ever, exclusively secret.

The idea of such a club was first mooted the previous year at a small gathering in the house of the actor and amateur criminologist Henry Brodribb Irving, the son of the legendary actor–manager Sir

Henry Irving. This was followed by a lunch in December 1903 at the Carlton Club which was the 'actual foetus of the Crimes Club', according to Arthur Lambton, the original Honorary Secretary until his death in the 1930s.

The founding members were Irving, Lambton, James Beresford Atlay (an authority on the case of the Tichborne Claimant and later the Wallace case), Lord Albert Edward Godolphin Osborne, John Churton Collins (professor of English at Birmingham University), and Samuel Ingleby Oddie, the future coroner of Westminster and a junior on the prosecution side in the Crippen case.

They soon found that many well-known people wished to join the club, and on 17 July 1904 these gathered for the first dinner at the Grand Central Hotel in London. Among them were A.E.W. Mason, Max Pemberton, George R. Sims, C.A. Pearson of *The Standard* and *Pearson's Weekly,* Fletcher Robinson, the begetter of *The Hound of the Baskervilles,* Dr Herbert Crosse of Norwich, and, of course, Sir Arthur Conan Doyle.

The general notion was to hold three or four dinners annually, on a Sunday evening for preference. Afterwards a talk was given on a celebrated crime, recent or historic. Arthur Lambton would take the chair, and after the talk or paper had been listened to with interest, there would be a general discussion. Very often the lawyers who had taken part in the case would air their views, giving the society a unique insight into the backroom secrets of crime and justice. It was for this reason that strict confidentiality was observed and total secrecy surrounded the proceedings – secrecy I have found difficult to penetrate.

'It is certainly,' wrote the novelist William Le Queux, 'the most exclusive and interesting club in London and its subscription is two half crowns yearly.' However, one of the founders, Ingleby Oddie, resigned in 1909. 'In the early days the dinners were enjoyable, for they were informal and all were genuine crime enthusiasts. The discussions of celebrated cases were just pleasant and very interesting after-dinner chats. Later, as numbers grew *Our Society* became, to my mind, too large and too formal. One's remarks had to take the form of speeches and papers prepared for reading to a large audience.'

Indeed, the original twelve of which Conan Doyle was one, grew to 40, then 60, 70, and nowadays 100 members. As these latter included such people as the Duke of Kent (a mere society figure rather than a criminalist), one can appreciate the dilution of the original intentions with which Our Society was founded.

Oddly this club and his membership of it is passed over by students of Conan Doyle (with the exception of Richard Lancelyn Green). What went on at these dinners was, however, of the greatest value to the creator of Sherlock Holmes. 'It was always interesting,' his friend Oddie recalled, 'to examine and handle exhibits from celebrated trials, to see photographs, and to learn what had become of famous persons tried and acquitted.'

These exhibits included a box of strychnine pills found on Dr Thomas Neill Cream, the multiple poisoner, when he was arrested in South London in June, 1892; Oddie also retained the repulsive impression which the mere photo of Cream made upon him. On another occasion John Churton Collins produced in triumph the right arm bones of John Williams the Ratcliffe Highway murderer, the subject of de Quincey's celebrated excursus in his essay 'On Murder Considered as one of the Fine Arts'. Collins and the journalist George R. Sims (creator of Dorcas Dene, detective) had taken them from the site of his 1820 burial in the East End of London when a mains was being laid in 1910.*

The papers, talks and comments before the society included Churton Collins on the Merstham Tunnel mystery; George R. Sims on Adolf Beck, who had been wrongly convicted twice and

* A recent investigation into the Ratcliffe Highway murders, by P. D. James and Tom Critchley, *The Maul and the Pear Tree* (new ed. 2000), suggests that Williams was in fact innocent. How this theory would have aroused the Crimes Club!

imprisoned on mistaken identification (Sims's articles in the *Daily Mail* had already secured £5,000 compensation for him); William Le Queux on the French multiple killer Henri Landru, whose detection he had taken part in, and on spies he had known; Arthur Diosy on Jack the Ripper, about whom he had woven a mystique of Black Magic; and, in later years, the man acknowledged as the father of modern forensic medicine, Sir Bernard Spilsbury, on his own career, on the mysterious death of Sir Edmund Berry Godfrey which had been laid at the door of the spurious 'Popish Plot' of the 1670s, and the equally mysterious and still unsolved murder of Mrs Caroline Luard; and Sir Edward Marshall Hall on Brides in the Bath killer George Joseph Smith (who was also the subject of a book by George Sims), and on the arsenic poisoner Frederick Seddon, who attempted to use Masonic influence to ward off the death sentence at the end of his 1912 trial.

One early talk Conan Doyle would have heard was that given on Sunday, 25 February 1906, by the Rev. Sam Jones about the tragic murder of Rose Harsent at Peasenhall, in Suffolk, four years previously. Despite the fact that all the evidence seemed to point to the guilt of William Gardiner, he was found not guilty at two trials. Jones, a vicar at nearby Bury St Edmunds, advanced the ingenious, if fanciful, solution that Rose's death had been an accident. All these cases are classics of their kind – there was nothing second rate about the crimes of the Crimes Club!

One of the strongest friendships Conan Doyle made at the Crimes Club – one he was to fondly invoke a quarter of a century later in Central Africa – was with John Churton Collins. Collins was an unusual personality who toiled for years in near poverty – scholarship is not a paying business – and was finally rewarded with the security of a professorship only at the end of his life. His devotion to the mysteries of crime was a lifelong passion; even his own end was mysterious, for he was found dead in a ditch, and the inquest returned an open verdict.

The Merstham Tunnel mystery – the curious death of Mary Sophia Money, thrown from a train on the London to Brighton railway line in September 1905 – aroused Collins's particular interest. He felt, quite rightly, that the police investigation had not been properly handled. True as that may have been, his own private investigations, though they took the matter a little further, were also without positive result. The case may, however, have given Conan Doyle a hint for the death of young Cadogan West, in 'The Adventure of the Bruce-Partington Plans', published in December 1908. (Sir Edward Parry, writing in 1924, concluded that poor Mary Money had been murdered by her brother Robert, who in August 1912 attempted to murder his wife and child in their Eastbourne lodgings, poured petrol over the bodies, and shot himself in the head as the flames devoured the room. His wife Florence had not been killed, however, and escaped the inferno. He had been living a double life for years, a life which has not been fully inquired into.)

Churton Collins prided himself on his memory. Conan Doyle, too, had excellent recall, trained as he was by the Jesuits in Stonyhurst. Collins came down to visit the Doyles at Hindhead one weekend in 1905. As an after-dinner test Conan Doyle asked him what he considered the finest passage in English prose. Collins obliged with a piece by Macaulay, and recited it word for word while Conan Doyle followed the text with his finger. Doubtless the evening also passed in cheerful talk of past horrors.

For other amateur criminologists one episode in the career of Churton Collins provided a warning, which Conan Doyle himself was often to overlook.

On 24 May 1906, the dead body of Mr Archibald Wakley, a young artist, was found in a passage at the foot of the stairs that led up to his studio on the second floor of a building in West Grove, Bayswater. The young man only worked there; otherwise he lived at home with his most respectable parents.

'Naturally everyone said "burglars" ' recalled Max Pemberton. 'So strongly did Churton Collins hold that opinion that he wrote two columns in a great daily paper and showed exactly how the thieves must have entered the building and left. A second article was promised but never printed, for the crime was suddenly revealed as a horrible affair about which the less said the better.'

Police inquiries made it seem more than probable that Wakley had been murdered by a soldier he had invited into his studio; but though the soldier was questioned the culprit was never brought to trial.

A homosexual artist beaten to death – 'rough trade' with a vengeance – was indeed a horrible affair, but the case illustrates the pitfalls facing the aficionado of crime who turns to detection. How often Sherlock Holmes had warned Watson against theorizing before one knew all the facts.

His friends and companions at the Crimes Club must inevitably have been of interest and great inspiration to Conan Doyle; alas, what he himself talked about at their meetings is still a secret of their unopened archives.

Arthur Lambton, however, in his memoirs *The Salad Bowl,* recalls what must have been one of Conan Doyle's own after-dinner stories from the earlier, more intimate, days of the club.

The question was whether many murders go undetected. Lambton thought they must be very few, but of those that did, many must be the work of medical men, who have an easy access to lethal poisons. In this connection he quotes a story 'that was told me by Conan Doyle ever so many years ago that is an exception to this rule. And here we have truth transcending fiction.'

There once resided in the country a young man who was studying medicine, and studying it very conscientiously, for he was most anxious to become a successful practitioner. He lived with a doctor and his wife as a paying guest, and in the course of time grew very much attached to his hosts, so much so that he became very concerned as to the health of the mistress of the house. She complained of perpetual headaches and nausea, and the boy could not help noticing the unhealthy appearance of her complexion. The case baffled him. Now it so chanced that he had in London a very distinguished relative in Harley Street, and this relative took an interest in him and extracted a promise that if ever he was in any difficulty in his work he was not to hesitate to seek his advice. Remembering this and in perfect good faith, one day without mentioning a word to anybody in the house, for he did not wish to add to any uneasiness that the wife's illness might occasion, he secretly secured some of the vomit, hermetically sealed it and despatched it to his relative for analysis. In due course he received the report from his London relation, accompanied by a very grave letter. The result of the analysis was that the unmistakable presence of arsenic had been found in the vomit. (I rather think that Marsh's test had not long before been discovered.) All unsuspecting, the boy called the husband aside and told him everything in awestricken tones. The husband listened to all he had to say, kept silent for a long time, looking at him in a very curious way, and then said in peculiar tones: 'Thank you, George, it's really too kind of you to take all this trouble. It shows how fond you must be of both of us. I can never thank you sufficiently.' And with that he went out of the room. A minute or two later the student was startled out of his life at hearing a revolver shot ring out upstairs. He darted up, burst open a locked door, and found his host had blown his brains out. Then slowly, he declares very slowly, the truth was borne in upon him. After the first shock of horror he decided that he had better run up to town and see his relative personally, and be entirely guided by his advice. The gist of this advice was, 'Say and do nothing'. No good purpose could be caused by creating a scandal. It was better that the wife (who, by the way, possessed a substantial fortune in her own right) should live on in a fool's paradise, for she was very fond of her husband. Accordingly this happened. An intelligent British jury brought in a verdict of suicide during temporary insanity, the widow completely recovered her health (and her complexion), and expended a considerable sum of money in erecting a tomb-stone, 'Sacred to the Memory of her Deeply loved husband', or as brilliant and witty James Atlay, the historian, remarked when he heard the story, 'Sacred to the Vomit'. Now to make this anecdote complete it is only necessary to state that the student married the widow. Perhaps he did. Next time I see Doyle I will ask him.

Was this a true story? The date suggested by Lambton would place it sometime in the 1840s – James Marsh's test for the presence of arsenic in human tissue was published in 1836, and came to wide public notice during the trial of Marie Lafarge for poisoning her husband in 1840. But perhaps he had in mind its more general use by forensic scientists in later decades.

But Conan Doyle himself had, like the student, passed many months in the 1870s and 1880 working with a succession of doctors in the North of England while studying medicine. Was this a story which one of them related to him, or was it even possibly drawn from his own experience? Investigation shows that none of the doctors he worked for died, only his friend George Turnavine Budd, and he not by suicide. So perhaps it was fiction after all, and might qualify as yet another of Conan Doyle's 'uncollected' crime stories.

Whatever the truth about the tale, it must have made a macabre contribution to one after-dinner *soirée* of the Crimes Club.

CHAPTER EIGHT

THE TRAIL OF JACK THE RIPPER

On Wednesday, 19 April 1905, Conan Doyle was one of a small group from the Crimes Club who met in the East End of London to follow up the trail of Jack the Ripper.

Conan Doyle had long been familiar with the story of the mysterious scourge of Whitechapel who had murdered a series of at least five women in the autumn of 1888 – the year that *A Study in Scarlet* was published as a book. These seemingly motiveless crimes had thrilled and shocked the whole country, indeed the whole world, and ripples of the wave of horror had even reached Conan Doyle in Southsea, so placid in its respectability.

During September 1889 the Hampshire Psychical Society was formed, with Dr Conan Doyle and Prof. William Barrett as Vice-Presidents. Doyle's close friend, who had first interested him in psychic matters, the somewhat eccentric General Drayson (the model, some think, for certain aspects of Professor Moriarty) was a leading light.

Conan Doyle's novel may even have influenced Jack the Ripper. On the wall of the murder room in Lauriston Gardens, the word *Rache* may have inspired Jack the Ripper to write his notorious wall inscription, 'The Juwes are not the people who will be blamed for nothing'.

A little later, in November 1889, a local paper suggested that Conan Doyle in his twin roles as crime novelist and spiritualist should attempt to trace Jack the Ripper by calling up the spirit of what some then thought was the latest victim of his dissecting knife! The mutilated trunk of a female had been found under a railway bridge in Pinchin Street on 10 September 1889. The head and legs were never found, and the woman was never identified. Even at the time the police did not connect this crime with Jack the Ripper, and though it then received sensational coverage in the papers, it is not now accepted as one of the series.

This piece of local facetiousness suggests that even at that early date Conan Doyle was known locally among his friends for his interest in real-life crime. What role spiritualism was to play in solving the mystery of Jack the Ripper we shall see in due course, and although nothing as sordid as the Whitechapel murders now appears in his fiction, Conan Doyle, like every other criminologist, remained fascinated by Jack the Ripper and the enigma of his identity.

On 2 December 1892 Conan Doyle visited the notorious Black Museum at New Scotland Yard, along with Dr Gilbert, the medical officer at Newgate, his brother-in-law E.W. Hornung who was later to achieve fame with his tales about ace 'cracksman' Raffles, and Jerome K. Jerome at the time editor of *The Idler*, but better known for his widely acclaimed *Three Men in a Boat*. This gruesome show, then housed in a cold, ill-lit room in the basement of the building on the Thames Embankment, contained relics of crime and murder going back several decades.

Of all the grim exhibits, Conan Doyle's attention was caught by a fading photograph of the disembowelled corpse of the Ripper's last victim, Mary Kelly, and by a letter and postcard written in red ink signed by him.

Sir Robert Anderson, sometime head of Scotland Yard, claimed that these communications, later removed from the Black Museum,* were the work of a journalist, but he refused to name him.

---

* They were returned anonymously in the autumn of 1988.

However, from internal evidence it is clear that they were really written by the murderer.

The letter is dated 25 September. By that date the Whitechapel murderer had killed two women: Mary Ann Nichols on Friday, 31 August in Bucks Row, and Annie Chapman called 'Dark Annie', on 8 September in Hanbury Street. (Two earlier murders, those of Emma Elizabeth Smith on 3 April and Martha Tabram on 6 August, had been bracketed with the Ripper murders but subsequently eliminated.) The killings had caused a sensation and the writer was exploiting this. The envelope was postmarked 'London East Central, 28 September 1888'. It was addressed to the Central News Agency office, which passed it on to the police, but the text was not released until after the double murder of Elizabeth Stride and Catherine Eddowes on 30 September. For Conan Doyle these letters brought the criminal vividly alive.

Dear Boss,

I keep hearing the police have caught me but they won't fix me just yet. I have laughed when they look so clever and talk about being on the right track. That joke about Leather Apron gave me real fits. I am down on whores and I shan't quit ripping them till I do get buckled. Grand work the last job was. I gave the lady no time to squeal. How can they catch me now? I love my work and want to start again. You will soon hear of me with my funny little games. I saved some of the proper red stuff in a ginger beer bottle over the last job to write with, but it went thick like glue, and I can't use it. Red ink is fit enough I hope ha ha. The next job I do I shall clip the lady's ears off and send to the police officers just for jolly – Wouldn't you keep this letter back till I do a bit more work, then give it out straight. My knife is nice and sharp I want to get to work right away if I get a chance. Good luck.

Yours truly,
Jack the Ripper

Don't mind me giving the trade name. Wasn't good enough to post this before I got all the red ink off my hands curse it. They say I'm a doctor now ha ha.

The postcard, postmarked 'London East, October 1', not only referred to the previous letter which was still unpublished, but also to details of the next two murders which were not as yet public knowledge by the time the card arrived at the Central News Office.

I was not codding dear old Boss when I gave you the tip. You'll hear about Saucy Jack's work tomorrow. Double event this time. Number one squealed a bit. Couldn't finish straight off. Had not time to get ears for police. Thanks for keeping last letter back till I got to work again.

Jack the Ripper

These communications had been sent to the editor of the news agency. An understanding of how news agencies work and their role in modern publicity implies a high level of education, which the demented style of the letters scarcely hides. As the denizens of the East End had already realized ('They say I'm a doctor'): Jack the Ripper was 'a Toff'.

The murders on 30 September – the Ripper's double event – of Elizabeth Stride in Berner Street just before 1 a.m. and of Catherine Eddowes in Mitre Square about half an hour later were followed by a pause. All doubts about there being a maniac at large were gone, and the population of London was thrown into a fever of fear and excitement.

Then on Friday 9 November Mary Jane Kelly, an Irish girl of about twenty-five, was butchered in her room in Miller's Court off Dorset Street. This was the last Ripper murder in the series of five. Then the killer, whoever he was, vanished as mysteriously as he had arrived.

What did Conan Doyle think at that time of the case? In the summer of 1894 he outlined to an American journalist just how Sherlock Holmes would have set about tracing the culprit.

I am not in the least degree either a sharp or an observant man myself. I try to get inside the skin of a sharp man and see how things strike him. I remember going to Scotland Yard Museum and looking at the letter which was received from the Ripper. Of course it may have been a hoax, but there were reasons to think it genuine, and in any case it was well to find out who wrote it.

It was written in red ink in a clerkly hand. I tried to think how Holmes might have deduced the writer of that letter. The most obvious point was that it had been written by someone who had been in America. It began 'Dear Boss', and contained the phrase 'fix it up' and several others which are not usual with Britishers. Then we have the quality of the paper, and a round, easy, clerkly hand. He was, therefore, a man accustomed to the use of a pen.

Having determined that much, we can not avoid the inference that there must be somewhere letters which this man has written over his own name, or documents or accounts that could readily be traced to him. Oddly enough, the police did not, as far as I know, think of that, and so they failed to accomplish anything. Holmes' plan would have been to reproduce the letters in facsimile and on each plate indicate briefly the peculiarities of the handwriting. Then publish these facsimiles in the leading newspapers of Great Britain and America and in connection with them offer a reward to anyone who could show them a letter or any other specimen of the same handwriting. Such a course would have enlisted millions of people as detectives on the case.

In fact the Metropolitan Police did issue facsimiles of both the letter and the postcard on a poster on 3 October 1888, asking anyone who recognized the writing to communicate with them or the nearest police station. Such answers as they received led nowhere. But they did not issue an analysis of the handwriting which might well have made tracing the writer easier. Even in 1894 this might have been done and the Ripper caught, but there is good reason to believe that by then the police knew the culprit was either dead or well out of the way in a lunatic asylum.

Among the members of the Crimes Club there was so great an interest in the case that Ingleby Oddie, then a lawyer, arranged with Dr Frederick Gordon Brown, the City of London Police Surgeon, the visit the scenes of the murders with Churton Collins, H.B. Irving, Dr Crosse, and of course, Sir Arthur Conan Doyle.

They were to be guided by Dr Brown himself and by City of London Police detectives familiar with the details of the crimes. In this they were lucky. Brown was one of the doctors who had been called to Mitre Square to examine the body of Catherine Eddowes, on which he later performed the post mortem. He told the Coroner that some anatomical knowledge was displayed by the killer's work, but whether this was from medical training or skill in cutting up animals was not clear. The entrails had been removed and deliberately placed on the right shoulder – which has since led some writers to see in this an example of Masonic ritual murder. Brown's notes on his post mortem as well as a set of mortuary photographs survive, from which the horror of the crimes can clearly be seen. From him Conan Doyle would have gained a direct and grim idea of the real nature of the murders.

The party met at the Police Hospital in Bishopsgate on a wet and dreary afternoon. At that date, long before the bombs of the Second World War, Whitechapel had changed little since the heyday of the Ripper. Here Conan Doyle, who had seen many aspects of life before now, was exposed to a new experience.

It was the Eve of the Passover, and the Jewish community of the East End was crowding into the narrow streets, especially Petticoat Lane. The party could not use their umbrellas or even keep together so great was the crush. It all seemed immensely curious and foreign, especially 'the strange articles of food'. As Oddie later recalled: 'Most of the married women wore black wigs, the idea being that they should conceal their charms from the eyes of all save their lawful husbands. Many of the women carried hens under their arms, on their way to have their throats cut by a priest according to ritual with a clean knife without a notch in the blade which was carefully shown to and inspected by all his patrons. There were other booths where chickens could be plucked; and others where cows could be milked into the women's clean jugs.' Moses, as Oddie observed, was acting as an unqualified assistant to the local Medical Officers of Health.

One theory about the identity of Jack the Ripper was that he might have been one of these Jewish ritual slaughtermen, and that the local Jewish community was hiding him. After the Mitre Square murder the inscription mentioned earlier was found in a hallway: 'The Juwes are not the people who will be blamed for nothing'. Nearby was a bloodstained fragment of the victim's apron cut off by the murderer on which he had wiped his hands. This writing was removed for fear of inciting anti-Jewish feelings, very much alive in Whitechapel after the trial of Israel Lipski the year before.

But 'the Juwes' are not the Jews, but the celebrated murderers of Masonic tradition* – yet another clue which has been taken up as pointing to some Masonic connection with the crimes.

The Crimes Club party also saw inside a doss-house and other cheap lodgings typical of the area, the sort of places that the victims of the Ripper lodged in, and for which they raised the rent by

---

* Jubelo, Jubela, and Jubelum, who, during the time of the building of Solomon's Temple, murdered Hiram Abiff, the Grand Master. In fact they are known as the 'ruffians' more frequently than the 'Juwes'.

walking the streets. According to John Churton Collins in his diary record of the walk:

> Conan Doyle seemed very much interested, particularly in the Petticoat Lane part of the expedition, and laughed when I said 'Caliban would have turned up his nose at this'.

But they had not come for local colour, but for local crimes. As they toured them, the sites of the Ripper murders all presented one common characteristic: they were dark, obscure and secret. Yet all were chosen to be easy to escape from. Bucks Row, Hanbury Street, Mitre Square and Miller's Court, all were provided with exits and with cover. Churton Collins records what he and Conan Doyle saw in Miller's Court where Mary Kelly died:

> This latter place was a dismal hole seen on a dark, wet, gloomy afternoon. It consisted of one very small room, with a small window, a fire, a chair and a bed. It was sombre and sinister, unwholesome and depressing, and it was approached by a single doorstep from a grimy covered passage leading from Dorset Street into a courtyard.

Here, behind the safety of a locked door, Mary Kelly was murdered and butchered, her nose, breasts and intestines cut out and placed on the table beside the bed.

This murder scene was also photographed by the police. Conan Doyle and his friends were shown the picture: 'a mass of human flesh,' recalled Oddie. 'In my twenty-seven years as a London Coroner I have seen many gruesome sights, but for sheer horror this surpasses anything I ever set eyes on.' That had been the last Ripper murder, on 9 November 1888. Were the earlier murders merely gratuitous, or were they all part of a pattern which led up to the death of the unfortunate Mary Kelly? She had been born in Limerick, Ireland, and lived in Wales until her husband was killed in a mine explosion. She had been in 'a fashionable house' in the West End of London, and claimed she had lived in France as the mistress of a mysterious protector who was never identified.

From there she had escaped into the East End, only to meet her death. Had someone been hunting her and her associates down, someone from her past? What is the significance of the fact that Catherine Eddowes, who had lived with a man named John Kelly, had called herself 'Kate Kelly'? Had she been killed by someone who knew only that he sought a woman called Kelly? What was the secret that these unfortunate women, all of whom lived in the neighbourhood of Dorset Street, shared in life and in death?

Dr Gordon Brown, the Crimes Club guide, had been, as mentioned earlier, the doctor who attended the corpse of Catherine Eddowes at Mitre Square. According to Churton Collins in his diary the next day: 'He was inclined to think that he [the murderer] was or had been a medical student, as he undoubtedly had a knowledge of human anatomy, but that he was also a butcher, as the mutilations slashing the nose, etc., were butchers' cuts.'

The suggestion that the Ripper might be some kind of medical man was an early and persistent one. Yet curiously (for remember we are in 1905) Dr Brown concluded that there was absolutely no foundation to the theory that the Ripper was a homicidal maniac doctor, whose body had been found in the Thames, though this was the theory at Scotland Yard. He was more of the opinion that the murderer suffered from a sort of homicidal satyriasis – that sexual perversion had led to the murders.

In fact there seem to have been two theories at Scotland Yard, and the homicidal maniac taken from the Thames was the one espoused by Sir Melville McNaughton and by Conan Doyle's friend Major Arthur Griffiths – both to be members of the Crimes Club. Sir Robert Anderson, writing five years later in 1910, said that Jack the Ripper was a low-class Polish Jew, later named as Aaron Kosminski.

What were Conan Doyle's own ideas, now that he had been given a chance to see the scenes of the crimes? By now he was as familiar as anyone with the details of the crime of the century. He is recorded as believing that 'Jack the Ripper disguised himself as a woman in order to escape from the scene of his crimes'. This notion perhaps arose from the finding of burnt-up women's clothes in the fireplace of Miller's Court.

One of the better-informed writers on the Ripper murders, Tom Cullen, wrote to Adrian Conan Doyle in 1962 to ask about his father's theories. Adrian replied:

> More than thirty years having passed, it is difficult to recall his views in detail on the Ripper Case. However, I do remember that he considered it likely that the man had a rough knowledge of surgery and probably clothed himself as a woman to approach his victims without arousing suspicion on their part.

Among Conan Doyle's fellow members of the Crimes Club, Jack the Ripper was an object of particular interest. Arthur Diosy, the Hungarian authority on things Japanese, for instance, was convinced that there was a Black Magic element in the murders, from the way new coins were set out near the bodies. Ingleby Oddie (who knew him from the dinners of 'Our Society') says that Diosy believed that the murders had been arranged in the form of a pentagram, a five-pointed star, and that this meant that the murderer was seeking a magical 'elixir of life', 'one of the ingredients of which must come from a recently killed woman'. Whatever the truth about the elixir, the locations of the murders can be constructed only into the most lopsided of stars. The police, in their dull practical way, were not convinced, although we do know that the murders ceased a week or two after Diosy took his ideas to Scotland Yard.

Meanwhile, in Edinburgh, Dr Bell and a medical friend were working separately on detailed reports of the crimes. 'There were two of us in the hunt,' Bell later recalled, 'and when two men set out to find a golf ball in the rough, they expect to find it where the straight lines marked in their mind's eye to it, from their original positions, crossed. In the same way, when two men set out to investigate a crime mystery, it is where their researches intersect that we have a result.'

From the suspects investigated by the police, Dr Bell deduced the name of the murderer. He wrote the name on a piece of paper and put it in an envelope. His friend had done likewise. When they opened the envelopes the same name was in each. They contacted Scotland Yard at once, and a week later the murders ceased. Was this merely a coincidence as I suspect it was with Arthur Diosy, or had they stumbled on a clue which in some way led back to the murderer? The murders ceased certainly, but Jack the Ripper was never brought to trial.

I don't think that Conan Doyle knew of this incident in the life of the original Sherlock Holmes till after Dr Bell's death in October 1911.

But to return to Conan Doyle's own original ideas about the Ripper. If the letters contained, as he suggested, American expressions, did that mean that the murderer was an American?

In fact, among the witnesses to the murder victims were some, including a policeman, who encountered a mysterious American accented seaman. As a result, sailors around the docks, and cowboys at the International Fair were questioned by the police without success. Was the Ripper really an American? It is an intriguing thought, but not a theory that has commended itself to many of the recent writers on the case.

Current theories about the identity of Jack the Ripper are that he was, variously:

- a Russian named Alexey Pedachencko
- an English barrister named Montague John Druitt, who had medical connections and was found drowned in the Thames
- a mad surgeon named Dr Stanley avenging the death from venereal disease of his only son
- a Jewish slaughterman
- a Jill the Ripper, possibly an abortionist covering up her mistakes
- HRH Albert Victor, Duke of Clarence
- James Kenneth Stephen, the Duke's tutor and cousin of Virginia Woolf
- a literary Black Magician, Dr Roslyn D'Onston Stephenson
- the Royal doctor, Sir William Gull, assisted by the painter William Sickert and his coachman John Netley
- and finally, William Sickert himself as the only principal.

These theories have nearly all been developed by writers since Conan Doyle's day – the first book wholly devoted to the mystery appeared only in 1929, Leonard Matters' *The Mystery of Jack the Ripper*. The evidence for these various theories is never completely convincing. Of them all, I myself incline to believe the last theory, which has been developed by the late Stephen Knight in his book *Jack the Ripper: the Final Solution* (1976), though his evidence has not always stood up to re-investigation by recent writers.

However, the whole of the Sickert case was re-investigated from the beginning by the American crime novelist Patricia Cornwell, who even went so far as to extract DNA from examples of Sickert's art works. From these fragments she was able to find what she believes to be a satisfactory match with DNA from material connected with the Ripper. Sickert was the Ripper. She considers the case closed.

Knowing those who write about the Ripper, this not likely to be true.

For there is now a chance that Conan Doyle was on the right track from the beginning. The Americanisms to which Conan Doyle drew attention would seem to support the claim that the Ripper was an Irish-American doctor, Francis Tumelty. The discovery of the attention which Dr Tumelty received in the American press as a prime Ripper suspect was revealed in *The Lodger* (1995) by Stewart Evan and Paul Gainey, the most remarkable breakthrough in Ripper research in recent years.

There is one last aspect of the case which did interest Conan Doyle and his friend and biographer the Rev. John Lamond, who shared his belief in spiritualism. For in his later life, with an increasing interest in the uses of clairvoyance, Doyle learnt more about the possible identity of Jack the Ripper. The case became part of the folklore of the spiritualist movement.

In July 1889 Scotland Yard received yet another letter purporting to be Jack the Ripper:

> Dear Boss
> You have not caught me yet you see, with all your cunning, with all your 'Lees' with all your blue bottles.
>
> Jack the Ripper

Whoever wrote this letter, and it may well have been the person who wrote the letters of 1888 that so impressed Conan Doyle, it remained secret in the files of the Metropolitan Police. But the passing mention of Lees is striking.

The reference is to the leading Christian Spiritualist, Robert James Lees. He had found favour with Queen Victoria, who was anxious to contact the departed Prince Albert, and had many other influential friends. At the time of the Ripper murders he had a troubling vision of one of them which he reported to Scotland Yard, but the police, pestered daily by cranks, ignored him. Another murder followed. Shocked by his visions Lees and his wife took a holiday abroad. On their return they were riding in a tram through Notting Hill when once again he became troubled. A man boarded the tram.

'That is Jack the Ripper,' he told his wife.

She did not take him seriously.

'I am not mistaken. I feel it.'

Leaving the tram, Lees followed the man down Park Lane from Oxford Street. At Apsley House the man caught a cab and disappeared into the Piccadilly traffic.

After the awful orgy of violence in Miller's Court, Lees concentrated his powers on his vision of the murderer. Then he took his 'information' to the police. Together with a police inspector he went to a house in the heart of fashionable Mayfair. There he challenged the wife of the resident, who confessed to worries about her husband's recent activities.

This man was Dr William Gull. Years later his daughter told Mr William Stowell, the distinguished pathologist, that one evening Lady Gull had been annoyed by the appearance at her house of a man calling himself a medium who had a policeman with him. According to her Gull himself then came downstairs and spoke of lapses of memory and of finding bloodstains on his shirt front.

Soon after, Gull made his will, and following a stroke, died in 1890. Or so it was said. Stephen Knight believed that he was in fact committed to an asylum under the name of Thomas Mason, dying only in 1892.

That Robert James Lees had tracked down the Ripper was, as the letter shows, a current rumour in 1889. The rumour made its way into print in 1895 in an American newspaper, though Gull was not actually named in this article. Although Lees' role was revealed in detail in the 1930s, it was not until the 1970s that the facts relating to Dr Gull began to filter out from several different sources. The story, however, was widely current in those spiritualist circles in which Conan Doyle and his friend Lamond moved. Though Conan Doyle felt that the police should make more use of clairvoyance in detecting recent crime, he was even more enthusiastic about its use in historical cases such as Jack the Ripper.

After all, the occult knockings involving the Fox sisters at Hydesville, New York State, in 1848 which began the modern spiritualist movement, led to the uncovering (it was then claimed) of the secretly buried body of a murdered pedlar. It was his tortured soul which was trying to communicate through the sisters with the living – or so the earliest spiritualists claimed, though the Fox sisters ended their lives in a maze of denial and counter-claim.

And there were, as Conan Doyle never tired of pointing out, many other very similar cases. But the manifestations of these occult forces properly belong to a later chapter of his life and this book.

The fictional use of Holmes and Watson to solve the Ripper murders – or indeed commit them – indulged in by modern writers as eminent in their field as Ellery Queen would undoubtedly have shocked and dismayed Conan Doyle.

Nevertheless, in those long conversations over their cigars and brandy the members of the Crimes Club found much food for thought and speculation in the topic of London's 'Autumn of Terror'. Several members were closely connected with the case: G.R. Sims, Sir Melville McNaughton, Lord Aberconway, Major Arthur Griffiths, Arthur Diosy, and even a relative of one of the putative Ripper suspects, the Duke of Kent.

Arthur Lambton, in his autobiography *The Salad Bowl*, recalls that in the early days of the club a certain member of the peerage wished to join. He offered to read a paper on the Whitechapel Murders. But the members knew a great deal about or, rather, against the noble lord, and did not wish to accept him. How could they put him off? J.B. Atlay drafted a letter for the Honorary Secretary to send in his own name:

Dear —————,

I am desired by the committee to thank you very much for your
kind offer to read a paper on the Whitechapel Murders, but you
will appreciate the reason we cannot accept it when I tell you
that the Whitechapel Murderer happens to be a very near and
dear relative of one of our most popular members . . .

CHAPTER NINE

THE PERSECUTION OF GEORGE EDALJI

It is my belief, Watson, founded upon my experience, that the lowest and vilest alleys of London do not present a more dreadful record of sin than does the smiling and beautiful countryside.

The Copper Beeches (1892)

Conan Doyle's wife, Louise, died on 4 July 1906. She had long been ill with tuberculosis, but her death left him emotionally drained. For several years he had been deeply in love with a younger woman, Jean Leckie, a relationship which he had kept honourably platonic. That empty part of his life that he had told his brother Innes about, was not filled. He would do nothing to cause Louise pain in what were clearly the last days of her life.

Now he was free to marry Jean, but only after a decent interval of mourning for Louise. However, his new marriage brought about a change in his relations with the children of his first marriage, and especially with his oldest child Mary, as Georgina Doyle has recently chronicled. His daughter (the 'Toots' of earlier years) felt repulsed. His son Kingsley, who he had decided should study medicine and become a cancer researcher – thus fulfilling his father's own career ambitions – was extremely secretive. He was a fine lad, but he 'lived behind a mask' and his heart was a mystery to his father.

(i) The Heart of Darkness

It was during this period of heightened emotional strain, in the second half of December 1906, that he received a letter from a young man, newly released from prison, claiming he was innocent of the crime for which he had been convicted: the vicious mutilation of a horse. The letter was brought to his attention by Major Wood, his personal secretary, his own Dr Watson.

Enclosed were a series of articles which he had just written for a Birmingham Sunday newspaper, which Conan Doyle read through with increasing interest. Something in this appeal caught his attention, setting it apart from the countless others he got every year. What the special appeal was has never been explained, but surely his memory must have gone back to the circumstances in which he had met his dead wife, when after the sudden death of her brother Jack, he found himself the victim of an anonymous letter, which hinted that he had poisoned him. Conan Doyle had been quite innocent: so might be this young man. For a long series of horrible letters from a truly poisoned pen were at the heart of the cruel persecution of George Edalji.

Conan Doyle threw himself into the case, acting out in real life the role of private detective and for the next nine months crusaded for the innocence of the young man.

He began by sending for the papers in the case, which included legal depositions as well as press cuttings. The affair, as he came to realize, was a complex one. And behind it, as he later discovered, lay an even more complex history.

It was a strange case, amply illustrating Sherlock Holmes' dictum about the hidden sin of the beautiful countryside. One is reminded, too, of Marlow's observation in Joseph Conrad's novella *The Heart of Darkness* (published in 1899), speaking of the peaceful English countryside in comparison with the sinister Congo, that 'This, too, has been one of the dark places of the earth'. But Conan Doyle, from his student years, knew the landscapes of the Midlands, the green fields rank with the outfall of coal mining and manufacturing, the English heart of darkness.

The setting for the case was South Staffordshire where, during the early months of 1903, the little village of Great Wyrley, lying between Walsall and Rugeley, was in a state of great excitement. A criminal was at large whose perverted taste it was to creep about the fields at night with a razor or sharp knife slashing cattle, sheep, and horses, leaving them in agony to bleed to death. The fear that this maniac might soon kill a child, as some of the letters warned, lurked in everyone's mind.

The first incident was on 2 February 1903, at Wyrley itself. A valuable horse belonging to Mr Joseph Holmes was found to have been ripped up during the night.

Two months later, on 2 April, a cob belonging to a Mr Thomas was cut up in a similar way. Within weeks, several sheep on the same day, and a horse belonging to a Mr Badger were terribly mutilated.

On 6 June two cows were attacked, and then three weeks later two horses belonging to the Quinton Colliery Company were also killed.

These were vicious crimes, eight in a series, and though the police were alert, they had no evidence to arrest anyone. Then, on 1 July they began to receive mysterious letters. Some were signed with false names, some with the 'signature' of a boy at Walsall Grammar School, which was six miles to the south of Wyrley by railway. This boy, fifteen-year-old Wilfred Guy Greatorex, was subsequently shown to be completely innocent.

The letters are remarkable for their length and unpleasant reading. In the first the writer made several references to the sea. These were to have great significance later in the search for the true author of the letters: 'I would like to go on a training ship like Tosh Hatton', 'let me go to the same training ship as Tosh Hatton', 'you must settle for me to go to a ship', 'I am leaving school soon and I would like to go to sea'. He also gloated over the disgusting details of the crimes. He claimed he was one of a gang, mentioning some by name. They enjoyed cutting up animals. 'He has got eagle eyes, and his ears is as sharp as a razor, and he is as fleet of foot as a fox, and as noiseless, and he crawls on all fours up to the poor beasts . . .'

Again: 'I have got a dare-devil face and can run well, and when they formed that gang at Wyrley they got me to join. I knew all about horses and beasts and how to catch them best. I had never done none before till those two horses near the line at Wyrley and they said I had drawn the longest lot and said they would do me in if I funked it so I did and caught them both lying down at 10 minutes to 3 and they roused up and then I caught each under the belly but they didn't spurt much blood and one ran away but the other fell . . . Now I will tell you who are in the gang, but you cannot prove it without me. There is one named Broell from Wyrley and a porter who they call Edgar at Wyrley station, and there's Edalji the lawyer . . . Now, I have not told you who is back of them all and I shall not unless you promise to do nothing at me . . . It is not true that we always do it when the moon is young and the one Edalji killed on April llth was full moon night'.

Conan Doyle hardly needed his training as a doctor or his insight as a writer to see that the author of these letters was a profoundly disturbed person. He revealed a deep-seated grievance against his community. Worse still; in a letter dated 10 July 1903: 'There will be merry times in Wyrley in November when they start on little girls, for they will do twenty wenches like the horses before next March.'

The police clearly had to do something, to arrest someone, or sooner or later it would be a matter of murder. But how, Doyle wondered, had the police come to settle on Edalji as the real culprit? Others had been named in the letters, but in Wyrley George Edalji, son of the Church of England vicar, was the odd man out.

His father, the Rev Shapurji Edalji was originally of a Parsee family in Bombay.* He was, simply, a Black Man.

Shapurji Edalji was born about 1841 and educated in Bombay and in England, and was the author of several learned little works on theology and language: *Lectures on St Paul's Epistle to the Galatians* (1879) and a Gujarati-English dictionary. He had come to England as a young man, and in 1874 had married a Scottish woman, Miss Charlotte Stoneman, the daughter of a Shropshire vicar. They had three children, two sons Horace and George, and a daughter, Maud Evelyn. Horace became a civil servant in the Revenue, George a solicitor and author, while Maud, according to one friend of the family was 'addicted to botanical research'.

Edalji had served in six parishes around England before coming to Wyrley in 1876, but the oddity of a 'black' vicar with his white wife and half-caste children in a rural parish in the ill-educated industrial heartland of England was bound to attract trouble. It was, after all, the duty of the English to evangelize the Blacks, not the Blacks to preach to the English. Some idea of the contemporary attitudes held about Black clergy can be found in Dorothy L. Sayers' novel *Unnatural Death* (1927), where the Rev. Mr Halleluja Dawson, a West Indian belonging to the Tabernacle Mission, is referred to by one of the minor characters in terms which would nowadays be difficult to print. Anti-semitism and racial prejudice were, as many books of the day reveal, commonplaces of respectable society.

---

* He was not a Hindu as many thought. The Parsees are the Indian followers of the prophet Zoroaster, refugees originally from Iran, chiefly settled in Bombay. They honour the sacred fire in their temples as a symbol of Ahura-Mazda, the good deity. Benevolence is the chief practical precept of their religion and they are responsible for many charities. In 1901 there were 94,000 of them in India.

A little earlier, in John Buchan's novel *Prester John* (1910), an African Free Church of Scotland clergyman is discovered by some lads stark naked on the beach near their village armed with a knife 'raising Satan' on a night near the full moon – a well-known time for evil madmen. This man had earlier been preaching 'nonsense' about Africans in the future having something to teach the British in the way of civilization. But the boys knew that 'the Bible says that the children of Ham were to be our servants'. The language and opinions would seem to echo those held by many around Great Wyrley.

In Wyrley George and his father were seen as 'foreigners'. George was gentle and humane, but very shy, avoided company and took long lonely walks. His strange appearance – his eyes bulged peeringly – looming up out of the gloaming could have been seen as alarming. Sinister rites at the full moon were easy to imagine. Certainly Mrs Edalji felt that racial prejudice in the community played a part. She told her supporters that their means did not allow them to go out much in county society. But then, would her husband have been welcome in the circles in which most clergymen of the Established church would have moved? Prejudice was not confined to cottages, but could also be found in the great country mansions.

And there had been incidents in the past, as the police knew. Their importance became clear to Conan Doyle later, though they did not form part of the evidence given in court. George Edalji was a marked man in the eyes of the local police.

George was a solicitor, with a practice in Birmingham. At Mason College (now Birmingham University) he had taken honours in his finals; he had won Law Society prizes; he had written a well-known book on railway law (*Railway Law for the 'Man in the Train'*, 1901). Though he was then poor and had to borrow money, a brilliant career lay before him, which must have fuelled local resentment. George was a small, frail, nervous youth

100

with a regular way of life; he did not smoke and he did not drink. But his peculiar appearance gave him an odd, even sinister, expression.

The police, prompted by the three letters (another accusing Edalji had been received on 15 July) kept a watch on Wyrley Vicarage, a large house standing in its own extensive garden. Elsewhere other officers patrolled the local lanes and fields, sometimes as many as twenty at a time. His name was already linked with the crimes. Soon after one of the previous outrages a reward of £25 was offered for information as to 'the originator of a supposed rumour linking young Edalji with the mysterious slaughter of animals' (*Westminster Gazette*). Oddly enough, one of the letters was posted in Wednesbury on a day that George and his sister Maud were away in Aberystwyth!

On the evening of Monday 17 August, Sergeant Thomas Parsons noticed a pony in a field beside the Great Wyrley Colliery. This was at eleven o'clock and the pony seemed fine. Squally rain came down at midnight, falling heavily at times till it cleared just before dawn.

At twenty minutes to six on the morning of 18 August, a lad named Henry Garrett, on his way to work at the mine, came upon the pony, its belly having been ripped up with a sharp blade. Garrett later testified in court: 'I was walking through that field by the colliery and saw a light brown pony by the hedge near the footpath. The horse came up to me and I noticed the cut in its side. It was the left side. Blood was trickling down slowly. Something like a lump of fat was hanging out. I told someone what I had seen. The pony went straight into the shed with the other horse.' But it had not been disembowelled. The sharp cut, though clean, was also shallow. 'The blood,' Henry Garrett testified, 'was dropping pretty freely.'

Garrett raised the alarm, and the police were called, followed by the local vet, Mr Lewis, at 8.30. The wound, he said, was quite fresh, done within the last six hours. (Though if it still bled at 7.30, less than two hours is more likely, for the wound would have begun to close up if it were any longer.)

This was the eighth incident of horse and livestock maiming, and it was quite enough. The police, led by Inspector Campbell from Hednesford raided the vicarage, arriving about 7.45. But by then George Edalji had left for Birmingham. (One of the letters had said 'Mr Edalji is going to Brum . . . about how it's to be carried on with so many detectives about, and I believe they are going to do some cows in the daytime instead of at night.')

Mrs Edalji and her daughter were at breakfast. As soon as they saw the shadow of the police helmets against the coloured glass of the hall door they knew the worst.

Inspector Campbell explained what had happened, and that he wished to see her son's clothes, and any weapons in the house. She brought out his clothes, and they also found a pair of boots stained with black mud. As for a knife, all she could produce was a botany spud. A further search revealed a set of razors belonging to the vicar: they were wet, and one had a dark stain.

George's blue serge trousers were stained with mud along the lower edge. The police found an old house-coat on which were darkish stains – perhaps blood, and whitish stains – perhaps the saliva of the horse.

'This coat,' announced Inspector Campbell, 'is damp.'

The vicar, who had come downstairs by now, felt it. It was dry. There were also horse hairs on it, said Campbell. The vicar took it to the window. He could see none. It was spread out on the desk, and the officer drew his finger down it. That wasn't a hair, but a roving thread from the fabric, the family protested. Nevertheless Campbell was allowed to take the coat away.

Meanwhile, the unfortunate pony had been put out of its misery by the colliery horse-keeper, and a section of the hide removed from the side of the gash, and taken back to the police station. When the police surgeon, a local practitioner named Dr John Kerr Butter, examined the coat at 9 p.m. there were hairs on it.

He removed twenty-nine from the coat and five from the waistcoat: 'I compared the hairs which I took from the jacket and vest with hairs taken from the piece of hide, and found they were similar in length, colour and structure under the microscope . . .' He was less helpful on the matter the stains. That on the razor was rust, the white marks on the coat were starch, other spots were food stains. Two stains on the cuff 'contained blood corpuscles that conformed to the character of mammalian blood' but they were not fresh and might have come from the pony or from underdone meat.

The left boot was down at heel, and Campbell thought it fitted a mark in the field. But that mark was not recorded or measured properly, or preserved. (The police did not seem to share Sherlock Holmes' views on the vital importance of footprints.) The field had, in any case, been milled over all morning by a crowd of morbid sightseers, and little sense could be made of any tracks there. Campbell did not mention the track-mark until late in the trial.

At some time around 11 a.m. that day (18 August), George Edalji was arrested at his office in Birmingham. He was warned he need say nothing, but that anything he did say would be taken down and might be used in evidence.

'I'm not surprised at this,' he said on the way to the station. 'I have been expecting it for some time.' These words were taken note of and at his trial were thought to reveal a guilty conscience.

At the station he was asked to give an account of his movements on the previous evening and night. What he said was straightforward. He had been 'out for a walk'.

He had come back from the office as usual about 6.30 p.m. He did some work at home, then he walked along the main road to Mr Hand's the bootmaker at Bridgetown, getting there at a little after 8.30 p.m. He was then wearing his blue serge coat, which was confirmed by John Hand. As his supper would not be ready until 9.30 p.m., Edalji walked around for a while. It had rained during the day but was not raining at that time. This, as Doyle noted, accounted for the mud on his clothes. It was black mud, shot up from the road. The mud in the field where the pony had been attacked was a yellow clay.

He returned to the vicarage, had his supper and went to bed. He shared a room with his father (and had done for seventeen years). The Edaljis' daughter was sickly, and her mother slept in the room in case there was any crisis in the night. George did not leave his bedroom until twenty minutes to seven the following morning.

This was confirmed by his father. The night had been wild, wet, and windy, and he had been racked with pain from his lumbago and spent a restless night. Sleeping lightly, he would have known if his son had left the room, as the door was locked at night.

Next day and the following Monday a preliminary hearing was held before the local magistrates. The evidence was stated and the police made out their case against George Edalji. On 4 September he was committed for trial at Staffordshire Quarter Sessions.

'I won't have bail,' Edalji told Constable Meredith. 'And when the next horse is killed it will not be by me.' On 21 September a horse was attacked – by one of Edalji's friends from the 'Wyrley Gang', the police suggested.

The horse belonged to Harry Green, the son of a local farmer. It was valued at £3. The police interviewed Green and he signed a confession that he himself had killed the horse. A week or two later, having got a ticket to South Africa, Green withdrew his 'confession' and claimed it had been bullied out of him by the police.

Local anger boiled over after the arrest of Edalji. The police had to take him by cab through a jeering crowd to the court at Cannock. The crowd attacked the cab, and tore the door off its hinges.

The trial of George Edalji opened at the Staffordshire Quarter Sessions on 20 October 1903 before the Assistant Chairman, a judge of limited experience. More properly, a case of such seriousness should have been held not before the local justices but by a Judge of the Assizes. And now the prosecution had developed a new line of attack.

At the Magistrates Court the police suggested that the crime had been committed by Edalji while he was 'out for a walk' between 8.00 and 9.30. But this was not helpful to their case. Witnesses had seen him; the bootmaker gave positive testimony. Furthermore, the pony had been seen uninjured at 11.30 p.m. If it had been wounded at that time then it should have been dead and not just bleeding the next morning.

Now a new case was to be advanced. It was submitted that Edalji had slipped out of the house between two and three o'clock in the morning unseen by his father or the patrolling police. He had walked half a mile to the field across the railway, mutilated the pony and returned by a different, longer route through the fields.

Had the vicarage been watched? Not exactly, said Sergeant Charles Robinson, there had been six men on duty the previous night but on the night of the crime only a general order had been in force, and no special precautions were taken. (But whatever precautions the police had or had not taken about watching the house, those within would have known nothing about them.)

The evidence of the footprints made an impression on the jury, despite the lack of method in the way the police had dealt with them; they had, according to Inspector Campbell, been measured 'with straw and a stick'.

But the key evidence related to the anonymous letters. A handwriting expert, Mr Thomas Henry Gurrin, testified that he was of the opinion that George Edalji had written the letters accusing himself of the cattle maiming. (Mr Gurrin's record was at best lacklustre; he had featured in the 1896 case of Adolph Beck, where his testimony convicted Beck, who would be proved quite innocent in April 1904.*) Against this the defence made little headway. Thinking that the prosecution's case was patently ridiculous and would not stand up, Edalji's counsel had made few preparations, and had no experts on hand to call. The police had it all their own way and, as is often the case, they were believed *because* they were the police.

The jury found Edalji guilty; the judge having defended the justice of holding the trial at Cannock (where local feelings ran high) rather than London (where a more balanced view might have been taken), sentenced him to seven years' penal servitude. 'Lord have mercy on us!' cried his mother in shock from the body of the court.

The Assistant Chairman of the Quarter Sessions, consulted later by the Home Office, said he and his colleagues were of the opinion that the conviction was correct. Yet to John Cuming Walters, influential editor of the *Manchester City News*, it was obvious from the first that Edalji was to be convicted, even though not one atom of substantial evidence was produced against him. He thought the Staffordshire justices acted on the principle that it was 'better to hang the wrong f'ler than no f'ler'.

The Wyrley Ripper was behind bars. Admittedly there had been another incident while Edalji was awaiting trial and another in November, and a further letter. But the authorities were confident that these were only a distraction by the 'Wyrley Gang' to confuse matters.

(ii) Conan Doyle Fights On

This then was the situation at the beginning of 1907 when Doyle read Edalji's letter and the details of the case in the cuttings from

---

* Beck was Jewish and circumcised. But when his look-alike was detained he was not. This crucial distinction between the two men passed without notice, an example of the inadequacies of police procedure at the time.

the Birmingham paper, *The Umpire*. 'As I read, the unmistakable accent of truth fixed itself upon my attention and I realized that I was in the presence of an appalling tragedy and that I was called upon to do what I could to set it right.'

Edalji was not without friends. At the time of his convicion 10,000 people, including several hundred lawyers, had signed a petition to the Home Office. In May 1904 his father published the correspondence he had had with an indifferent Home Office. Mr R.D. Yelverton, the former Chief Justice of the Bahamas, had never ceased to argue the weakness of the case. More recently he had renewed his attack aided by Mr Voules, the editor of the radical paper *Truth*. This may have succeeded in convincing the Home Office to release Edalji in October 1906. But was he innocent or guilty? Still under police supervision, he could not work at his profession: he had been struck off the Solicitors Roll and now worked as a humble clerk. The very volume of protest seems to have ensured that the local authorities became even more firmly convinced of his guilt. In the current cant of our own day they thought Edalji was 'in denial'.

Conan Doyle arranged to meet Edalji early in January 1907 in London. The rendezvous was in the foyer of the Grand Hotel at Charing Cross. Doyle was late. As he arrived he recognized at once the coloured man who was his guest. Edalji was reading a newspaper to pass the time, holding it at an angle close to his face. Surprised, Doyle realized he must be *nearly blind*.

He introduced himself and asked 'Aren't you astigmatic?'

'Yes,' Edalji admitted. He had never worn glasses, as even the strongest lens could not alter what was basically a deformity of the eyeballs.

'Surely this was raised at your trial?'

Edalji had wanted to call an oculist, but his counsel felt the case against him was so 'ridiculous' it was not worth the trouble.

Thinking over all the evidence he had read, Doyle realized that it was impossible for this young man to have made his way anywhere in the dark. But he must check, and be sure. He sent Edalji to Mr Kenneth Scott, a leading eye specialist. Scott diagnosed that Edalji had eight dioptres of myopia, which was worse than Doyle, himself a trained ophthalmic doctor, had thought.

Conan Doyle had already been in touch with the Rev Shapurji Edalji, and he now made arrangements to visit Wyrley, to see for himself the vicarage and the scenes of the crimes. His sympathies were confirmed by what he saw there. 'What roused my indignation and gave me the driving force to carry the thing through was the utter helplessness of this forlorn little group of people – the coloured clergyman in his strange position, the brave, blue-eyed, grey-haired wife, the young daughter, baited by boors and having the police who should have been their natural protectors, adopting from the beginning the harshest tone towards them and accusing them, beyond all sense and reason, of being the cause of their own troubles and of persecuting and maligning themselves.'

Doyle at least visited the vicarage; this was more than the Chief Constance had ever done. He arrived for breakfast, and over that meal began to put together the background to the case, to hear just what lay behind the prosecution, indeed, persecution.

The Edaljis had married in June 1874. George had been born in 1876. Shapurji had taken over the parish from his wife's uncle, who had been vicar there for many years. 'He was,' wrote John Cuming Walters of the *Manchester City News*, 'in a queer little colliery villager on the borders of Cannock Chase, the residents in which were mainly groups of old families who had nothing to do with neighbouring communities. Most of the men were miners, but there was a gipsy band also in the locality. A queer aloof district in all respects.' Edalji, 'a patriarchal gentleman' Walters adds, and his wife were noted for their kindliness of heart and their charity. They had lived peacefully at Wyrley from 1876 until 1888. That year there had been an outbreak of obscene graffiti scribbled up on the walls around the village attacking the family. A former maid, who they had been compelled to dismiss for an offence, was questioned about these libels, but she was not charged because of lack of evidence.

The girl left Great Wyrley, but more messages, in a different hand, began to appear. These came as notes thrown through the windows. In the local shops tradesmen received fake orders from the Edaljis.

The worst period was between 1892 and 1895. Controversial letters began appearing in the county papers above Shapurji Edalji's name which he had not sent. Other letters were sent to individuals outside the village, including one to the headmaster of Walsall Grammar School. The letters made a particular target of the Rev Shapurji, his wife, son and daughter. Then there were the practical jokes.

Bogus advertisements were inserted signed by the vicar. Postcards were sent to other clergymen; in Essex one received a card simply signed 'S. Edalji'.

> Unless you apologise at once and by telegram for the outrageous hints you give in your sermons concerning my Chastity, I shall expose your adultery and rape.

Rubbish was scattered across the vicarage lawn; once a large key was left on the doorstep of the house: it had been stolen from the Walsall Grammar School. The Chief Constable of Staffordshire, Captain the Hon. George Alexander Anson, accused George of having stolen it. The police formed the fixed idea that the problem had its origins inside the vicarage – and that George was responsible. Anson was convinced that the young man would end up in prison.

The vicar was driven to share the details of his persecution with a wider public, writing to *The Times* and other national newspapers in August 1895. Though it may well be the key document in a series of crimes that continued in the Wyrley area down to 1934, this letter has not, I think, been reproduced before.

A STRANGE HOAX

TO THE EDITOR OF *THE TIMES*.

Sir, Some unknown person has sent for the last three years, and still continues to send, a large number of letters and postcards in my name to clergymen, solicitors, detectives, managers of newspapers, and tradesmen generally asking them to do a number of things for me. He has forged my signature, and his handwriting and style of composition are such as to make one believe that his communications must be genuine. Clergymen are asked to come and take funerals for me or visit some dying person, who, it is alleged, is wishing to see them. Solicitors are informed that if they called here without delay they should have some valuable information from me. Detectives are asked to call here, when they would be commissioned by me to undertake some secret and delicate business. Managers of newspapers all over the country are requested to insert in their papers notices of births, marriages, and other matters for which there is no foundation whatever. Tradesmen of almost every description are requested to send to my house wines, spirits, medicines, books, furniture, clothes, musical instruments, and a host of other things. In numerous cases the requests contained in these fictitious communications have been complied with; the people to whom they were addressed have either called personally or sent the things asked for. They have thereby been put to a great deal of unnecessary trouble and expense. The person who is engaged in this evil business seems to have no regard for the time, convenience, or interest of any one. All he seems to care for is to gratify his own desire for fun or revenge.

110

I beg leave, therefore, to caution all persons against accepting, without inquiry, any letters or postcards which may come to them with my name and address. As such forged communications are sent every now and then by the forger to all parts of the United Kingdom, including Ireland, the editors of all the papers in the country would confer a favour not only upon myself but upon the public at large if they would reproduce this letter in their columns, or in some other way caution their readers against the frauds.

I am, Sir, your obedient servant,

S. EDALJI, Vicar of Great Wyrley.

Great Wyrley Vicarage, Walsall, Aug. 14

These extraordinary hoaxes went on for three years. The police were convinced that the culprit was young George Edalji. This was absurd, said his father, for he had been with them when letters had been shoved under the door.

But Captain Anson, a brother of Lord Lichfield, the major landowner in the county, a family connected with the highest in the land, including royalty, was quite adamant. He was a man who believed strongly in the value of his own opinions; and in later years liked to share them with the wider world. He did not care much for 'Black Men'. About the key – young George was at school in Rugeley and did not attend the Grammar School – Anson wrote: 'I may say at once that I shall not pretend to believe any protestations of ignorance which your son may make about the key.' Later he added he hoped to get the culprit 'a dose of penal servitude'.

In December 1895 there appeared a bogus advertisement in a Blackpool newspaper, signed 'S. Edalji'. And then nothing. Silence, calm and serenity returned to Wyrley. For seven years

111

there was peace, until February 1903, when the cattle maiming began.

This was an appalling history, which had not been revealed at the trial, and which put the police attitude and the current livestock rippings into a very different perspective. For nearly two decades the little family had been at the centre of cruel crimes the police had done little or nothing to clear up.

From the vicarage, Doyle set out to explore the supposed route. To get from the house to the scene of the last mutilation at the colliery, he had to cross the full breadth of the London and Northwestern Railway, an expanse of rails, wires and other hazards, with thick hedges to be forced apart on either side. 'I, a strong and active man, in broad daylight, found it a hard matter to pass.' On the route from the vicarage a steep, dark and dirty flight of steps and a tunnel would also need to be negotiated.

As for the fields, could an almost blind youth have found his way around an area with which he was not familiar? And Edalji tackling a horse; the suggestion was ludicrous.

On his return to London Doyle wrote up the case in a series of articles which he negotiated with *The Daily Telegraph* to publish free of copyright. They were widely reported in many papers, even in America, and were later published in pamphlet form. The articles caused an immediate sensation.

Others had argued for Edalji, but this was Conan Doyle, the creator of Sherlock Holmes; Conan Doyle, the national hero. The Home Office was forced to listen.

He went through the evidence against Edalji, relentlessly demolishing the police case, spotlighting the abundant racial prejudice which the case revealed. Perhaps the ill-educated villagers might be excused, but there was nothing to mitigate the attitude of Captain the Hon. George Anson; his prejudice had infected the whole police force.

This was an English Dreyfus case. Both the French soldier and Edalji were rising young men in professions, ruined by handwritten evidence, the one a Jew, the other a Parsee. The Dreyfus case had caused an outcry in France. Now what did England say about the Edalji case?

Also there was the attitude of the Home Office to be explained. Mr Yelverton had presented his evidence, and what did they do? Evidently they were shaken, and they compromised. After three years of imprisonment they let Edalji go. Who had decided that he was free man but a guilty one? This demanded an answer.

> But the door is shut in our faces. Now we turn to the last tribunal of all, a tribunal which never errs when the facts are laid before them, and we ask the public of Great Britain whether this then is to go on.

The controversy was instant and immense. Conan Doyle secured the support of Churton Collins, his friend from the Crimes Club, who aroused Birmingham University. And the Rt. Hon. Sir George Cornewall Lewis, the most eminent solicitor of the day, a man involved in countless celebrated cases of the Victorian era, came to the aid of Edalji, using his discreet influence 'behind closed doors'.

The Home Office, it seemed, did not care to explain – do bureaucrats anywhere ever care to justify their actions? – but the Home Secretary, Mr Herbert Gladstone (son of the late Prime Minister), did agree the case would be re-examined. There was no Court of Appeal in those days. With no machinery existing for a retrial, instead he elected to appoint a committee.

Conan Doyle was delighted. He believed he was on the trail of the real culprit and would soon have the evidence. The committee consisted of Sir Arthur Wilson, the Rt. Hon. John Lloyd Wharton, and Sir Albert De Rutzen (a relative of Anson's, by the way). They delivered their report in May 1907.

113

They could not concur with the verdict of the jury. George Edalji, they decided, had been wrongly convicted. On the other hand, with what appears to be a desperate attempt to save face, they insisted Edalji had written the letters. 'Assuming him to be an innocent man,' the committee concluded, 'he has to some extent brought his troubles on himself.' In others words, as John Walters observed at the time, Edalji was 'probably' guilty of something else for which he had not been tried; so he was graciously granted a free pardon for what he done, and deprived of compensation for 'probably' doing the other thing of which he had not been convicted. He had served three years for nothing and was now told he deserved no sympathy. They had, however, to admit that the police investigation was focused not on investigating the case, but on gathering 'evidence' against Edalji, of whose guilt they were already convinced. All of which was contrary to the principles of British justice.

George Edalji was granted a pardon, but denied any official compensation for his three years in gaol. In contrast Captain Anson was in 1907 made a member of the Royal Victorian Order, an order of knighthood in the gift of the king and government. What better way of showing what the highest in the land felt about the Edalji case.

This compromise caused further contention. The Law Society, influenced by Sir George Lewis, restored Edalji to the Solicitors Roll. *The Daily Telegraph* raised a subscription of £300 for him – he used the money to repay an aunt who had covered the cost of his defence.

Conan Doyle stormed the Home Office. But the verdict was final and the officials referred him to the report. Doyle could not consider it final. Justice was not seen to be done. Another article followed for *The Daily Telegraph*: 'Who Wrote the Letters?' The answer to his own question was the result of assiduous detective work between January and August 1907.

(iii) The Real Culprit?

'So far,' Conan Doyle later wrote, 'my work had been satisfactory. Where I caused myself great trouble was that in my local exploration at Wyrley I had come across what seemed to me a very direct clue as to both the writer – or rather writers – of the letters, and also of the identity of the mutilator – though the latter word may also have been in the plural.'

'I became interested, the more so as the facts were very complex and I had to do with people who were insane as well as criminal.'

Then Doyle began to get letters – a fact which left the Home Office still convinced that Edalji was the author of them all; Conan Doyle began to think the bureaucrats insane. Those letters put him on the trail of the culprit, but before the evidence was complete he brought what he had learned to the attention of the police and the Home Office, to emphasize how much he needed their goodwill and co-operation. This he did not get. Quite the contrary.

Doyle's detective work had been demanding. On 27 January 1907 he wrote to his mother: 'All my energies have gone towards the capture and exposure of the real offenders. These are three youths (one already dead), brothers by the name of Sharp. The case I have against them is already very strong but I have five separate lines of enquiry on foot, by which I hope to make it overwhelming. They are decently educated men as is evident from the letters.'

How he had traced them was a Sherlockian adventure in itself.

One of the letters Conan Doyle received contained a sneering reference to the Headmaster of Walsall Grammar School: '. . . you blasted fool don't you know he was at school with that blasted Greatorex lads Will and Anthony and he hated them like poison. There was no education to be got at Walsall when that bloody swine Aldis was high school. He got the bullet after the governors were sent letters about him. Ha, ha.'

The name of Edalji surfaced again and again.

'The proof of what I tell you is in the writing he put in the papers when they loosed him out of prison where he ought to have been kept along with his dad and all black and yellow faced Jews . . . Nobody could copy his writing like that, you blasted fool.'

Doyle collected these obscene missives eagerly. Certainly their author was insane, a suitable case for treatment. But each specimen added to the dossier of evidence going back more than a decade.

'On the evidence of the handwriting,' he later wrote 'I have come to one conclusion. I contend that the anonymous letters of 1892 to 1895 were the work of two persons: one a decently educated man, the other a foul-mouthed semi-literate boy. I contend that the anonymous letters of 1903 were nearly all written by that same foul-mouthed boy, then grown into a man in his twenties. On further evidence I contend that Foulmouth not only wrote the letters, but did the mutilations.

'But to say this is to put the end at the beginning. Let us go back. Let us take the facts in the Wyrley mystery as they are presented to us, and see what inferences we can draw from them.

'At the beginning, one point is so obvious that I wonder it has escaped notice. This is the extraordinary long gap between the two sets of letters. Letters, childish hoaxes, abound up to the late December of '95. Then, for nearly seven years, nobody gets an abusive letter. To me this did not suggest that the culprit had changed his whole character and habits overnight, reverting to them with equal malice in 1903. It suggested absence; that someone had been away during that period.

'Away – where? Look at the very first letter in the outburst of 1903. In it the writer makes no less than three glowing allusions to the sea. He recommends an apprentice's life at sea [see passage on page 98]; his mind is full of it. Taken in conjunction with the long absence, may we suppose that he had gone to sea and recently returned?

116

'Note, too, that the final hoax against the Edaljis in '95 is a bogus advertisement in a Blackpool paper. This is perhaps a coincidence; anyone may go to Blackpool for a holiday; but it is also the pleasure-resort of Liverpool – a sea port.

'Suppose, for the sake of argument, we take this line on a working hypothesis. Where are we to look first for traces of this hypothetical person? Surely in the records of Walsall Grammar School!

'Walsall Grammar School, clearly, is the connecting link between the two sets of letters. In Group A, a scurrilous message is sent to the headmaster of that time. A large key, stolen from Walsall Grammar School is left on the Edaljis' doorstep. In Group B, the false signature on the letters is actually that of a pupil at Walsall. I, myself, in 1907, received a letter which breaks out into irrelevant ravings against the headmaster of fifteen years ago.

'My first step in the enquiry lay at Walsall. I must enquire whether there had been at the school, during the early nineties, a boy who (a) had a particular grudge against the headmaster, (b) was innately vicious, and (c) subsequently went to sea? I took this obvious step. And I got on the track of my man at once.'

On his visit to Walsall Doyle talked to Mr J.A. Aldis, the former headmaster. At once a name was thrown up.

At Walsall Grammar School, from 1890 to 1892, there had been a boy named Royden Sharp. His school record, as sent to Conan Doyle by Mr Aldis, was a bad one:

Xmas 1890. Lower I. Order 23rd out of 23. Very backward and weak.

Easter 1891. Lower I. Order 20th out of 20. Dull, homework neglected.

Midsummer 1891. Lower I. Order 18th out of 18. Caned for misbehaviour in class; tobacco chewing and prevarication and nicknaming . . .

Xmas 1891. Lower I Order 16th out of 16. Unsatisfactory, often untruthful; always complaining or being complained of. Detected cheating and frequently absent without leave.
Easter 1892. Idle and mischievous, caned daily, falsified schoolfellows marks and lied about it. Midsummer 1892. Played truant; forged letter and initials; removed by father.

Doyle now had a name and an inkling of the character that went with it. Royden, he learned, had a taste for knives, for ripping up cushions in the train to school so that the horsehair spilled out. His father had had to pay compensation more than once for straps which he had cut off the carriage windows. At Walsall there was one boy, Fred Brookes, with whom Royden Sharp had a bitter feud. The Brookes family (like the Edaljis) were the victims of hate mail between 1892 and 1895.

After he was taken away from school, Royden Sharp was apprenticed to a butcher, where he learned to kill and cut up animals.

Still he proved troublesome. At the end of 1895 he was sent to sea as an apprentice. The ship sailed from Liverpool – a fact which Doyle later confirmed. Early in 1903 Sharp came back from the sea, for good, and was living with his family at Wyrley during that year of attacks on cattle and horses.

Doyle later ascertained that for ten months in 1902 Sharp had served on a cattle boat on the Irish trade. He knew how to approach and handle animals: a vital talent, Doyle pointed out, for the cattle slasher. 'Compare this man with the studious and purblind Edalji'. And it was the cattle boat that provided a vital clue.

The name Greatorex had also surfaced in the letters. From this family Doyle obtained a sample of Royden Sharp's writing, a letter written to young Greatorex in 1901.

Moreover, Mrs Greatorex recalled visiting the Sharp house,

which faced out over the fields, in July 1903. She and her husband were old friends of the family. At that date the cattle-slashing craze was at its height.

Mrs Greatorex was talking to Royden Sharp about the incidents. He grew gleefully confident. From a cupboard he produced a large horse-lancet and showed it to her.

'Look,' he gloated, 'this is what they kill cattle with.'

Mrs Greatorex was shocked, and slightly sickened 'Put it away,' she said, adding: 'You don't want me to think you're the man, do you?'

This horse lancet came into the possession of Conan Doyle – how he never explained, but readers of Sherlock Holmes can well imagine some clever ruse, probably by one of the Greatorex family, to get it.

In his dossier, later submitted to the Home Office, Doyle explained the curious features of this instrument.

'Now the wounds in all the outrages up to August 18th were of a very peculiar character. In every case there was a shallow incision; it had cut through skin and muscles, but had not penetrated the gut. Had any ordinary cutting-weapon been used, it must certainly in some instances have penetrated far enough to pierce the cut with its point or edge. Note that the blade of the horse-lancet is like this:

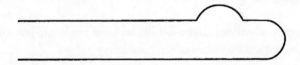

'It is very sharp. Yet it could never penetrate more than superficially. I submit this very large horse-lancet, obtained by Royden Sharp from the cattle boat as being the only kind of instrument which could have committed all the crimes.'

More details came to hand. Conan Doyle could show that John

Sharp, the elder brother had collaborated in the letters of 1892–95, and that the Edalji family had long been the focus of their dislike. One other brother was now dead, but John Sharp had become an architect and had emigrated to California. And from California Doyle now began to receive hate mail; the letters came from the town where John Sharp lived. He wrote and asked the police to investigate. There was a John Sharp, but not his John Sharp; the letters were the work of a crank in the same boarding house. Doyle had to accept this, though only half-convinced.

Among the many threatening letters and cards Doyle received here are extracts from two in May 1907.

'. . . Desperate men have sworn their Bible oath to scoop out your liver and kidneys . . . and there are those who say you have not long to live. I know from a detective of Scotland Yard that if you write to Gladstone and say you find Edalji is guilty after all, and you were mistaken and promise to do no more for him, they will make you a lord next year. Is it not better to be a lord than to run the risk of loosing kidneys and liver? Think of all the ghoulish murders that are committed. Why then should you escape? . . . I have given you the tip . . . May you live for ever and those devils not cut your tongue or tonsils out . . .'

And again, on 27 May 1907:

'I hope you will not have a deathly accident but live to learn the truth, but I won't answer for your safety a day . . .'

In January, fresh from Wyrley, Doyle had written that he had five lines of inquiry in hand. They slowly closed around Royden Sharp and his brothers. From the Greatorex family he had examples of the Sharps' handwriting, both of John, the architect, and Royden, the Foulmouth. While he continued to crusade in the press through June and August, Doyle asked Dr Lindsay Johnson to examine them. Johnson had been called by the defence in the Dreyfus affair and had an international standing in the field. Johnson's method was to enlarge the writing on a screen, so that the minutest of characteristics stood out; even the pulse rate could be measured. From the evidence of the text, and from Johnson's analysis, he showed that Royden Sharp was the principal author, and his brother the secondary author.

Conan Doyle drew up a report: 'The case against Royden Sharp for the committing of the outrages upon cattle from February to August 1903, for which George Edalji was condemned to seven years penal servitude at Stafford Assizes November 1903'.

'This seems to me,' he concluded, 'to be a complete case and if I – a stranger in the district – have been able to collect it, I cannot doubt that fresh evidence would come out after his arrest. He appears to have taken little pains to hide his proceedings and how there could at any time have been any difficulty in pointing him out as the criminal is to me an extraordinary thing.'

But Doyle had not counted on the almost universal reluctance of the police authorities to admit they have got the wrong man. Doyle submitted his report to the Home Office, and the Home Office consulted the Staffordshire Police – that is to say Captain the Hon. George Anson. Having taken Anson's advice, they naturally rejected Doyle's report.

'It will hardly be believed,' he wrote years later, 'that after I had laid these facts before the Home Office they managed to present the House of Commons with an official legal opinion that there was not a prima facie case while a high official of the Government [Herbert Gladstone] said to me: I see no more evidence against these two brothers than against myself and my brother. The points I mention are taken from the paper I laid before the Law Officers of the Crown, which lies before me as I write, so the facts are exactly as stated.

'I had one letter in sorrow and also in anger from the Stafford-shire police complaining that I should not have libelled this poor innocent young man whose identity could easily be established. I do not know what has become of Sharp or how often he has been convicted since, but on the last occasion of which I have notes the magistrate said, in condemning him to six months imprisonment, his character was extremely bad, he having been convicted of arson, of stealing on three occasions, and of damage. On his own confession he had committed a deliberate and cruel theft from his aged mother and it was impossible to overlook the seriousness of the case. So much for the inoffensive youth whom I had libelled.'

That was in 1924. Royden Sharp, I understand, died a few years later; he was certainly dead by 1933. During his lifetime Conan Doyle never named Royden Sharp in public. But in a pamphlet published in 1914, Captain Sir George did, in order to defend the defamed young man! J.D. Carr, Conan Doyle's first biographer, like Doyle, had never seen Anson's admission, and so he used the pseudonym 'Peter Hudson' in his book. In 1964 Pierre Nordon named him from Conan Doyle's notes on the case, making the identity of the culprit completely public. Sharp's name was repeated in a play by the poet Roger Woddis about the case presented locally at the Victoria Theatre, Stoke-on-Trent in 1971.

And George Edalji? He received no compensation for his three years in gaol. On 25 November 1907 his name was restored to the Solicitors Roll by Order of the Master of the Rolls. He moved to London and from 1907 to 1941 practised in Borough High Street, and from 1941 to 1953 in and around Argyle Square, W.C.

George E.T. Edalji died on 17 June 1953, aged 85, at Welwyn Garden City, Hertfordshire, where he lived with his unmarried sister Maud, who died a decade later.

The behaviour of the local police in the Edalji case leaves a sour taste in the mouth even today. That they found support in the Home Office and the Courts is only to be expected: it is what invariably characterizes a miscarriage of justice. But George Edalji was luckier than some in that he got his measure of final justice, and thanks to Conan Doyle his innocence was established and his name cleared.

That, however, is not how things are seen by some in Staffordshire. A local historian, Mr Michael Harley of Walsall, surprised me during my research by claiming that he hoped to prove that Edalji was guilty. He is firmly convinced that the police, in their wisdom, had got the right man. He feels that Conan Doyle's kind heart led him astray, and that the supple George Edalji fooled him.

According to Michael Harley, many strange rumours about Edalji circulated in 1903, though they were never part of the evidence offered against him in court. Though it was claimed by his friends that he led an exemplary life, neither drinking nor smoking, Edalji did gamble, according to local report. He was short of money, had written begging letters, and the cattle slashings arose from a bet that he could 'do up' so many animals in a year.

Michael Harley has brought a sharp eye to bear on the vicarage and its life. He believes that the family closed ranks in support of George, and to deceive Conan Doyle. All, that is, except the mysterious elder brother Horace, who left home earlier, and was ashamed of what later happened at the vicarage.

Can this be true? I doubt it. The rumours about Edalji must have originated with the police. There is no evidence of an objective kind to support or document the claims. There is really no answer to Conan Doyle's case that Edalji was too blind to kill and maim animals in the dark, nor does any theory about his gambling, his bets with locals, or his need for money, explain any of the evidence relating to the earlier obscene letters and the practical jokes, and the fact that the slashings went on long after he had gone to live in London, until 1914 in fact. If there is a case to be made, Mr Harley will have many incredulous people to convince when he publishes his evidence, not all of which he has shared with me. Though his book was announced for publication in London in 1992, it has not yet appeared. Another local writer, Paul Lester, has supported this case against Edalji in part.

Richard Whittington-Egan, who is perhaps one of the most distinguished living historians of crime in Britain, in 1985 edited Conan Doyle's articles and letters on the Edalji affair. He is not wholly convinced by Conan Doyle's theories about the case. He accepts that Edalji is innocent, but that to the local people he may well have appeared as some kind of bogey-man.

> And yet they knew that their bogey-man was a sober solicitor. Presumably they did not recoil from the darker visage of his father, Shapurji, returning from some pastoral mission. But Captain Anson was no rustic simpleton. His fixed belief in the guilt of the parson's son must have had some solid bedrock. Something more than wildfire gossip and calumny. This vital *ratio* Conan Doyle failed to elicit from Anson, and his defence case was consequently tainted from start to finish by areas of ambiguity. Although it was not Conan Doyle's finest hour, yet he was never seen in a more noble light, fighting and suffering, not infallible, but unimpeachable and adamant in his cause.

This surely is ill-founded. To have raised an ambiguity about the case was to raise a doubt which should have favoured Edalji. And why, if something serious was known about the young man, was it not brought forward at his trial, if, as is suggested, it underlay the police case against him?

There is in fact an element in the Edalji case which has never been revealed until now. Some light on why the Chief Constable and the police were so convinced about George Edalji's guilt – the vital *ratio*, so to speak – is thrown by a private memo written by Herbert Gladstone (now among his papers in the British Library), which he wrote out on the evening of 6 June 1907.

Secret

Tonight at dinner I met Mr Hazell – MP West Bromwich. Confidentially he told me that he was with Mr Vachell in the Edalji case. Both he and V. were convinced that E. wrote two letters. When the trial was on, a member of the E. family – he thinks it was G.E's brother – brought them a letter which had been found in one of G.E.'s drawers. It was brought as a specimen of G.E.'s handwriting and the idea was that an expert should be called to show it was different to the anon, letters – it was actually brought as G.E.'s own writing.

The letter was a long one of several pages. It contained several scraps of paper atrocious in character.

The letter was addressed to the servant maid at the Vicarage. It was full of things unmentionable. It told her to put the scraps under the doormats and about the house. On the scraps were abusive remarks – 'Curse Edalji' – and so forth. The letter was not posted. Vachell and he decided to suppress the letter as most damaging to the case. It would seem that by accident the letter was left in the drawer. Mr H[azell] told me that when he met Vachell in Jan (or Feb?) when Martin Moulton letters were known to have begun, V. said to him 'he is at it again' – meaning G.E.

Gladstone finally noted 'Hazell said that nothing could have been worse than the content', yet he thought that the prosecution 'ought not to have had a conviction on the evidence'.

This letter, it must be observed at once, came into the hands of Edalji's lawyers from Horace Edalji, the mysterious brother, and its connection with George Edalji was never proved.

If Horace was willing to compromise George in this way with his own lawyers, it is almost certain that he would also have passed material to the police, material which they might have been able to use as 'background' on Edalji but not produce in court. Hence the Chief Constable's strange certainty about George Edalji's guilt.

If Royden Sharp was actually responsible for the slashings – as now seems reasonably certain, was Horace Edalji also involved? Was he in fact one of the letter writers of the late 1890s? And when the police came making inquiries did he connive at framing George to protect himself? That Horace later moved away from home and changed his name suggests strongly that he had some guilty secret.

Never in the course of the inquiries, as Conan Doyle noted, did Captain Anson himself come to the vicarage to see the vicar and his family. The reason is now clear. The source of his 'information' was the local inspector, Mr Campbell, but Anson could not face the vicar without the danger of blurting out in conversation what he had been told about what had come into the hands of the police from Horace Edalji.

The disclosure of this secret memo casts an even more terrible light on the Great Wyrley affair. George Edalji was prosecuted, indeed persecuted, by the police on the basis of evidence given in secret by a witness with whom he was never faced. This is contrary to the Common Law of England and the dictates of natural justice. Conan Doyle was right. The Edalji case still demands a resolution.

Horace Edalji became a civil servant, working as a tax inspector in Scotland. He married Anne Gertrude Magee, an Ulster woman, at Hereford in 1910. Adopting her name he moved as Horace Edward Magee to Belfast, and later to Dublin, where he lived in the prosperous suburb of Blackrock. After changing his name he broke completely with his family. He died in a Dublin nursing home in 1953.

In the end Horace took the real secret of Great Wyrley vicarage to his grave. But for Conan Doyle his brother George might never have had justice.

When Maud Edalji died she left in her will 'all my papers connected with the case of my brother George E. T. Edalji who was falsely accused of horsemaiming in 1903' to the Law Society. They are some of the key collections relating to the case, but seem never to have been consulted by previous writers on the case. I am informed by the Law Society librarian that they cannot now be found. It is a mystery whether they were ever received; though Sir Compton Mackenzie claimed an official of the Law Society destroyed them to protect the reputations of some of the lawyers involved.

Contrary to the feelings of some, and the controversy that continues about the case, the Edalji affair *was* Conan Doyle's finest hour as a detective.

Quite how right he was became clear in the decades after George Edalji was restored to respectability. He never came to the notice of the police again, in contrast, as Conan Doyle pointed out, with the later career of Royden Sharp. Recent writers such as Michael Harley and Paul Lester have drawn upon the previously secret Home Office files, but these merely enlarge upon the official case made at the time. Local investigations have turned up little in the way of real evidence against George Edalji relevant to charge of letter writing or animal maiming.

John Walters summarized the matter very effectively in 1933:

(1) The letters signed 'Greatorex' were written, probably out of personal spite, to annoy the Edalji family.

(2) They could not have been written by a member of the family, as their only effect was to cause pain to that household.

(3) The maiming outrages were the work of a culprit, or culprits, who had no connection with the 'Greatorex' letter-writer.

(4) The police, impotent and exasperated, wrongly connected the two widely different events; the cattle-maimers, to avert suspicion, encouraged the false idea.

(5) George Edalji, being suspected of writing the 'Greatorex' letters, was now suspected of being the mutilator of cattle; the police looked no further, local prejudices prevailed, and the miscarriage of justice ensued.

Though George had removed himself to London, the maimings and poison-pen letters continued. Not for weeks or months, but for years. There were cases in August 1907, and October 1908. A young butcher named Hollis Morgan, originally from Great Wyrley, was arrested but the case was dropped. There were six more outrages in August 1912. Anson refused to connect these with the Edalji crimes. There were yet more maimings in July 1913 near Walsall, and two cases at Wednesbury. The Great War came and went; the maimings ended but the letters continued. Even after George's father, who had remained on as vicar at Great Wyrely, died in May 1918, the slashings did not end.

The letter-writer had announced he was retiring for the duration of the war in 1914. But in September 1919 he wrote again claiming he would be back at work. These years represent an aspect of the conditions at Wyrley which many writers, some local, prefer to avoid.*

As we have seen, George Edalji had been exonerated of the maimings, but the Home Office committee thought that he had been responsible for the letters, and so had brought his troubles on his own head. This was as much as they could do to preserve the dignity of the Chief Constable.

* It should not be overlooked that the animal slashings in Staffordshire were not, as some seem to think, unique. A correspondent in the letters column of *The Daily Telegraph* claimed they were the commonplace work of bored rural thugs. They are akin perhaps to the bestiality that city people so often ascribe to backward folk in rural places. Charles Fort and others have collected unexplained records of strange attacks in England dating back to as early as 1810, when sheep in Ennerdale on the Borders were attacked. In 1874 there were attacks in Ireland, around Cavan and elsewhere. Nearer to Edalji's period: in 1904 at Newcastle, Hexham, Falkirk, Tyneside, Tunbridge Wells, Sevenoaks, and in 1905 near Badminton, Hinton and Gravesend; in 1906 around Royal Windsor Park, and in 1925 at Edale in Derbyshire. Some of these were thought to be by animals, such as a set of Canadian sleigh dogs that escaped in Liverpool! Others may well have been by sexual perverts. More recently strange attacks on animals have been recorded across the Americas. What made the Edalji case unique was the combination of the maimings and letters.

But after George was long gone from the district, never again to come to the attention of the place, Royden Sharp continued his career as a troubled and troubling young man, as Conan Doyle pointed out. The letters, and indeed the maimings, continued. These were claimed to be the work of the Wyrely Gang, led by someone who called himself 'G. H. Darby'. These activities were dealt with in a 1914 pamphlet to which Conan Doyle and Anson contributed. Anson insisted that they had nothing to do with the Edalji series. Doyle agreed because the earlier series had nothing to do with Edalji. Eventually the maimings ended, but poison-pen letters continued, and the police made better efforts to investigate.

Finally at long, long last, in November 1934 a local man was convicted.

Enoch Knowles, 57, a Darlaston labourer, was sentenced at the Stafford Assizes to three years' penal servitude for sending menacing and obscene letters through the post.

There were several charges against Knowles in relation to letters to women, the letters usually being dispatched after they had given evidence in the Courts. They contained threats to kill and were 'filthy in tone'.

Mr A.J. Long, who prosecuted, said that a judge and a journalist, among others, had been threatened with violence, and in one case, when writing to a woman, Knowles described himself as 'Jack the Ripper of Whitechapel'. The police lawyer then continued:

The case had now let light on some things that had worried the authorities in the country for some years. In 1903, when Knowles was only 26 years of age, there was a case at the Quarter Sessions at Stafford of a man tried for maiming horses at Great Wyrley. The case attracted wide interest. The accused man was sentenced to seven years' penal servitude, but later was granted a pardon. I am not suggesting that the Home Secretary was affected in any way by the letters Knowles wrote.

Following that case, long continued, all sorts of people who had been connected with the case got letters, and the letters indicated that in spite of the conviction the maiming would go on. Letters were received giving the times and places where maiming would take place. Most of the letters purported to come from a person who signed himself 'Darby, Captain of the Wyrley Gang'.

Knowles had gone into the army in 1916. After the war ended he got married in 1919. Matters were all quiet for over a decade. But then in 1931 he got involved in a county court action, and he apparently was overcome by his 'curious desire' again, sending letters to a bailiff who had been involved in his case.

Later he wrote to people on matters that had nothing to do with him at all. On one occasion he wrote a very cruel letter to a member of the Royal Family. The police and the Post Office authorities had been for years trying to find out who was writing these letters. Knowles's guilt was eventually established when a postcard from him to some relatives was compared, in the post office, with the obscene communications.

For the defence it was submitted that Knowles, who pleaded guilty, had written the letters at times when he had been worried or not in the best of health. In passing sentence the judge said he took into account Knowles's age and previous good character. What did not emerge in court was the full connection of Knowles with the events going back to 1903 and earlier. Was he, with Royden Sharp, a member of the slashing gang or gangs? Certainly there were copy-cat slashings, but there was also a strong continuity. Are we to take from the lawyer's mealy-mouthed account of the Edalji case that in 1907, at the time when the local police and the Home Office were insisting that Edalji wrote the letters, they were aware that another poison-pen was at work?

Edalji responded to this conviction with an article in the London *Daily Express*, a national paper friendly to Conan Doyle. With all his distinguished supporters dead, there was no renewal of his claim for compensation. But with the conviction of a man for obscene letter-writing over the years since 1903 the final rotten prop supporting the official case fell away.

Those writers who still claim that in some way Edalji was guilty are motivated by a distorted sense of local patriotism. The case they make, based largely on recently released official files, is merely a restatement of what was said at the time of the original scandal. We have heard it all before. Nothing new that shows the guilt of Edalji of any crime has been produced.

They should remember John Cuming Walter's description of Great Wyrley as 'a queer and aloof district'; and bear in mind the Holmesian dictum quoted at the head of this chapter: 'It is my belief, Watson, founded upon my experience, that the lowest and vilest alleys of London do not present a more dreadful record of sin than does the smiling and beautiful countryside.'

Conan Doyle had been a doctor in several country districts with scattered with charming homesteads. He knew what he was talking about. 'But the reason is very obvious,' as Holmes explains to Watson.

'The pressure of public opinion can do in the town what the law cannot accomplish. There is no lane so vile that the scream of a tortured child, or the thud of a drunkard's blow, does not beget sympathy and indignation among the neighbours, and then the whole machinery of justice is ever so close that a word of complaint can set it going, and there is but a step between the crime and the dock.

131

'But look at these lonely houses, each in its own fields, filled for the most part with poor ignorant folk who know little of the law. Think of the deeds of hellish cruelty, the hidden wickedness which may go on, year in, year out, in such places, and none the wiser.'

CHAPTER TEN

STOLEN: THE IRISH CROWN JEWELS

The detectives might well say that it is an affair for a Sherlock
Holmes to investigate.

> Sir Arthur Vicars, in an interview published by
> the Dublin *Daily Express,* 15 July 1907

Conan Doyle's mother had always had an immense interest in the
history of her family and of the Doyles in Ireland. In sorting this
out, she had appealed for help to the Chief Herald of Ireland, Sir
Bernard Burke. He was succeeded in 1892 by her second cousin,
Sir Arthur Vicars, Ulster King of Arms, who also was a leading
authority on the genealogy and history of Irish families. From the
resources of his ancient office in Dublin Castle, the oldest government department in the country, he provided the Doyles with a
detailed family tree, for which they were very grateful.

So it was with great distress that Conan Doyle read in the papers
early in July 1907 that Sir Arthur's office in the Bedford Tower in
Dublin Castle had been robbed, and the Irish Crown Jewels which
were in his keeping removed from the safe by means of a copied
key. The robbery had taken place on the eve of a state visit by
Edward VII and caused a sensation throughout Europe. The
jewels, it should be explained, were part of the regalia of the
knightly Order of St Patrick, having been presented to the knights

by William IV in 1830. The motto of the Order, founded in 1783, was *Quis Seperabit* – 'Who would Separate' – a regal symbol of the union between Ireland and Great Britain, a union which many in Ireland were dedicated to breaking. Was the robbery an ordinary crime, or had it a political motive?

Conan Doyle wrote at once to his cousin, asking if he could give any advice. There is a suggestion in *The Leprachaun*, a Dublin satirical paper of the day, that Conan Doyle may have gone to Dublin in person, though there is no evidence of this elsewhere. Indeed, he protested to one correspondent at the publication in the press of 'the Statement that I had volunteered to investigate the Dublin Castle [robbery]'. He was afraid that such a report 'might hamper my efforts in the Edalji Case by giving the impression that I was a universal busybody'.

And indeed suggestions to the effect in other papers were denied. Vicars was heartened by his private support, and gave Doyle all the details about the robbery, as they were then known. He told Doyle his chief suspect was Ernest Shackleton's brother. He added that 'Scotland Yard told me that the brother who is an explorer well versed in advertising himself was a bad lot financially too'. Doyle, however, had met and admired the explorer. But his brother was a different matter. The affair was a mystery with sinister political and sexual undertones. Piece by piece, from Vicars and other sources, Conan Doyle put together the background to the case.

Sir Arthur Vicars, an effete, scholarly man, had been appointed to his post in 1893. As Ulster King of Arms, he held office directly under the king, and was not a government employee. He was a fussy person, deeply involved in the medieval enchantments of his special field. He had appointed his own assistants from a curious collection of individuals. His mother was Irish, and he had installed his Irish-born nephew Peirce Gun Mahony as Cork Herald; Francis Shackleton, the brother of the Antarctic explorer Sir

The young creator of Sherlock Holmes – Conan Doyle during the
Southsea years around 1884.

Dr Joseph Bell, Conan Doyle's teacher at Edinburgh University, who helped inspire the methods of Sherlock Holmes.

Conan Doyle at the entrance to 1 Bush Villas, Elm Grove, Southsea, where the first Sherlock Holmes story was written a year after the sudden death of Jack Hawkins.

A LOST WOMAN
MARY KELLY
IN MILLER'S COURT

Mary Kelly, Jack the Ripper's last victim, in Miller's Court.

George Edalji, showing the prominent eyes which caught Conan Doyle's attention on first meeting him.

(Left) Edalji's father, the Rev Shapurji Edalji, who was originally from a Parsee family in Bombay, married an Englishwoman and became vicar of Wyrley. *(Right)* One of the horses slashed in the Edalji affair.

Wyrley Vicarage, the home of the Edalji family.

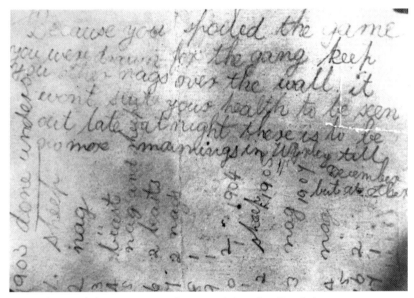

Part of one of the mysterious letters, giving details of the
mutilations, sent to the police under false names in the Edalji affair.

Police searching a field near Wyrley for clues in the Edalji affair.

Dr Crippen and Miss Ethel Le Neve in the dock at Bow Street.

The dining-room where Miss Marion Gilchrist's body was found.

(Left) Oscar Slater in 1928, after his pardon and release from prison the previous year following Conan Doyle's successful campaign. *(Right)* Miss Marion Gilchrist, the victim for whose murder Oscar Slater was wrongly imprisoned.

George Joseph Smith, the Bluebeard of the Bath, and 'ruthless beyond all conjecture' according to Conan Doyle. This was the official police photograph taken in Brixton prison.

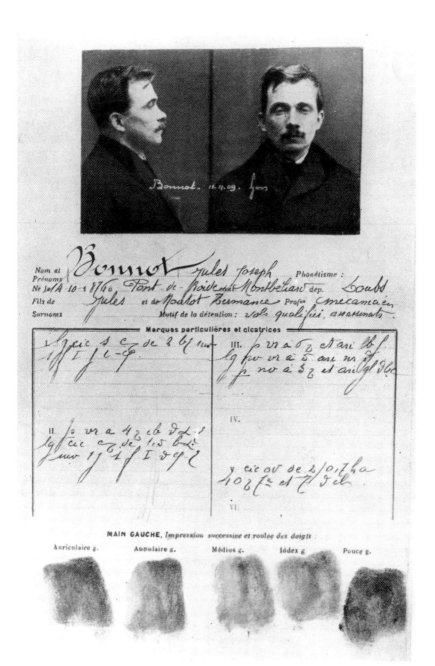

Police photo and chart of Jules Bonnot, known as 'The Motor-Bandit', and formerly Conan Doyle's chauffeur.

(Left) Jules Bonnot in his chauffering days. On 26 April 1912 he was fatally wounded in a shoot-out with French police. *(Right)* Major-General Charles Luard before his wife's murder.

The summer house, called the Casa, where Mrs Luard was murdered. Some of the circumstances of the Luard case inspired Conan Doyle's 'The Problem of Thor Bridge'.

Norman Thorne's hut at Crowborough, near Conan Doyle's home in Sussex.

 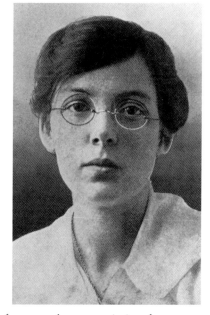

(Left) Norman Thorne, the chicken farmer, whose conviction for murder worried Conan Doyle. Thorne was hanged at Wandsworth Prison on 22 April 1925. *(Right)* Elsie Cameron, whose remains were found in Norman Thorne's chicken run.

Daily Mirror

THE DAILY PICTURE NEWSPAPER WITH THE LARGEST NET SALE

MAJOR
BLAKE
FINED
£250

No. 7,207   THURSDAY, DECEMBER 16, 1926   One Penny

MRS. CHRISTIE'S DRAMATIC DASH TO SECLUSION

Mrs. Christie entering a waiting motor-car on arrival at Manchester.

A friend mounting guard over Colonel and Mrs. Christie's carriage at Leeds.

Mrs. Christie (right) with her sister, Mrs. Watts, changing trains at Leeds.   Part of the crowd that waited in rain for Mrs. Christie at King's Cross.

Mrs. Agatha Christie, the novelist, who was found at a Harrogate hotel after being miss. | brother-in-law, she travelled in the London train from Harrogate, but changed to the

Newspaper headline announcing Agatha Christie's discovery. Conan
Doyle believed the Christie case 'offered an excellent example of the
uses of psychometry as an aid to the detective'.

Bartolomeo Vanzetti *(left)* and Nicola Sacco *(right)*, who were wrongly convicted of murder and robbery, and electrocuted on 23 August 1927. The foreman of the jury commented at the time, 'Damn them, they ought to hang anyway.

Demonstration to free Sacco and Vanzetti. Conan Doyle observed, 'it is impossible to read the facts without realizing that the two Italians were executed not as murderers but as anarchists.

Conan Doyle, in later life, at the desk where much of his detective work, fictional and real, was thought out.

Ernest Shackleton, as Dublin Herald; and the wealthy Francis Bennett Goldney, F.S.A., later a notorious Conservative Mayor of Canterbury, as Athlone Pursuivant.

Then and later there were rumours of Vicars being associated with a ring of homosexuals in high government circles in Ireland and London 'involving the highest in the land'. This aura of suppressed scandal made the affair of the Crown Jewels dangerous for many leading people, right up to King Edward himself.

The actual facts of the robbery were clear enough. The jewels – whose care was a constant source of worry to Sir Arthur, or so he claimed – were kept in a safe in the library of the Bedford Tower in which the Office of Arms was located, and not, as required, in the strongroom on the same floor. Anyone calling to see Vicars would be shown into the library. The jewels were last seen when Vicars showed them to a visitor on 11 June. On 6 July Weirs, the Grafton Street jewellers, sent back one of the collars which they had been altering. Vicars asked William Stivey, the office messenger, to put the collar in the safe, giving him the key to it from his chain. Stivey departed, but then Vicars rightly thought better of what he had done and was following him downstairs, when Stivey appeared in the doorway of the library, an anxious look on his face.

The safe, he said, was already unlocked.

Opening it, Vicars was dismayed to find that the regalia, and some of his own family jewellery, were gone. The thief had taken his time, carefully undoing a ribbon on one of the pieces, and folding the tissue paper before replacing it in the various boxes. The loot included the Grand Master's Diamond Star, the Grand Master's Badge, five collars of the Companions, and some smaller pieces. The Star was of eight points, in Brazilian diamonds, in the centre of which was a shamrock (symbol of Ireland) on a ruby cross (symbol of England) with a blue enamel background. The Badge was equally splendid, also in diamonds, emeralds and rubies.

The official valuation was £31,500, about £3,500,000 in today's money. As pieces of historical interest much more might be paid for them than the mere value of the stones. But even broken up, they represented a spectacular haul.

This then was no minor criminal coup, Conan Doyle realized. As King Edward was due in Dublin in a few days, Vicars was exhausted by the preparations, but was aware of the significance of what had happened. When he was told of the loss, the King's language was extreme, though he remained polite in public. Was this a calculated insult by Irish Nationalists or Republicans? Or was it, as has been suggested more recently, the work of a group of Irish monarchists, hoping to restore an Irish king?

How the jewels had been stolen was the first question. On Wednesday 3 July Mrs Mary Farrell, the office-cleaner, had mentioned to Vicars that the door to the Bedford Tower had been left unlocked one night, and on another occasion the door to the library and the strongroom had been left open as well. Vicars had mislaid his own keys, among them the key to the front door. It turned up in his suburban Clonskeagh house a few days after the robbery was discovered. But Vicars at the time seemed unconcerned at these odd events: his mind was fixed on the royal visit. Now, as a direct consequence of the theft, royal disfavour set about destroying him.

The investigations had been begun by the Dublin police, whose headquarters were across the Castle Yard from the Bedford Tower. But as Conan Doyle learnt, they made little progress, aside from a sneaking suspicion that Vicars himself might be involved. Vicars realized this and it scared him.

Soon, however, the assistance of Scotland Yard was also called upon, in the person of Chief Inspector John Kane. His inquiries were thorough, but when he presented his report to the Dublin authorities, actually naming a suspect, he was rebuffed. He returned to London. Who Kane suspected is not known for certain, as his report has never been traced. Vicars himself seems to be a likely candidate. This was an odd result, for Kane himself had eliminated from his investigation the names of several people whom rumour connected with the case.

Some time earlier Mrs Farrell had been surprised to see a mysterious stranger in the Bedford Tower. She told the police that he was Lord Haddo, the son of the Viceroy, Lord Aberdeen. At the subsequent inquiry she refused to name the man she had seen. Second thoughts? Or had she been 'got at'? Lord Haddo, in any case, was officially cleared.

Rumour, always so vital in Dublin, spoke of stag parties, of orgies and unnameable vices. The name of Vicars was connected with Frank Shackleton and a Captain Richard Gorges in these rumours. But at the time of the robbery, Shackleton, like Lord Haddo, was out of the country; or rather, at the time of the discovery of the theft, for the actual date of the theft was unknown.

Failing to find a culprit, the authorities were determined to make a scapegoat of Vicars. He refused, on legal advice, to have any part in the private and unsworn Commission of Inquiry into the theft. In October 1907 he was dismissed from office on the King's direct orders. His life was in ruins. In the years that followed, convinced that Shackleton and Gorges were the men responsible, Vicars tried persistently to clear his name.

In this he had the support of Conan Doyle. During the South African War, Doyle had known Shackleton and heard of Captain Gorges, a hero of Spion Kop, and he had not liked what he heard. Their reputations had been sexually unsavoury. Shackleton, as a businessman, sailed close to the wind – eventually he was to be jailed for fraud. Conan Doyle's interest centred on Shackleton, as Vicars now believed that he had been drugged on 30 June and his keys copied. But as Shackleton had covered his tracks well, and established an alibi by being out of the country when the robbery was discovered, Conan Doyle believed he must have had the help of either Peirce Mahony or Captain Gorges. On the whole Gorges seemed the more likely criminal.

In May 1920, when Ireland was passing through the Troubles, the matter of the Crown Jewels arose again for Sir Arthur Vicars. Conan Doyle was once more contacted, and their letters show that as far as Conan Doyle was concerned the case was solved: Shackleton was the culprit. But by this time, having served a prison term for another offence, he had disappeared from public view and finally died anonymously in 1939.

Also in May 1920 Vicars' home, Kilmorna House in County Kerry, was raided by armed men; the incident was later described in the House of Lords. But though it passed off safely, it set Vicars' mind on making a will. Hence, in part, his consultation with Conan Doyle. How could he expose the criminal?

His solution was to accuse Francis Shackleton by name in his will as the thief, and to denounce what he saw as the 'wicked and blackguardly acts of the Irish government' who were 'backed up by the late King Edward VII whom I had loyally and faithfully served'.

This sensational passage was not admitted to probate, and the actual will itself was sealed by order of the Keeper of Public Records until a recent date. The law had long been quite clear that the text of a will could not be used, as Vicars had used it, to publish libels on the Head of State, the Irish Government, or private individuals.

A year later, on 14 April 1921, Sir Arthur Vicars was murdered. Kilmorna House was again raided by armed men, set on fire, and the baronet shot to death on the lawn before it. Around his neck was hung a label: 'Spy. Informers beware. IRA never forgets.'

The IRA issued a statement that it was not responsible for the crime, and after the Treaty, when the estate was being divided up by the Land Commission the new Irish government saw to it that no local man was given any share of the Kilmorna lands. An editorial in the *Manchester Guardian* commented that Vicars' murder was 'one of the most horrible in the black recent records of crime and counter-crime in Ireland.'

The death of his distant cousin was a horror Conan Doyle could do nothing about. He had supported and advised Sir Arthur with his ready sympathy for every victim of injustice, though he would not have countenanced such a passage as that in Vicars' will. There was nothing he could do in a public way to assist Vicars, but he had helped in an oblique way. The robbery at Dublin Castle served a different purpose for him when he used it as the basis of 'The Bruce-Partington Plans', published in *The Strand* in December 1908, seventeen months after the robbery in Dublin.

The plot of the story, set back in 1895, hinges on the theft of the plans for a top-secret submarine from a safe in Woolwich Arsenal to which only three people had keys. As at Dublin Castle three keys, to the outer door, the inner door and the safe itself, would be needed to steal them. With this outline from the case of the Irish Crown Jewels he combined elements from the Merstham Tunnel mystery in which his friend Churton Collins had been so concerned.

The papers were stolen from their official guardian, Sir James Walter [Sir Arthur Vicars], by his younger brother Valentine Walter [Frank Shackleton]. He had been detected by young Cadogan West, who followed him from Woolwich by train and was murdered by the German agent Oberstein in circumstances suggested by the fate of Miss Money on the Brighton line. The motive was, as always, money.

As Holmes explains to Col. Walter, every essential of the case was known. Valentine was hard pressed for money (as was Shackleton), and took an impression of his brother's keys. Cadogan West had some previous reason to suspect him, and his accusation led to his own death.

This story had a strange sequel. At the end of July 1914 Peirce Mahony was found dead beside a lake near his home in Wicklow. His shotgun had gone off, it was thought, while he was climbing over a fence, and he had received both charges in the heart.

In their unsurpassed account of the Irish Crown Jewels affair, Francis Bamford and Viola Bankes suspected there might have been more to this than an accident. 'As a result of his interference Cadogan West was murdered, and his death arranged to look like suicide. Had Sir Arthur Conan Doyle, borrowing a framework of fact to construct a work of fiction, written more truly than he ever guessed? Did something happen in the summer of 1914 which made it necessary for someone connected with the loss of the Crown Jewels to remove the potentially dangerous Mahony from the scene? And did that someone, taking a leaf from the case-book of Sherlock Holmes, stage a murder to appear like a case of suicide?'

In 1916 Captain Gorges, then in jail for manslaughter, made a veiled admission to a fellow prisoner that he had been involved in stealing the jewels and could assist in their recovery . . . Nothing was done to follow this up. Gorges survived, with his secrets, into the 1950s. And though there was a recent flurry of interest after the death of one of Mrs Farrell's family, when the police and officials from the National Museum searched a field in the Dublin mountains without success, nothing more for certain has been heard of the Irish Crown Jewels. In the 1920s there was a tentative offer to the new Irish government to return them, but this came to nothing, and in fact the jewels may by this time have been broken up and sold.

There is no doubt that Vicars and Conan Doyle were essentially right in their solution to the crime. In a letter to a friend Vicars once commented that Herbert Gladstone 'the other day told me he suspected the thief & he was right – I could give you his name in confidence – he is the only gentleman in this Govt. of cads . . .'. Conan Doyle, after his experiences with Gladstone over the Edalji case, might not have agreed with that verdict. But in any event, Gladstone proved as unhelpful as every other politician, and Vicars and Conan Doyle were never formally able to expose Frank Shackleton.

CHAPTER ELEVEN

THE LANGHAM HOTEL MYSTERY

Crime, Conan Doyle recognized, was properly a matter for the police, at least in the first instance. But disappearances were another matter. He had always been attracted by such mysteries. In a notebook kept in Norwood he scribbled down a passing notion: 'Idea of the Beggar near Change and the strange disappearance of Mr Easton Brown.' This eventually became 'The Man with the Twisted Lip'. I suspect that Mr Brown, like the beggar, was a real person, but have found out no more about his disappearance.

Relatives or friends of such vanished persons often turned in despair to Conan Doyle after the police had failed them, as is so often the case with the thousands who go 'missing' every year. There was one case where a man had disappeared though he was known to have gone to Sweden. When his relatives approached Conan Doyle, they were told (strangely enough) that he would be found in a certain part of London, and to their amazement his theory proved correct.

Of another such case, in 1907, we have more details. It concerned a young officer who vanished from his room in the Langham Hotel in Portland Place, a hotel very familiar to Conan Doyle himself. He received a letter from a Mrs Bellew, who told him that her favourite cousin, Henry Armstrong, had vanished in

London. He had gone out to a show, returned to his hotel, and had been seen entering his room. He was not seen to leave it. He just vanished.

Having given the affair some thought, within the hour Conan Doyle answered Mrs Bellew's appeal by return of post.

Dear Mrs Bellew,
Your cousin is in Scotland. Look for him in Glasgow or Edinburgh, and I guarantee you will find him.

Arthur Conan Doyle

Here for once Conan Doyle in his own words relates what happened.

'Few of the problems which have come my way have been very similar to some which I had invented for the exhibition of the reasoning of Mr Holmes. I might perhaps quote one in which that gentleman's method of thought was copied with complete success. The case was as follows: A gentleman had disappeared. He had drawn a bank balance of £40 which was known to be on him. It was feared he had been murdered for the sake of the money. He had last been heard of stopping at a large hotel in London, having come from the country that day. In the evening he went to a music-hall performance, came out of it about ten o'clock, returned to his hotel, changed his evening clothes, which were found in his room next day, and disappeared utterly. No one saw him leave the hotel, but a man occupying a neighbouring room declared that he had heard him moving during the night. A week had elapsed at the time that I was consulted, but the police had discovered nothing. Where was the man?

'These were the whole of the facts as communicated to me by his relatives in the country. Endeavouring to see the matter through the eyes of Mr Holmes, I answered by return mail that he was evidently either in Glasgow or Edinburgh. It proved later

143

that he had, as a fact, gone to Edinburgh, though in the week that had passed he had moved to another part of Scotland.

'There I should leave the matter, for, as Dr Watson has often shown, a solution explained is a mystery spoiled. At this stage the reader can lay down the book and show how simple it all is by working out the problem for himself. He has all the data which were ever given to me. For the sake of those, however, who have no turns for such conundrums, I will try to indicate the links which make the chain. The one advantage which I possessed was that I was familiar with the routine of London hotels – though I fancy it differs little from that of hotels elsewhere.

'The first thing was to look at the facts and separate what was certain from what was conjecture. It was all certain except the statement of the person who heard the missing man in the night. How could he tell such a sound from any other sound in a large hotel? That point could be disregarded, if it traversed the general conclusions.

'The first clear deduction was that the man had meant to disappear. Why else should he draw all his money? He had got out of the hotel during the night. But there is a night porter in all hotels, and it is impossible to get out without his knowledge when the door is once shut. The door is shut after the theatre-goers return – say at twelve o'clock. He had come from the music-hall at ten, had changed his clothes, and had departed with his bag. No one had seen him do so. The inference is that he had done it at the moment when the hall was full of returning guests, which is from eleven to eleven-thirty. After that hour, even if the door were still open, there are few people coming and going so that he with his bag would certainly have been seen.

'Having got so far upon firm ground, we now ask ourselves why a man who desires to hide himself should go out at such an hour. If he intended to conceal himself in London he need never have gone to the hotel at all. Clearly then he was going to catch a train which would carry him away. But a man who is deposited by train in any provincial station during the night is likely to be noticed, and he might be sure that when the alarm was raised and his description given, some guard or porter would remember him. Therefore, his destination would be some large town which he would reach as a terminus where all his fellow passengers would disembark and where he would lose himself in the crowd. When one turns up the timetable and sees that the great Scotch expresses bound for Edinburgh and Glasgow start about midnight, the goal is reached. As for his dress-suit, the fact that he abandoned it proved that he intended to adopt a line of life where there were no social amenities. This deduction also proved to be correct.'

Lady Conan Doyle added a little to this, for her husband had shared his deductions with her. 'He told me that the vanished man would reappear either in Glasgow or Edinburgh in three days time. He was so certain he wrote it in a letter to the boy's family. On the third day a telegram told my husband that it had turned out precisely as had been deduced.'

Other cases that came to his notice were not so easily resolved. In 'The Problem of Thor Bridge', published in 1922, Dr Watson alludes to unfathomed cases that left even Sherlock Holmes bewildered. 'Among these unfinished tales is that of Mr James Phillimore, who stepping back into his own house to get his umbrella, was never more seen in this world.' Conan Doyle had in mind a real event, as he reveals in his memoirs. 'I heard of such a one in America which would certainly have presented a formidable problem. A man of blameless life starting off for a Sunday walk with his family, suddenly observed that he had forgotten something. He went back into the house, the door of which was still open, and he left his family waiting for him outside. He never reappeared, and from that day to this there has been no clue as to what befell him. This was certainly one of the strangest cases of which I have ever heard in real life.'

According to the author Wallace Klinefelter, this 'had happened in America where Doyle heard of it while on one of his lecture tours. Although requested to apply the methods of Sherlock Holmes, he refused.' Such a bizarre event better belongs in the records of Charles Fort than those of everyday life.

What drives perfectly respectable people to disappear still remains a mystery. Every year thousands vanish, like the young officer in this case. It has been calculated, on the basis of official records, that over 60,000 people 'disappear' every year in the United States alone. Their worried families are unlucky enough not to have a Sherlock Holmes – or even a Conan Doyle – to assist them. Sometimes it is a matter of murder; more often than not it is the secret unspoken desire to begin life all over again in another place as another person.

CHAPTER TWELVE

THE VANISHED DANE

In the summer of 1909 Conan Doyle received a letter from a young nurse, Miss Joan Paynter, of the North Western Hospital in Hampstead in north London.

> I am writing to you as I can think of no one else who could help me. I cannot afford to employ a detective myself as I have not the money, neither can my people for the same reason.
>
> About 5 weeks ago I met a man, a Dane. We became engaged and although I did not wish him to say anything about it for a little while he insisted on going down to Torquay to see my people . . .

Here, it seemed, was a case much like his own story 'A Case of Identity' written in 1891. It will be recalled that in the story the young man who made love to the young lady disappeared, and was eventually unmasked as her stepfather, anxious that she should not marry, losing him the use of her annuity. Here the young man gave her gifts, persuaded Miss Paynter to give up her nursing job at the hospital, and then, when all the preparations for the wedding had been made, disappeared 'like a soap-bubble'.

He had known that the girl had no money. Nor was it a case of sexual exploitation, for there was no seduction or attempted seduction. It was a mystery, and it frightened her.

The frantic Miss Paynter got in touch with Scotland Yard, and they seemed to believe that the amorous Dane might have got into the hands of sharpers. But they failed to trace him.

The Danish police were contacted, but they too failed. If he had not been murdered or kidnapped, he must have gone off on his own accord. But where was he? And what was his game?

> Please don't think it awful cheek on my part, I feel so
> awfully miserable and it was only this morning that I
> thought of you, please do all you can for me and I shall
> be eternally grateful.

Could any chivalrous knight refuse such a plea? Here was an opportunity 'to show that the general lines of reasoning advocated by Holmes have a real application to life'. In this case, Doyle notes in *Memories and Adventures* (1924), 'I was able, by a similar process of deduction, to show her very clearly both whither he had gone and how unworthy he was of her affections.'

Working from the information Miss Paynter was able to give him in a second letter, Conan Doyle eventually contacted the sailor's cousin in Copenhagen, an employee of the Danish East Asia Company, and learned from him something of the man's real character. While he seemed superficially attractive, he was in fact an adventurer she was better off without.

Miss Paynter, in a letter from Torquay dated 7 August 1909, thanked Conan Doyle:

> I don't know how to thank you sufficiently for all your
> kindness, please accept my most grateful thanks for all you
> have done for me. As you say, I have had an extraordinary
> escape, and I dread to think what might have happened if he

hadn't gone away when he did. I am returning the letter [from the cousin in Copenhagen] and will certainly let you know at once if I ever hear of him again.

This case left his biographer, John Dickson Carr, in a quandary. 'But how did the investigator manage this? We have only her side of the correspondence. Where, in those letters, was the clue which seemed so plain to him? It is as exasperating as that case in which Holmes recognizes the truth by the depth to which the parsley had sunk into the butter. The biographer, who risks justified abuse for telling so incomplete a story, can only report that there appears to be no sign of a clue anywhere.'

But in this case Conan Doyle was anxious to preserve the honour of a lady. In other cases, he was more forthcoming about how he arrived at the truth.

CHAPTER THIRTEEN

WAS CRIPPEN INNOCENT?

The murderous medical man always arouses a peculiar frisson of horror. So it was not surprising that Conan Doyle should have followed with fascinated interest the case of Dr Hawley Harvey Crippen in late 1910.

On 18 October Conan Doyle travelled up to London from his Sussex home to attend the opening in the Central Criminal Court at the Old Bailey of the sensational trial of Dr Crippen for the murder of his wife, the failed music hall artiste, 'Belle Elmore'. Crippen was said to have disposed of her remains in particularly ghastly circumstances.

Through the barrister Edward Marshall Hall, Conan Doyle obtained a seat in Court One. The little man in the dock, he was shocked to see, listened with patient equanimity to the horrendous evidence in the case, and even managed to regard with quizzical interest the fragment of abdominal skin, said to show an appendix scar, which was passed up to him for his inspection. (He was photographed secretly in court by Arthur Bennett, one of the few such photos ever taken in a British court.)

This was a case which had seized upon Conan Doyle's imagination, not only because of the macabre details, but because all the resources of modern science and technology had been brought into play in the pursuit and capture of the accused. The trial also saw the emergence in the public area of a new hero of detection in the person of Dr Bernard Spilsbury.

Hawley Harvey Crippen was an American dentist – a graduate of my own Alma Mater, the University of Michigan in Ann Arbor. His career had not been a distinguished one. He had drifted from city to city in the United States, finally coming to London with his wife Cora in 1900. She had ambitions to grace the stage as a singer, but she was, alas, a performer with little natural talent. However, she could, with her more than ample figure, dress the part of Belle. As the possibility of the limelight retreated, the Crippens took lodgers into their house, 39 Hilldrop Crescent, in North London's Camden Town, to help pay their way. Crippen himself was obliged to rise early to see to their needs before going out about his own business in the City. It was a dreary existence, and the troubles of his trade as a supplier of patented American nostrums did little to enhance it.

Crippen was, then, the classic little man with a domineering wife, who sought a little love in the arms of one of the secretaries at Munyon's Remedies, the drug company where he worked. She was twenty-seven-year-old Ethel Le Neve, a pleasant, obliging girl, and their relationship was no secret to his colleagues.

Then, at the beginning of 1910, Belle disappeared. She had gone back to America, Crippen told their friends. Then her death in California was announced. Her friends were vexed and mystified. After Ethel appeared in public wearing Mrs Crippen's jewellery and furs, two of them, a Mr and Mrs Nash, went to the trouble of making inquiries in California. Dissatisfied, Nash took his suspicions to Scotland Yard, and soon Chief Inspector Walter Dew was calling on Dr Crippen at Hilldrop Crescent.

When he called at Munyon's the following Monday to make further inquiries, Dew found that Crippen too had disappeared. A search was now made of the house, and on 13 July when the paving in the cellar was raised, the remains of a human being wrapped in a pyjama jacket were discovered. A warrant was immediately issued for the fugitives.

Crippen and Le Neve had crossed to Antwerp where they caught the liner S.S. *Montrose* to Canada. On board the ship they were soon suspected by its captain, a keen amateur detective, who noted the gun bulging under 'Mr Robinson's' jacket, and the far from convincing disguise of the woman masquerading as his son, 'John'. By means of Marconi Radio Telegraphy Captain Kendall alerted the authorities, and Crippen and Le Neve were arrested on arrival by Dew who came aboard the ship at Father Point, just off Quebec, disguised as a harbour pilot.

Meanwhile, Bernard Spilsbury was at work on the remains uncovered from Crippen's cellar. These were now identified from the scar tissue from an old appendix operation and the pyjama suiting buried with the remains. At the trial the date and purchase by Crippen were proved. The detailed medical evidence from Spilsbury seemed to clinch the case. Mrs Crippen had been poisoned by the rare drug hyoscine, the first time it had been used for murder. Crippen had openly purchased five grains of the drug on 17 January 1910.

And yet Conan Doyle and some of those who attended the five days of the trial realized that the 'Guilty' verdict left a great deal of the case unexplained. Crippen impressed all those who came in contact with him at this time. As a Catholic perhaps Doyle's moral awareness was playing a part? Was Crippen shielding Ethel who, at a separate trial, had been acquitted? What had happened at Hilldrop Crescent? Was this mild man, so anxious about his lady friend, really a vicious murderer?

The brief for the defence was to have been offered to Edward Marshall Hall, but as he was away on holiday it was sent elsewhere. As a result Crippen's defence was badly handled by Alfred Tobin. After the verdict there was a wave of sympathy for him. Marshall Hall had a distinct idea of how he would have conducted the defence in order to get Crippen's conviction reduced to manslaughter.

He developed his theory fully in a talk he later gave to the Crimes Club. Conan Doyle invited him down to Windlesham, where they debated his ideas over port and cigars in the billiard room after dinner. Could Crippen have been innocent? Conan Doyle wondered.

Marshall Hall believed that Mrs Crippen was domineering woman with an insatiable sexual appetite. Poor little Crippen, caught between Ethel and Cora, found it all too much for him. He bought the hyoscine to act as a sedative and sexual depressant, but alas he miscalculated the dose. As none of the drug was found in his possession, it was assumed that he had given her all five grains. But was this the case? Did he intend to kill Cora, or merely to knock her out, while he enjoyed a night of illicit love-making with Ethel?

Finding her dead, Marshall Hall went on, Crippen should have called another doctor or the police. If he had done so he would have escaped the gallows; he might not even have been tried. But he panicked, and cut up the body, burying it in the cellar and throwing the head off the Channel Ferry (as everyone thought). It was this horrid butchery which really convicted him. Marshall Hall explained to Conan Doyle that had he been able to this make this plea himself, he would have hoped to have got Crippen off.

Others have disagreed. Their mutual friend and former member of the Crimes Club, Ingleby Oddie, was a junior barrister on the prosecution team. He thought Crippen was certainty guilty, though he may not have planned to cut up the body. He overdid the hyoscine dose, and brought about delirium and hysterical screaming. To silence Cora he then shot her. There were, Oddie claimed in his autobiography, tales of screams and a sound like a slamming door from the neighbours. He was then forced to dismember the body, as he could no longer pass off the death as mere heart failure.

Travers Humphreys, who led for the prosecution with Sir Richard Muir, thought that in another country Crippen might have had the benefit of extenuating circumstances. In France, for instance, it might have been seen as a crime of passion. But not in England. In England, on 23 November 1910, Crippen went to the gallows, taking with him the dark secrets of Hilldrop Crescent. Conan Doyle felt little sympathy for him, and yet there may well have been an echo for him in this case of that other, closer, death that still haunted him from Southsea in March 1885.

CHAPTER FOURTEEN

THE CASE OF OSCAR SLATER

'The whole case will, in my opinion, remain immortal in the classics of crime as the supreme example of official incompetence and obstinacy.'

Sir Arthur Conan Doyle, in
The Spectator, 25 July 1914

In the summer of 1912 Conan Doyle was approached by the lawyer acting for a prisoner serving a life sentence for the brutal murder of an old lady of eighty-two in Glasgow in December 1908.

He was sent a copy of William Roughead's edition of *The Trial of Oscar Slater*, from which he learnt the disturbing facts of the affair, and felt compelled to take up the case. He did not find Oscar Slater himself, a German pimp and shady jewel merchant, an attractive figure – he could not sympathize with him as readily as he had with George Edalji, but the cause of proving him innocent was to involve Doyle for sixteen years.

Oscar Slater's trial constituted an even graver miscarriage of justice than the Edalji affair, one which to this day is not resolved. Here, for the first time, I will make explicit the full facts of the case as they were known to Conan Doyle, but which have never been related before.

155

(i) *Murder in Queen's Terrace*

On the rainy night of Monday, 21 December 1908, Helen Lambie, a maid employed by Miss Marion Gilchrist, left the second-floor flat at 15 Queen's Terrace, West Princes Street, Glasgow, to buy an evening paper. This was not an errand she did every night, but usually when her mistress was expecting visitors she did not want the maid to see.

It was then seven o'clock. Sometime in the next ten minutes Miss Gilchrist was murdered.

In the flat below lived Mr Arthur Adams and his mother and five sisters. He was not on intimate terms with Miss Gilchrist, but as she had long been anxious about burglars, he had arranged with her that she could knock on the floor if she needed help in an emergency.

At five minutes to seven Mrs Rowena Liddell, Mr Adams's sister, noticed a man leaning against the railings outside the house as she came in. He was very respectable, but had a distinctive long nose with a most peculiar dip: 'You would not see that dip among thousands'. (He could have been waiting for one of her sister's music students, though there was conclusive evidence later that someone had been watching the house for several weeks.)

In the flat, Helen Lambie collected a penny for the paper, leaving on the table a half-sovereign for the shopping to be collected on her return. She left Miss Gilchrist sitting at the table in the dining-room, her back to the fire, reading a magazine. On the way down the street Lambie paused to chat to a policeman on duty.

Suddenly the Adams household were startled by three sharp bangs on the ceiling. Adams went out into the close and up the stairs. He gave at least three long, almost rude, rings to the bell. The door to the close had been open. Her door was locked, but the gas was turned up in the hall. As he stood there he heard the sharp sound of wood breaking. He returned to his own flat, but his worried family urged him to go upstairs again as the noises were continuing – 'the ceiling was like to crack'.

Again he rang the bell. There was now no sound from within. While he stood there irresolute, Helen Lambie returned. On her way up from the street she too had been surprised to find the close door open, wet footprints on the stair, and now Mr Adams at the door. He said he had heard a noise. She thought it might have been the clothes rack in the kitchen, which was held up by a system of pulleys, collapsing. She opened the door and entered the hall. Adams stood waiting at the threshold.

From the spare bedroom at the end of the hall, a man emerged. He came down the hall, passing Helen Lambie, who said nothing to him but went on into the kitchen. He passed Adams, and then once outside, sprinted down the stairs. Lambie had shown not the slightest surprise at seeing him: a crucial point in the case. She went into the kitchen, where the clothes rack was in order.

'Where is your mistress?' Adams asked. Lambie went into the dining room, and screamed out, 'Oh, come here.'

Miss Gilchrist was lying on the floor by the dining table, head towards the fireplace. A skin rug had been thrown over her. Lifting it, they found she had been brutally beaten about the head. This is how William Park described it later: 'The head had been severely battered, both eyes smashed in, and there were horrid gashes and cavities on the sides of the head, with other awful injuries to the face.' Blood was everywhere. And yet the old lady was still alive, dying only as they knelt beside her.

Adams and Lambie ran downstairs. It was now ten minutes past seven. While the distraught girl wailed to the Adams family, Arthur Adams himself ran out into the street. Nobody like the fugitive he had seen leave the flat was now in sight. The murderer had disappeared into the black Glasgow night.

He returned with a policeman and his own doctor, Dr Adams. Dr Adams made an examination, and concluded that Miss

Gilchrist had been beaten with the chair that stood nearby, and that the seat would have kept the blood to some extent off the clothes of the killer. But only to some extent. Arthur Adams and Lambie had not noticed blood on the clothes of the man in the hall.

Helen Lambie now ran off to the house of Miss Margaret Birrell, a cousin of the victim, to break the awful news to her. What passed at her house, 19 Blythswood Drive, where Lambie arrived at seven-fifteen, was later to be the subject of dispute. As it did not form part of the evidence at the trial we can pass over it for now.

On her return, Miss Lambie was questioned by the police, who had now arrived in force at the flat. Officially, she now said she was not certain she could identify the man in the hall.

The first policeman on the scene was Superintendent William Douglas, Western Division, and later Mr John Ord, Superintendent of the Glasgow CID. Whatever she told Douglas at first, Helen Lambie later told Ord that the only thing that seemed to be missing from the apartment was a single diamond crescent brooch.

Aside from her claim, there is no other evidence at all that any jewellery was stolen that evening. There were pieces worth upwards of £3,000 in various parts of the flat. If robbery was the motive, it was curious these too were not looted.

All the man had left behind was a box of Runaway matches and a spent match used to light the gas in the spare bedroom. There the police found a small wooden box, in which papers were kept, which had been broken open (the sound of breaking wood heard by Arthur Adams?), and the papers it contained scattered on the floor. There was no blood on the box or the match.

Yet the police now took robbery to be the motive and issued an alert. They were looking for: 'A man between 25 and 30 years of age, 5 feet 8 or 9 inches in height, slim build, dark hair, clean shaven; dressed in light grey overcoat and dark cloth cap. Cannot be further described.'

It seemed odd to Conan Doyle, having reviewed the evidence thus far, that Miss Gilchrist should have admitted the man. The doors were arranged that she could open the close door to the street mechanically and see who was coming up the stairs. If he were a stranger she could then lock her own door. There was no sign the flat had been broken into. Whoever he was, Miss Gilchrist herself had let her killer in.

But how, Conan Doyle considered next, had the police got on the trail of the man they now arrested? Apart from those given by Lambie and Adams, they obtained another, more detailed, description a few days later from a fourteen-year-old girl named Mary Barrowman of a man she claimed to have seen running from the house. (Her statements that she was in West Princes Street are hard to reconcile with Adams's claim that the street was empty, and her employer's later claim that she was mistaken about the day.) Another witness, an intelligent school teacher named Agnes Brown, claimed that she had seen two men running away from the area on the night of the murder. One resembled the man seen by Adams and Lambie, the other was more heavily built. She was not called as a witness at the trial.

Then on Christmas Day the police received information that a German Jew named Oscar had been offering around for sale in his drinking clubs a pawn ticket for a diamond crescent brooch. The police visited his flat and learnt he and his mistress had gone to Liverpool with the intention of sailing to America.

Oscar Slater was pursued, eventually being arrested in New York. There at an extradition hearing, Adams, Lambie and Barrowman identified him as the man they had seen. There was no other evidence against him, beyond the fact that he was 'identified' and that he had 'fled'. The brooch in the pawn office was proved to have been his own property, and not to have been stolen from Miss Gilchrist.

From the facts laid out before him, Conan Doyle concluded

that the identification was tainted: Slater had been pointed out to the witnesses in a corridor before the hearing in New York, and Lambie and Barrowman had been coached in what to say.

But as so often in cases of miscarriages of justice, Oscar Slater's defence was badly handled. The police built 'a case' against him. His way of life, as a pimp, gambler and jewel dealer was what convicted him, not the evidence. The jury, after being misdirected by Lord Guthrie, the judge, returned a verdict of guilty.

This was such a clear travesty of justice that 20,000 people signed a petition against his execution. Oscar Slater was reprieved and sent to Peterhead Prison for life.

There the case might have ended. The prison chaplain, John Lamond, a friend and biographer of Conan Doyle, heard Slater's claims to be innocent without a qualm. It never occurred to him that Slater might, in fact, have been falsely convicted. All too many people assumed that if Oscar Slater was in prison that was where he deserved to be.

Conan Doyle, basing himself on the evidence in Roughead's book, wrote a pamphlet about the case which was published in August 1912. It was not well received, and though he won a few solid supporters, the general reaction was to dismiss the matter.

He received a letter from one member of the jury, who said he had not been convinced by the evidence. It had not been shown at the trial how the murderer had got into the flat, and if the murder had been committed as the Crown claimed, there ought to have been blood on Slater's clothes: 'I had the feeling all through the trial that there was a missing link somewhere.'

This letter was printed by the *Daily Record* in Glasgow, which added that many people believed the real murderer was still walking the streets of the city, albeit conscience-stricken. Such people could, so the paper said, point him out.

Time passed. Then at the end of March 1914 Conan Doyle received a letter from a Glasgow solicitor named David Cook. He

160

was acting for a detective on the Glasgow police force named John Trench. Detective Lieutenant Trench alleged that when Lambie had called on Miss Birrell minutes after the murder, she had named to her the man she saw in the hall. Miss Birrell had warned Lambie not to say anything about this to the police. And though Trench himself had been to see Miss Birrell the evidence had been suppressed.

This added a whole new element to the case. Cook and Trench, supported by Conan Doyle, campaigned to have an inquiry. This was eventually held. It was unsworn and Miss Birrell and Helen Lambie denied Trench's allegations, especially about the identity of a person referred to as 'A.B.', who was supposed to be the man in the hall that evening. Slater stayed in prison. Worse, Cook and Trench almost joined him. They were arrested on a charge of receiving stolen property, and though they were acquitted, their lives were ruined. This was in 1915, and the arrest came the day before Trench was to sail to the Dardanelles. John Trench died in 1919; David Cook two years later.

Time passed again. Conan Doyle spared little thought for Oscar Slater during the war years and after. In 1925 a fellow prisoner smuggled out of prison an appeal from Slater to Conan Doyle pleading with him to take up the case again. This he did, but once again the authorities turned down any hope of an inquiry.

A new figure now entered the case: William Park, a determined Glasgow journalist. Park found new evidence, that the brooch which had played a major part in the arrest of Slater was not stolen and that a new witness who saw a man running away from Miss Gilchrist's house on the night of her murder said he was not Slater. Encouraged by Conan Doyle, Park wrote a book about the case called *The Truth about Oscar Slater*. However, work on the subject had warped Park's judgement, and he was drinking heavily. Through his own firm, the Psychic Press,

Conan Doyle published the book in 1927, adding a preface of his own.

The book caused a sensation. Once again there were calls for an inquiry. The *Daily News* published an influential series of articles taking the case against Slater apart. In October 1927 Helen Lambie, interviewed in America where she now lived, withdrew her official evidence, and a month later, Mary Barrowman also stated that she was now uncertain of her evidence. This was sufficient. On 14 November 1927, Oscar Slater was released from Peterhead Prison.

An appeal followed and, though in the usual way of lawyers, some of the evidence which was brought forward in support of Slater was not accepted, it was admitted that aspects of the trial had been unfair. Slater was pardoned, and a close-fisted government paid him £6,000 compensation. He retired to Ayr, where he lived quietly, dying in 1949. He and Conan Doyle later had a falling-out over the matter of who should pay for the appeal, but this was sorted out in the end to mutual satisfaction. Conan Doyle did not like Slater, but he was convinced that he had nothing to do with the murder of Miss Marion Gilchrist.

Conan Doyle and his friends likewise had no doubts about the identity of the 'man in the hall', a man who could reveal the whole truth about the case.

His name was Francis James Charteris.

(ii) Why Miss Gilchrist Died

One thing is certain: Marion Gilchrist was not killed for her jewellery by a common thief. She was killed by someone she knew, for reasons buried deep in the history of the Gilchrist family and their relations, who included the prominent Charteris family.

For Conan Doyle the solution to the case lay in the events of that December evening and the strange behaviour of Helen Lambie in meeting 'the man in the hall', and in the text of Miss Gilchrist's will.

Miss Lambie, it will be recalled, did not challenge the man who came out of the spare bedroom and passed her as she was on her way into the kitchen. She did not challenge him for the simple reason that she knew well who he was.

After she had found Miss Gilchrist dying, she ran off to see Birrell. To her she poured out the horrible details of what had happened. What follows is their actual dialogue.

'Oh, Miss Birrell, Miss Birrell, Miss Gilchrist has been murdered, she is lying dead in the dining-room, and oh, Miss Birrell, I saw who did it.'

'My God, Nellie, this is awful. Who was it, do you know him?'

'Oh, Miss Birrell, I think it was Dr Charteris. I am sure it was Francis Charteris.'

'My God, Nellie, don't say that. Unless you are very sure of it Nellie, don't say that.'

But Nellie Lambie was sure, and probably frightened. Later she repeated her claim to the police and that night Detectives John Pyper and James Dornan visited Miss Birrell. From them she heard that Helen Lambie had repeated the charge. Miss Birrell told her friends and also a member of Glasgow Corporation, who contacted Chief Superintendent Ord.

The next day another detective, none other than Lieutenant John Trench, called on her and took a statement. (This visit is confirmed in his police diary.) When he gave the statement in to Ord, his superior seemed to be impressed.

'This is the first real clue we have got.'

But later he told Trench: 'I have been ringing up Douglas and he is convinced that Dr Charteris had nothing to do with it.' Superintendent William Douglas was in charge of the Western Division of the city, where the murder had taken place.

It now became the official police line that Helen Lambie could not identify the man; though later she agreed to identify Oscar Slater as the man she had seen when police faced her with him in

New York. She was a good girl, of a class that did what it was told. At least, what it was told by senior policemen in Glasgow in 1909.

Miss Birrell had told Trench that 'Miss Gilchrist was not on good terms with her relations. Few, if any, visited her.' Dr Charteris was one of those few, as Helen Lambie was later prepared to admit at the secret inquiry, even as she denied the story of what happened on the night of the murder.

Marion Gilchrist was a curious woman, with a strange past. Rumour in Glasgow suggested that she had made a fortune as a dealer in stolen jewellery, though no concrete evidence of this has ever been uncovered. Certainly she was rich, and afraid of something.

During the months before the murder there had occurred some strange events. In September, an Irish terrier, which had been a present, died. Miss Lambie thought it might have been something it ate; Miss Gilchrist was convinced it had been poisoned. In November she changed her will. And from 1 December neighbours had been aware of a man watching the flat. Some twelve people saw the man, at different times and in different clothes. From the confused details of their evidence – some said he was foreign-looking, others that he had a moustache – it may well be that two men were involved.

When Miss Gilchrist's death was officially registered on 23 December, the information was provided by another relative of hers, Mrs Mary McCall, who had come up from her home at Boscombe Court in Bournemouth in the south of England. None of her local relatives in Scotland had, it seems, been prepared to come forward.

At probate Miss Gilchrist's estate was valued at £12,000. To her sister she left the life income of £2,000, which was to go to charities after her death. To other nieces and their children, £2,200 as legacies. After some other bequests, including £20 to Helen Lambie, what remained of the estate, £6,280, went to an illegitimate daughter, Mrs Maggie Galbraith Ferguson, whose own daughter was named, significantly enough, Marion Gilchrist Ferguson.

Originally much of Miss Gilchrist's money had come from her father, and her peculiar way of life had only added to family tensions about the inheritance.

Her brother James had died some years before. His widow Mary had married Matthew Charteris, Professor of Materia Medica and Therapeutics at Glasgow University, who had died in 1897.

His father had been a plain schoolmaster, but his brother, the Very Rev. Archibald Hamilton Charteris, Professor of Biblical Criticism at Edinburgh University, had been since 1870 one of the Royal Chaplains in Scotland.

Matthew Charteris had three sons. The eldest was Archibald Hamilton Charteris, then Professor of International Law at Glasgow University, and later at the University of Sydney. The youngest was a soldier, later Brigadier-General John Charteris. And the middle son was Francis James Charteris, like his father, a medical man. He eventually became a professor at the University of St Andrews.

The Charteris family was distinguished and well connected, indeed one of the more prominent families in Scotland.

Francis James Charteris was not related by blood to Miss Gilchrist, but was loosely viewed as being her nephew. He was born in 1875, making him about thirty-three at the time of the murder. All the witnesses agreed that the man they saw was a respectable young man in his middle thirties. He had studied medicine at Glasgow and Leipzig before opening a medical practice in Glasgow. How could such a person come to be suspected of involvement in a brutal murder?

The explanation which Charteris gave was a simple one. The following facts were his version of what happened that night, on the case. But they were not revealed during his lifetime.

At the time of the murder Francis Charteris was attending the birth of a baby boy. Later that evening he received a police message asking him to break the news of the murder to his mother. Going by the flat in West Princes Street he called in. There he found the police questioning an incoherent and confused Helen Lambie. Seeking to make clear to the police her impression of the man she had seen, she said 'He was like Dr Charteris there.'

It was this remark, according to his friends, that Detective Trench took up mistakenly, and from it grew his disgraceful action in 1914, which led to his dismissal. Charteris was the mysterious 'A.B.' whose identity had so puzzled everyone in the report of the inquiry.

It is said, unbelievably, for his own relatives gave evidence at the inquiry, that Dr Charteris was unaware of the rumours about him until 1951. These, as rumours will, became enlarged. He was said to be a drug addict, a drunkard, the owner of a brothel in Garnethill, and the organizer of shocking orgies at his lodgings as a student.

An addition was made to the legend to explain the initials used at the inquiry. It was said there were two men, one of whom was an Austin Birrell, another relative of Miss Gilchrist's. He was said to have gone off his head and to have wandered about Glasgow in the 1930s mumbling about his remorse for the brutal crime.

Some of this information came out after Dr Charteris died on 4 July 1964. In 1969 another effort was made to clear the name of John Trench, but the application was dismissed by the Glasgow magistrates. *The Glasgow Herald*, which had been no friend of Oscar Slater, attacked Trench again in an editorial by Alistair Phillips. Trench's moral offence was still inexcusable. 'What he did, by inflating his own sketchy and inaccurate second-hand knowledge of the early interrogations, was to impeach a respectable Glasgow physician who patently, and to the satisfaction of the procurator-fiscal and the very senior officers on the scene, had nothing to do with the crime.'

It seems that even today in Glasgow there is one law for the shady pimp and another for the Royal Chaplain's nephew.

Trench's knowledge was not second-hand: he had taken part in the inquiry. He had interviewed Miss Birrell himself and had reported the matter to his superiors. That surely was the whole point of his claim. Nor does the account which Dr Charteris gave square with the events as recorded at the time and as recounted at the inquiry.

It was admitted at the inquiry that the alibi of 'A.B.' – Dr Charteris – had been investigated, which was odd indeed if his name had not been connected with the murder. He claimed that he was attending a birth at the time: we have no evidence that this was true. More crucially, Helen Lambie identified him, not to the police later in the evening as he relates, but to Margaret Birrell within minutes of the murder.

Conan Doyle had few doubts about his guilt. And certainly, on the basis of what we now know, it would seem that a more searching investigation should have been made. One was certainly begun, as we can see both from the testimony of John Trench and the comments in the papers in December 1909, which had hinted that a 'sensational arrest' was to be expected.

There are still those, as Conan Doyle knew in his time, who believe, contrary to all the evidence, that Oscar Slater had something to do with the crime. It is surely time that this rumour was scotched. I hope that by naming Dr Francis Charteris as one of those implicated in the murder of Miss Gilchrist, something will finally be done to clear the names of Oscar Slater and John Trench from the tragic consequences of the cover-up initiated by the police to protect the well-connected Charteris family.

I believe Francis Charteris and another relative went to the flat that night, perhaps by arrangement, perhaps not. Miss Gilchrist admitted them because she knew them. His companion knocked Miss Gilchrist out while Dr Charteris went to search for family papers in the spare room; Miss Gilchrist showed signs of reviving. His companion (clearly a disturbed personality) then beat her to death with the chair. While Charteris continued his search, his partner in crime left the flat and perhaps hid on the upper flight of stairs as William Roughead surmised, until the coast was clear. (Or escaped through the kitchen window with the aid of a convenient drainpipe, as some evidence suggests.) Surprised by the entrance of Helen Lambie and Mr Adams, Dr Charteris, whom Helen recognized from a previous visit, walked coolly out of the flat, before running down the stairs and into the night, to be swallowed up in mystery.

That was what Conan Doyle believed. And as I said earlier, this book is intended to represent his views, while not ignoring other sometimes contradictory views. It may now be too late to prove him right, but some redress should be given to the tarnished reputation of Detective-Lieutenant John Trench. It is never too late for justice.

The case of Oscar Slater still arouses the fiercest controversy. Indeed, like other controversies, such as the assassination of President Kennedy, a flood of information is tending to rub out the simple outline which Conan Doyle accepted.

In 1993 Thomas Toughill, who had been for a time a policeman in Hong Kong, reinvestigated the affair in the light of all the documents, including released official files. He was a keen supporter of Trench's position and detailed much more evidence about the Charteris family than was available to Conan Doyle down to 1928 or to me when I was writing originally in the late 1980s.

But to show no case is ever closed, the distinguished writer and criminologist Richard Whittington-Egan published in 2001 a detailed rebuttal of the Trench *v.* Charteris position. His book was, again, based on a very careful appraisal of the evidence, and on what he had gleaned by further local investigation.

While all are agreed that Slater was innocent, of this crime at least, neither is agreed on other matters. Whittington-Egan concludes that the murder was committed in the course of a robbery, and that rumour in the city was later able to put a name to the crime. This, however, still seems unconvincing to me. Burglars always work quickly, ransacking the premises, throwing the contents of drawers around the rooms. There was none of that in the Gilchrist case. There was a very limited search of a bureau by one intruder, and a brutal attack on Miss Gilchrist by a second.

If the case comes down to the Charteris family as against common burglars I still think that Conan Doyle and Trench were right. The Scottish establishment covered up the case until 1928, protecting one of their own, and pinned the crime on Slater. Toughill thinks that they never wished for the return of Slater from New York. Perhaps it would have been better for him if he had not been so trusting of the Scottish authorities.

Those concerned with this ongoing debate, as opposed to Conan Doyle's view of the case, will be able to read Toughill and Whittington-Egan for themselves, and make up their own minds. Conan Doyle's own papers relating to the Oscar Slater affair, covering the years 1914-29, were bought (for £30,000) at Christie's in May 2004 by the Mitchell Library in Glasgow, to be added to their existing holdings on the case. Doubtless on the basis of this hoard of 145 items, other writers will in their turn rebut Whittington-Egan and Toughill. However, I suspect the papers will serve only to reinforce the views of Trench and Conan Doyle, which I have summarized. Our hero's point of view will not, I think, be too easily discounted.

One final point: there can be little doubt that Conan Doyle's reputation and standing sank in the eyes of many influential people. His son Adrian told the critic and journalist Stuart P. B. Mais that in 1927 Conan Doyle was passed over for the offer of a peerage by Stanley Baldwin owing to the strong opposition from Queen Mary and the Archbishop of Canterbury, Dr. Randall Davidson. What reason could they have had? Conan Doyle had dismayed many Anglicans with his views over both spiritualism and divorce. But was there more?

The Archbishop Randall Davidson was a Scotsman, born in Edinburgh of Presbyterian parents; an Anglican convert, he had been close to the Royal Household since 1882. It strikes me that their personal and public connections with Dr Charteris's uncle, the Very Rev. Archibald Hamilton Charteris, a Royal Chaplain for Scotland (1870–1908), might indeed have prejudiced these two and others in the Scottish Establishment against Doyle.

Was this rejection of Sir Arthur Conan Doyle by his country to be a legislator the final injustice of the Slater affair?

CHAPTER FIFTEEN

INTO THE VALLEY OF FEAR: CRIME IN AMERICA

America for Conan Doyle was something of a second homeland. Just as he admired her people and many of their institutions, so too he was fascinated by American crime, so different from what he knew in Britain and Europe.

From his first novel *A Study in Scarlet* in 1887 to the last of his stories published in 1930 ('The Last Resource'), American crime runs through his work, providing new themes and ideas. The visits he paid to America gave him new experiences as well, further stimulating his imagination. The cases which interested him constitute in themselves a minor chronicle of American crime, a black reflection of the American values he admired.

The sensational background to *A Study in Scarlet* dealt with the Mormon murders in Utah in the early years of that now settled state. Doyle called his 'Avenging Angels' Danites, even though that Mormon faction truly belonged to an earlier period in the tangled Mormon history, and never actually existed in Utah. But he accurately reflected contemporary views of the followers of the Prophet Brigham Young. And there were murders – Danite or not. He drew some of his information from John. H. Beadle's *Brigham Young's Destroying Angel* (1872), later bolstered by *Polygamy: Life in Utah, or The Mysteries and*

171

Crimes of Mormons (1904), a copy of which was in his crimes library at one time.

Visitors to modern Salt Lake City must find it hard to believe that in the nineteenth century this prosperous, vital city was the object of awed wonder for its polygamy, its new-fangled creeds, its prophetic leaders – and its terrible crimes committed in the name of God, such as the Mountain Meadows Massacre when Mormons dressed as Indians attacked a westward-bound wagon train killing men, women and children. The view expressed by Doyle in his novel, of tyrannical elders seizing the prettiest young women for their harems, of opponents being murdered by masked bands, of strange disappearances, was one largely shared by his readers. Nor was it too far from the truth.

When Conan Doyle was on his fourth trip to America in 1923, a trip which took him to the Far West at last, he visited Salt Lake City, where he was favourably impressed by the Mormons. One of the elders of the Church of Jesus Christ of Latter-Day Saints, Bishop Charles W. Nibley, resented the fact that Conan Doyle should be welcomed at all, let alone allowed the use of a hall to speak in, and given money when he was the author of a base book about their ancestors. Conan Doyle referred to the episodes which had inspired him as 'a passing stain on the early history of Utah'. But he refused to apologize, as the facts were true enough and could not be denied.

The passion and prejudice which had marred the rise of the Mormons was not, as Conan Doyle realized, an exceptional thing. America espoused freedom and liberty of conscience, but again and again these have had to be fought for at a great cost. And often enough, as he realized, the freedom of one American was the slavery of another.

Conan Doyle had written his novel without visiting the United States. He used the article on the Mormons in the *Encyclopedia*

Britannica and the numerous articles and reports of the affairs of Utah that filled the newspapers and magazines in the 1880s. But it was these very strong American elements worked into the first Sherlock Holmes novel that began to make his name known on the new continent, and which led to the commission from an American publisher to write *The Sign of Four* in 1889, and so to a further series of Holmes short stories in 1891. When he did arrive in America to lecture in the autumn of 1894 it was as a famous writer, the man who had just had the nerve to kill off Sherlock Holmes.

On his three-month trip he gave everywhere the same basic lecture, 'Readings and Reminiscences', and it proved very popular. He had nothing of the snobbish Englishman about him. His Irish temperament, his Scottish accent, his British reserve, all appealed to his audience.

Sherlock Holmes naturally featured in his talk, for he told the familiar anecdotes about Dr Bell and read from the stories. His leisure was limited, and he saw very little outside of the lecture halls and the hotels in which he stayed with his younger brother, Innes, who was travelling with him. Now and again dinner and a bed were provided by a friendly citizen.

Of real crime there was little enough, nothing that he and his biographers have cared to mention. But they have overlooked one interesting episode. Doyle's progress from city to city was widely reported. The whole continent was aware of him and wide awake to Sherlock Holmes. He was due to lecture in Toronto at the end of November.

While he was in Chicago, Conan Doyle received a letter from Hector Charlesworth, an enterprising journalist with the *Toronto World*, asking him to give his opinion of a recent murder case in that city. Enclosed were a set of cuttings from the paper dealing with the case. Conan Doyle replied on 19 October:

Dear Sir,

I shall read the case, but you can realize how impossible it is for an outsider who is ignorant of local conditions to offer an opinion.

Thanking you I am,
Faithfully yours,
A. Conan Doyle.

He read through the cuttings and discussed them with his brother Innes, his 'Watson' companion of the Southsea days. The case outlined in the cuttings was certainly bizarre enough.

On the evening of Saturday, 6 October, 1894, Frank Westwood, the eighteen-year-old son of a fishing tackle manufacturer, answered the door of his family home in the respectable suburb of Parkwood. From the shadows outside a figure fired one shot. As Frank staggered back into the hall, his mother came hurrying down the stairs attracted by the disturbance.

'I'm shot,' the boy said simply, and made his way upstairs to his bedroom. His father, meanwhile, had come down with his own revolver and fired it off into the area around the house. This failed to attract attention, so he telephoned the police, who arrived minutes later, at around eleven o'clock.

On the following Thursday Frank Westwood died. He had told the police that he did not recognize his attacker but thought it was a dark, slender young man. The odd circumstances of Frank's father firing his own gun that evening suggested to the police that this might have been an internal family affair: both Mr Westwood and his eldest son were suspected of the crime. Local rumour linked the killing with a woman, or a woman in disguise. Weeks passed without any advance in the police case. A government reward was offered, but produced no new evidence.

Hector Charlesworth, who had been working on the story for the *World*, thought it might be a good publicity stunt to seek

Conan Doyle's opinion. A local 'Sherlock Holmes' in Parkwood had already made an inept intervention in the affair; perhaps the master himself might be able to solve it.

He was delighted with Conan Doyle's reply, promising that his opinion would be published in due course, and that Conan Doyle might 'yet embody the facts in an interesting novel'.

Conan Doyle's letter was published on 29 October. A month later, on 26 November, he arrived in Toronto to lecture at the Massey Hall, and at his request, Hector Charlesworth hurried around to the house where he was staying to bring him up to date on the Westwood case. By this time there had been developments.

The murderer had eventually been betrayed to the police by a pickpocket and was taken into custody. Arrested, 'the slender young man' turned out to be a mulatto girl named Clara Ford.

Her preliminary examination before the magistrates was to take place the next day, so that many of the details of the case were still unknown. It was reported that under cross-examination she had volunteered her confession. Conan Doyle, however, commented:

I was very much interested in the account of the affair given in the copies of the *World* that were sent to me. It is a strangely absorbing mystery, and I discussed it at length with my brother after reading it. However, without a knowledge of local conditions, I couldn't attempt to set up an opinion against those of your law officers. I can quite understand how, in the first instance, the public may have thought that the family knew something more of the affair than they stated, but I concluded that the father's story was so unusual that it must be true. As to the present prisoner, Clara Ford, I cannot offer an opinion, I never met with such a case as hers. The system of closeting a prisoner with an officer and cross-questioning her for hours, savours more of French than English methods of justice.

Doyle was right to be cautious about her 'confession'. Clara Ford was a seamstress who had become infatuated with young Frank Westwood, though he rejected whatever overtures she made. Out of jealousy she shot him, then fled along the waterfront and hid in a room over a restaurant frequented by blacks in the city centre. There she might have merged into the background indefinitely, but Clara could not keep her mouth shut. She boasted of her exploit, of her revenge on the white boy who had spurned her. She was turned in by the pickpocket she thought was a friend. Under arrest, she pleaded guilty to the charge.

But Clara Ford soon found friends who hired an expensive lawyer named E.F.B. Johnston on her behalf; 'a group of sentimentalists' sneered Hector Charlesworth. At her trial, Clara claimed that the police told her she would go free if she confessed. Realizing how wrong she had been she withdrew her confession, pleaded not guilty and, in what the presiding judge, Chancellor Sir John Boyd, called 'the most disgusting example of the weakness of the jury system' he could recall, was eventually acquitted. The case remained sensational to the end. A murder in travesty, became a travesty of justice. This was on 4 May 1895, by which time Conan Doyle was back in England.

Clara Ford took advantage of her fame, and travelled with 'Sam T. Jack's Creoles', a burlesque show, billed as the damsel who had killed a man in pursuance of the 'unwritten law'.

Conan Doyle himself believed in the 'unwritten law' – witness the titled lady, the widow of a great statesman, who shot the society blackmailer Charles Augustus Milverton (in a Sherlock Holmes story published a decade later in 1904). But the psychology of the Clara Ford case interested him. The travesty of male disguise had been used by Irene Adler in his first story for Strand in 1891. Can Clara Ford have been a reader of Sherlock Holmes? Miss Adler could easily have gunned down Sherlock Holmes on the doorstep of 221B Baker Street just as Clara had Frank Westwood. Doyle returned to the theme in another odd story, 'The Man with the Watches', in which a young man goes about dressed as a girl. These are odd depths in Conan Doyle, but as a doctor he had seen some odd phases of life. As a man of chivalry, he would have hated Frank Westwood for insulting a black woman, but the murder seems to have arisen from a personal obsession of a sexual nature, too obscene for the kind of popular fiction Conan Doyle was obliged to write.

At the time of the Westwood murder the Chief Inspector of Criminal Investigation for the Government of Ontario was the legendary John Wilson Murray. The memoirs of his extraordinary career as a detective, published in 1904, were among the few modern works which Conan Doyle later added to his criminal library.

The admiring interest he had in Murray may have been partly due to the fact that the detective was born in the city of Edinburgh – in 1840. As a lad, Murray had run away to sea a couple of times, eventually joining the US Navy for the duration of the Civil War. After the war he joined the Secret Service, then the police department of Erie, Pennsylvania. His abilities brought the offer of a job with the Canadian Southern Railways, and from there Murray passed into the Ontario Police. At thirty-five he controlled a huge area of Southern Ontario, one hundred thousand square miles of rough country. His tenacity in pursuit of criminals earned him the nickname 'Old Never-Let-Go'.

John Murray combined just those qualities of determination and sheer deductive genius which Conan Doyle admired in a detective, and which he had made the heart of Sherlock Holmes.

The Blenheim Swamp murder of 1890 was a classic of Murray's career and of Canadian crime – a crime with suitably sinister overtones to appeal at once to Conan Doyle. And because the victim was a prominent Englishman, the British papers gave a vast amount of attention to the case, making Murray a household name.

On 21 February 1890, the body of a youth, little more than a boy, was found by the Elridge brothers, Joseph and George, woodmen in the remote swamp. He had been shot twice and there seemed to be few clues. His soft hands and fine features suggested a person of good breeding. His suit and other clothes were English, though there were no identifying tags or marks on them. A photograph and a description were routinely circulated.

The area of the swamp was painstakingly searched for clues. Nothing. But Murray would not give up. Back he went again to search on his hands and knees. Then, at last, he found a clue: a cigar holder with an amber mouthpiece marked 'F.W.B'.

Among the people who came in to the mortuary to examine the body were a couple named Mr and Mrs Reginald Birchall, who said they had crossed the Atlantic with a young man who called himself Francis W. Benwell. They had parted company at Niagara Falls.

Murray suspected the Birchalls were lying. He could find no trace of Benwell at London, Ontario, the city they claimed he was heading for, so he went back to Niagara Falls. There, acting on his hunch, he had the Birchalls arrested. Then the evidence he needed emerged.

A young man named Douglas Pelly came forward. He had travelled with the Birchalls and Benwell from England. He, like Benwell, had answered an advertisement for a partner in a Canadian ranch. Benwell and Birchall had gone to look at this property in February, but only Birchall returned, explaining that Benwell had gone on to visit friends elsewhere.

Murray asked Pelly if there had been anything suspicious about the Birchalls' behaviour. Indeed there had been: on their visit to the famous falls he had had the feeling that Reginald Birchall attempted to shove him over the edge.

From Scotland Yard Murray obtained details about the background of the Birchalls, who in the past had gone under the names of Lord and Lady Somerset. Tracing their route from Niagara, Murray followed their trail while in company with Benwell to Eastwood, where he found a girl who had seen them together and a while later had heard shots. A farmer named Charles Buck was also interviewed who had seen Birchall alone an hour later, and yet another girl, Mary Swazie, who had seen 'Lord Somerset' on the platform of the Eastwood railway station. From England the detective learnt that the Birchalls had tried to dun Benwell's father for £100.

The case was complete. Though Mrs Birchall was eventually released, her husband was tried, convicted and hanged on 14 November. From the single slender clue of the cigar holder Murray had built up a complete case, piece by piece. It was an achievement of which Sherlock Holmes would have proud, and one which greatly impressed Conan Doyle.

'I have never shown any special cleverness at unravelling mysteries other than imaginary ones, and have never had a share in the solution of any problem of great public interest,' he told Hector Charlesworth before he left Canada. This, of course, was soon changed.

When next Conan Doyle came to North America it was as the champion of George Edalji and Oscar Slater. And it was from America that he was to draw inspiration for what John Dickson Carr, himself a distinguished detective story novelist in the locked-room genre, considered to be the very best of all detective novels, *The Valley of Fear*.

The origins of the novel went back to a visit Conan Doyle received in April 1913. William J. Burns, then known as America's greatest detective, came down to spend the weekend with the Doyles in Windlesham. Burns, with his reddish moustache and genial eye, 'the easy and polished manners of a diplomat over something else which can be polished – granite', charmed the author.

Burns was a long-time admirer of Sherlock Holmes and his fictional 'practical methods'. He demonstrated to Conan Doyle the latest thing in detective aids, the Detectaphone, by means of which the hidden detective could listen in to conversations in another room. Doyle relished the tales Burns had to tell him of his own experiences, and of other celebrated detectives like the men of Pinkerton's National Detective Agency.

Burns, as Conan Doyle learnt, had enjoyed an amazing career. His father, a tailor, had been Police Commissioner of Columbus, Ohio, in the 1880s, which gave the younger Burns (also a tailor in his twenties) the opening to try his hand at detective work. With a natural talent as a sleuth Burns helped the local police solve many mysteries, and his reputation as an amateur detective grew apace. In 1885 he helped the state government clear up a notorious election fraud in Columbus, Ohio.

At the start of the 1890s, Burns joined the United States Secret Service, founded during the Civil War by Allan Pinkerton. His achievements were legendary in this post. In 1894 he tracked down a counterfeiter named Brockway who had enjoyed a twenty-five-year career. In 1896 he broke a ring of Costa Rican revolutionaries who were financing their schemes by forging US and Costa Rican bank notes. Then in September 1897, after three prisoners had been taken from a Ripley County Jail and shot, and two more lynched, the Governor of Indiana called in Burns when local police failed to discover the culprits. Working undercover as an insurance agent Burns soon compiled a list of those responsible for carrying out that extra-legal 'justice'.

Further secret service work involved a complex investigation into public land frauds in Washington, Oregon and California. Burns ruthlessly pursued the trail of those involved from local officials up to a senator. In San Francisco there was a three-year investigation into corruption which sent local Union-Labor Party boss Abe Ruef to jail. He was now called by the press 'the American Sherlock Holmes'.

In 1909, with his son Raymond as partner, Burns established the William J. Burns National Detective Agency in New York. The company, with local offices across the continent, took on the protection of the 11,000 member banks of the American Bankers' Association. This was, for Burns, mere routine work.

A bomb planted in the offices of the *Los Angeles Times* in 1910 resulted in the deaths of 21 people, and it was thanks to Burns and his Agency that the Irish brothers John J. and James B. McNamara and Ortie McManigal of the International Association of Bridge and Structural Iron Workers were tracked down and brought before a court. Although defended by the great liberal lawyer Clarence Darrow, the trio confessed and were jailed. This case was another part of the long and bloody battle between the detective agencies hired by the employers and the newly organized American trade unions.

Burns, during his visit to Windlesham, also recounted for Conan Doyle the extraordinary feat of Pinkerton agent James McParland, in penetrating the Molly Maguires, a secret organization among the Irish miners in Pennsylvania which derived its name from the custom of wearing women's clothing as a disguise. This episode took hold of Conan Doyle's imagination, and he began to turn over in his mind the possibility of using it as the basis of a new novel.

After Burns had planted the seed of the idea, Conan Doyle developed a plot loosely based on James McParland and his adventures. More details were easily obtained, as Allan Pinkerton himself had written about the investigation (in *The Molly Maguires and the Detectives*) and the activities of the Molly Maguires were well documented. It seemed like a good vehicle for a Sherlock Holmes story – set in 1895, but harking back to the Pennsylvania mining towns of 1875.

Having completed *The Valley of Fear*, as the novel came to be called, during the winter of 1913 and the spring of 1914, Conan

Doyle played down the Irish aspect of the story – it did not do to offend the sensibilities of the Irish-American community. Later, on publication, the German names were also changed, to Swedish ones. It was the first tale of Sherlock Holmes for ten years, and was widely welcomed when it appeared in book form in 1915.

Conan Doyle did not lose touch with Burns. The following April (1914) he and his wife accepted an invitation by the Canadian Pacific Railway to visit Jasper National Park in Alberta, and while passing through New York he and Burns met again. Burns came down the river to meet Conan Doyle on his liner, along with eager press representatives.

Among them was Mr Brennan, a director with the Mutual Film Corporation, who pressed Doyle into action as a 'star turn' in his company's continuing weekly film serial *Our Mutual Girl,* for a supposed 'real-life' detective consultation about the whereabouts of the missing heroine, Margaret, played by Norma Philips. A mild action yarn with romantic overtones, about the misadventures of a young rural girl as she makes her way from the country to the city, the film was tied in with a serialized magazine story, which in turn yielded several advertising franchises. This role as 'a consulting detective' was one of the few film appearances of Sir Arthur, but the only one in 'a detective' role.

By now Burns himself with his International Detective Agency was involved in a criminal affair which had excited the whole nation, and which touched a nerve in Conan Doyle as well – the case of Leo Frank.

Frank, a well-educated Jew with a young wife, was the Factory Superintendent of his uncle's National Pencil Company factory in Atlanta, Georgia, in the heart of the Old South. One of the company's employees was a maturely developed thirteen-year-old named Mary Phagan. On Saturday, 26 April 1913, while most of the city was at a parade, Mary went down to collect her pay from Frank, who was alone in the factory; the following day she was found beaten and strangled in the factory basement by the night watchman, a negro named Newt Lee.

Lee and Frank were obvious suspects. A note found by the body supposedly (but impossibly) written by the dead girl referred to the tall negro.* But the odd circumstance that Frank had telephoned the factory on the Saturday night to ask if anything was wrong – a thing he had never done before – drew the police interest to the Jew, an interloper in traditional Georgia. All those anti-Northern, anti-Jewish prejudices which lie only a little way below the surface of the Southern sensibility bubbled up.

There was no real case against Leo Frank, and he was convicted largely on the evidence of James Conley, another negro employed by National Pencil. The trial of Leo Frank took place amidst great publicity and the pressure of local public opinion was clearly against him; though there was never any evidence of rape, nor any charge of it, the image of the ravished white maiden despoiled and murdered by the pervert Jew had taken hold of the local people's imaginations.

The friends of Leo Frank hired William Burns to investigate. Burns sent his local agent to the scene and soon followed himself. He was nearly lynched by a crowd at Marietta in the course of his inquiries. The local police did not share Burns's opinion that Frank was innocent, and there was increasing resentment against both Leo Frank and William Burns.

Burns traced letters written by Conley in which he confessed between various obscene phrases, to having murdered Mary Phagan. There is little doubt now that this prize witness for the State of Georgia was the real murderer. Another employee in the factory, terrorized into silence by Conley, told *The Tennessean* in 1982 that Leo Frank did not kill Mary Phagan, as he had seen 'Jim Conley holding the victim's body'.

* The text was: 'Mam, that Negro hire doun here did this i went to make water and he push me doun that hole a long tall negro black that hoo it was long sleam tall negro i wright while play with me.'

Despite threats on the life of Governor John M. Slaton if he should take such an action, Slaton commuted Leo Frank's death sentence to life imprisonment. Dissatisfied by this apparent 'injustice', a mob, calling themselves the Knights of Mary Phagan, took Leo Frank from his cell – where he had already been attacked by the guards – and lynched him. The culprits, all well known locally and easily identified from photographs, proudly posed for at the scene, were never arrested. 'Southern justice' had had its way. Jewish groups and others, despite the new evidence, have never succeeded in having Leo Frank's name cleared.

Conan Doyle followed the Leo Frank case with great interest, as Burns wrote to him about it in 1915 – a volume dealing with the evidence in the case was among the select books in his crime library. And he followed Burns's later career as well, though this became less glamorous. In 1917 William Burns was found guilty of entering a law office to copy letters for a client: he was fined.

In 1921, Burns was appointed by President Harding's Attorney-General to be director of the Federal Bureau of Investigation. In May 1924, he was obliged to resign, tarnished by association with the 'Tea Pot Dome' corruption scandal. A further tussle with the law followed when Burns worked for Sinclair Oil in 1927. The company retained Burns to put the jury under surveillance in the case in which their president, Harry Sinclair, was on trial for bribing the Secretary of the Interior. Sinclair was acquitted and the Burns Agency was fined $1000 for 'jury-tampering'. Burns had fallen in esteem by taking public office and the talents of the detective had been corrupted by American political life. It is significant that Conan Doyle does not mention Burns after 1924. A cloud of scandal now hovered over the 'Sherlock Holmes of America'.

In May 1914 Conan Doyle, accompanied by his family, passed through New York on their way to the Canadian West. As mentioned above, again he met William Burns and through him was able to inspect several American prisons such as the Tombs in New York City (on 28 May) with two of Burns's staff and Sing-Sing on the Hudson (30 May). He was interested to see 'a jovial English forger' styling himself Sir John Gray, better known to the police however 'Paper Collar Joe'. Conan Doyle thought the Tombs a beautiful place, with 'fine appointments' and perfect discipline. He was not impressed with the conditions which prevailed in Sing-Sing, though he admired the reforming efforts of the governor, an Irish-American named Lang.

He was refused permission to see the prize prisoner there, a Lieutenant Becker, a corrupt policeman awaiting death for murdering Herman Rosenthal, the owner of a gambling den, who was going to expose him. Instead Conan Doyle himself was locked in a cell for five minutes. The experience left him claiming the prison should be burned down. It was a hundred years behind the times, he was reported by the London *Times* as saying, and was a disgrace to America compared with what existed in Britain. 'Probably a third of the prisoners are defectives whose cases called for medical treatment, or care in an asylum. Perhaps another third are young men who ought never to have been put with hardened criminals, and the last third men for whom such places as Sing-Sing have to exist.'

He thought that crime in the United States was like the country itself – cosmopolitan. He had heard it said that the crooks in New York were the cleverest and most resourceful in the world. There were perhaps fewer violent crimes in England because of the fear of the death penalty. 'Even so I should say we have all the criminal enterprise in England that we want.' However, as a final comment on the city, Conan Doyle was impressed with the police, 'a marvellous lot of men' who were much improved on those he had noticed twenty years before. Now they were young, vigorous and responsible; but then the USA was a country for young men.

The rest of his journey through Canada to visit Jasper National

Park was free of criminal connections, so far as I can find out. However, on the voyage back to England, Conan Doyle met William A. Pinkerton, son of the famous Allan, who now headed his father's agency. Inevitably the talk drifted not only onto crime, but also onto the Molly Maguires. Doyle had already completed *The Valley of Fear* and it was to begin running in *The Strand* in September. But when he read the novel in 1915 Pinkerton was furious, feeling that Conan Doyle had made use of a private conversation. Of course, this was not the case. Pinkerton did not realize that the novel had been completed on the basis of Burns's information long before they met, but the friendship between the two men cooled, despite a series of warm letters from Conan Doyle.*

When it appeared in the summer of 1915 *The Valley of Fear* was greeted with joy by Conan Doyle's admirers, especially in America. Publication in the midst of a great war did not seem to affect the popularity of the book at all.

Conan Doyle himself returned to America in April 1922, this time to lecture on spiritualism, though he still found some time for criminology. One person he met was Edward Morrell, who had been tortured in San Quentin and had gained psychic powers which inspired Jack London's cruel and sordid novel *The Jacket* (known in America as *The Star Rover*).

Having read of its iniquities in Joseph Fishman's *Crucibles of Crime* (1923), Conan Doyle visited Chicago Jail on his next American trip in 1923. He was again shocked at what he saw, and equally shocked at the public indifference to the problem – a dangerous indifference. Crime breeds crime, 'the small sinner

* In addition to hunting down Butch Cassidy and the Sundance Kid, the firm was asked by William's old friend Winston Churchill, then Home Secretary, to provide the security for the Coronation of George V in 1911. It also provided guards for the Prince of Wales on his American visit to protect him from Irish Republicans.

becomes the large sinner, and sooner or later the community pays the price,' he said. The jail had no light or air in the building. He thought the architect should have been in it! He left in a depressed state to write an article about it.

Penal reform is still very much an issue, and Doyle's impressions and reactions are still valid. He wrote about what he had seen for the *Chicago Daily News*, the editor of which hoped to effect some change in the system. But Chicago was then entering one of the most lawless periods in the history of the United States: between 1920 and 1931 the wave of organized crime masterminded by Al Capone threatened to overwhelm the city completely.

The jail in Chicago dated from 1840, though one section was built in 1890. It was dark, airless and grim. The prisoners had little or no work, and all kinds were mixed together, first-time offenders with old lags. It was appalling. The efforts of John Howard and Elizabeth Fry which had reformed British prisons had made no impact on America. In England, Doyle had been very impressed by a visit he had made to the Borstal institution for young offenders at Maidstone, supervised by a governor of the military type and run along the lines of a very strict public school. The first of these experimental reformatories had been opened at Rochester, Kent, in 1908.

It should not be thought that Conan Doyle was sentimental about criminals. For the habitual criminal he recommended imprisonment for life. It was for the first offender that Doyle reserved his concern, especially the young first offender, who he felt should receive all the aid he could to set him straight.

The detection of the criminal, the intellectual exercise which Sherlock Holmes delighted in, is only one aspect of crime. Punishment and the remaking of the criminal, things of little interest to the reader of novels, awoke the conscience of Conan Doyle. The serious purpose of criminology shades over into the more complex area of penology.

The prohibition era of America in the 1920s, with its criminal gangs and citizen vigilantes inspired Conan Doyle's very last story to be published, in 1930. 'The Last Resource' pulled its punches by being the vision of a future possibility, but the details were sharply drawn from the current American reality of violent crime and political reaction. However, Conan Doyle's solution, that the good citizens take the law into their own hands and machine-gun the gangs to death, is prescient of the Fascist solution to Europe's problems. Conan Doyle, though, died in 1930, and some horrors he did not live to see. From first to last, American crime provided Conan Doyle with vivid images for his fictional recreations.

Readers have often wondered why Sherlock Holmes never uses fingerprints. When they are referred to by a police officer, he remarks casually that he had heard something about them, almost as if they had been invented on the Moon.

The idea of fingerprints as a means of identification was an old one, but it was placed on a proper scientific basis only by the studies of Sir Francis Galton, who published his *Finger Prints* in 1892. A revised version of Galton's system was developed by Edward (later Sir Edward) Henry in India in 1897; the following year his *Classification and Uses of Finger Prints* became the definitive textbook on the subject for many decades to come. In July 1901, Henry became the first chief of Scotland Yard's new Fingerprint Branch.

One classic American case which impressed Conan Doyle and which is relevant here concerned the robbery of the express train to New Orleans in 1894. This had been investigated by the Brooklyn journalist Solomon Solis Carvalho, who then edited the *New York World*, and specialized in sensational suicides and murders. Carvalho detected the alleged robber by the imprint of his thumb on one of the seals of the rifled packages. This, Conan Doyle told an Indianapolis journalist in October 1894, was 'one of the cleverest detective bits in real life, or even in fiction'. It was also one of the earliest uses of fingerprints, though it seems to be unknown to historians of the introduction of fingerprints.

In fiction the interest in fingerprints inspired Mark Twain in the writing of *Pudd'nhead Wilson* (1894), where the identity of the twins is resolved by their fingerprints. He had earlier alluded to the use of fingerprints in *Life on the Mississippi* (1883). Conan Doyle was impressed by the idea as well. What he did not know was that the jury in the New Orleans express train robbery trial did not accept the evidence, that the criminal was acquitted, and then sued the *Sun* for damages. 'Sherlock Holmes', commented the *Indianapolis Journal* (16 October 1894), 'would never have lost a case in such a way.'

But Conan Doyle was right to appreciate – long before the authorities or even juries did – the significance of fingerprints in the detection of crime. It was not until 1905 that an English Court accepted fingerprint identification in a case of murder. The methods of Sherlock Holmes were, it seems, more convincing to the man in the street than to the science of criminalistics.

CHAPTER SIXTEEN

THE BLUEBEARD OF THE BATH

Like Sherlock Holmes, Conan Doyle was an omnivorous and thorough reader of the newspapers, taking several a day. Cuttings, as often as not relating to crime, were sent to him by a clippings agency, and again like Sherlock Holmes, he filed the most interesting.

In January 1915, a month in which the real news of the day was the terrible losses on the Western Front, several newspapers, including the *News of the World*, carried reports of the verdict which had been returned by a jury in Kentish Town, north London, in an inquest on a young bride who had been found drowned in her bath.

Her name was Margaret Elizabeth Lloyd, born Lofty. She had married John Lloyd at the Bath Register Office on 17 December 1914. Later that day she and her husband had taken a room at 14 Bismarck Road, Highgate. Mr Lloyd on arrival had made particular inquiries about a bath, and was pleased to hear the boarding house was fitted with one.

The Lloyds had then visited Dr Stephen Bates, who had prescribed a sedative for Mrs Lloyd's headache. The following day Mrs Lloyd visited the offices of Mr Arthur Lewis, a solicitor, for the purpose making a will in favour of her husband. That night Mrs Lloyd asked for a hot bath at 7.30. Ten minutes later the landlady, Mrs Blatch, heard splashing in the bath, followed by the curious sound of hands slapping the side of the bath. A deep sigh was audible – then there was silence. Wondering about this, she heard the organ in the sitting-room on which Mr Lloyd was playing *Nearer My God to Thee* – a hymn which many then associated with sinking of the *Titanic*.

As Mr Lloyd came down the stairs and went out, the landlady continued with her various kitchen duties. Some minutes later the door bell rang; Mr Lloyd had returned.

'I've bought some tomatoes for Mrs Lloyd's supper. Is she down yet?'

They found Margaret Lloyd dead in the bath. The police were called, the usual formalities gone through, and on 21 December Mrs Lloyd was buried. The inquest opened the following day and was adjourned to 1 January, when the jury found that Mrs Lloyd died from suffocation by drowning in the bath water; death by misadventure.

Poor Mr Lloyd applied for probate of his wife's estate through Mr W.P. Davies, a solicitor in Shepherds Bush, in the west of London. Customary technical procedures delayed the grant, however, until 11 January.

The reports of the inquest were widely noticed, by Conan Doyle among others. A mysterious death always gained Conan Doyle's attention, but as he read the report from Kentish Town, a recollection stirred in his memory. The pattern seemed familiar. As Sherlock Holmes had observed to Watson the very day they met, a crime will always have its parallel somewhere.

More than a year previously, he recalled, in December 1913, there had been a very similar case in Blackpool, the seaside resort on the west coast of England. The newspaper cutting about the case had been kept, and was soon turned up. It made interesting reading.

On 10 December 1913, a Mr and Mrs George Smith had taken

rooms with Mrs Margaret Crossly at 16 Regent Road, Blackpool. Mr Smith was anxious to know first if the house had a bath; in fact he had turned down other accommodation only because there was no bath. That same day the couple had called on Dr George Billing. Mr Smith explained that his wife had a severe headache from their long journey, and she was given a prescription for tablets and some stomach medicine.

On the evening of Friday, 12 December, Mrs Smith asked if she could have a bath, and Mrs Crossly filled it for her. The bathroom was situated on the floor above and immediately over the kitchen. To their puzzlement, Mrs Crossly and her family became aware of water, presumably from the bath, dripping through the ceiling and running down the kitchen walls. At that moment Smith called down the stairs, 'My wife can't speak to me – go for a doctor.' Dr Billing was called in, but Mrs Smith was already dead; drowned. An inquest held on the following day returned a verdict of death from misadventure. It had all been a dreadful accident. On 15 December the funeral of Mrs Alice Smith was attended by her mother Mrs Elizabeth Burnham and her brother Norman Burnham. Smith bade goodbye to them on the following day, and three days later received the insurance money on his wife's death. They never saw him again.

Conan Doyle was struck at once by the coincidence of the two brides dying in similar circumstances. As a doctor he knew what would happen if someone had a fit or a heart attack in the bath. For someone to drown the head would have to pass completely under the water, and the legs would have to be doubled up or extended over the end of the bath. It did not seem possible that an adult could drown in a bath. A sinister pattern of deliberate murder began to suggest itself. Could there be other cases, so far unnoticed?

Conan Doyle felt there was nothing he himself could do in this case, so he communicated with a friend of his at Scotland Yard, Detective-Inspector Arthur Neil. By coincidence, Alice Smith's father Charles Burnham had also read the report of the Highgate inquest in the *News of the World* and had sent that report, together with a clipping of the Blackpool inquest report on his daughter, to the Aylesbury police through his solicitor. Joseph Crossly, the son of the Blackpool landlady, had in the meantime also read the report of the Lloyd inquest. He sent copies in turn to the police at Scotland Yard.

Inspector Neil is said, by American writer Albert Ullman, to have called on Conan Doyle to discuss this information. Further-more Mrs Lloyd's husband seemed to have disappeared without trace, and Conan Doyle thought this most peculiar.

'It occurs to me that you might put more men on his track,' he is said to have told Neil. 'If these deaths are not sheer coincidence, then this business isn't finished.'

'You mean . . . ?'

'Oh yes, yes. If murder has been committed, then you will have a creature to deal with who will be as rapacious a human as a pike that escapes being devoured by its parents – ruthless beyond all conjecture. No time is to be lost.'

Neil then asked the Highgate Coroner to delay the issue of the form certifying the cause of death to the insurance company which had covered Mrs Lloyd's life. Eventually, he reasoned, the missing husband would have to apply in person, or through his solicitor to obtain the necessary form if he was to lay hands on the money due on his wife's death. Having shown himself, the police could then trap this 'rapacious pike', as Conan Doyle had called him.

The Assistant Commissioner of CID was incredulous that the reports were linked. But he generously allowed Inspector Neil to make inquiries about the death of Mrs Lloyd, or Miss Lofty as she should be called, as that incident lay within the Metropolitan area.

On 19 January, 'in consequence of information received', Neil contacted the Aylesbury police and the Post Office. Two days later he had received reports about Mrs Alice Smith, or Burnham, and the following day Miss Lofty's bankbook, with its details of her finances. The facts seemed to support the suspicions of Conan Doyle, Charles Burnham and Joseph Crossly.

On 1 February the man known as Lloyd called at the office of Davies the solicitor regarding the settlement of his 'wife's' estate; there he was arrested. John Lloyd was held on a charge of falsely entering facts about his marriage to Miss Lofty at Bath on 17 December; in short, he had married her bigamously. That, however, was merely a holding charge, while a more thorough inquiry was begun.

A third murder, though the first in his chronology of killing, came to light only when Smith was under arrest. This was the death on 13 July 1912 of Bessie Mundy in a bath at Herne Bay, where she and Smith were living as Mr and Mrs Williams. The house they rented was without a bath, and Smith had gone to a local ironmonger and bargained over the cheapest bath in stock, knocking half a crown off the price. This was installed in an empty room, but not fitted. A visit was made to a local doctor to establish that poor Mrs Williams (whom the neighbours thought very healthy) suffered from fits of epilepsy. The same doctor, called in three days later when Mrs Williams was found dead in the bath, accepted that she had drowned during an epileptic fit.

The police were astonished to find that Smith had married Miss Mundy in 1910 at Weymouth, had absconded with all her cash a few weeks later, had met her again by chance on the street at Weston-Super-Mare in March 1912, and had been reconciled to her, and to the rest of her money. His charm and powers of persuasion were formidable.

Now her body was exhumed and examined by Dr Bernard Spilsbury. In his report to the police he noted, 'I am of the opinion that we have not, so far, discovered the full list of this man's crimes.' But charges of murder were laid only in relation to the deaths of Alice Burnham, Margaret Lofty and Bessie Mundy.

Police investigations were made in 40 towns, statements taken from 150 witnesses, 112 of whom were called to the eight-day trial at the Old Bailey which opened on 22 June 1915. This was to be the longest and most important trial in England since that of Palmer the poisoner in 1860. There were 264 exhibits, including the three baths from Herne Bay, Blackpool and Highgate.

Much of the evidence related to the devious and manipulative aspects of George Joseph Smith's marital adventures.

It was clear that some of those whose hearts and possessions Smith had plundered, Beatrice Thornhill, Edith Pegler, and Alice Reavil among them, had narrowly escaped with their lives, but the police were by no means sure they had traced the full extent of Smith's murders. Of those that were revealed, all took place on Friday night/Saturday morning; each time Smith had gone out to buy food for supper − fish at Herne Bay, eggs at Blackpool, tomatoes at Highgate; all made use of a bath.

There was little his counsel, Edward Marshall Hall, could do to save Smith. He was convicted and sentenced to death on 1 July 1915. After his appeal was dismissed, he was executed at Maidstone Gaol on Friday, 13 August.

Throughout the ordeal of his arrest and trial Smith showed little emotion. He was a man quite without ordinary feelings. He had wanted to bury Alice Burnham in a plain deal coffin in a common grave at Blackpool. Joseph Crossly had protested that he himself would never bury his wife in such a way, no matter how poor he was. Smith was not impressed.

'When they are dead, they are dead,' he answered, a harsh, if sound, philosophy.

Conan Doyle's friend the journalist G.R. Sims dubbed Smith 'The Bluebeard of the Bath'. By contrast with the millions killed in the Great War, the number of Smith's victims may seem paltry. Conan Doyle by now was deeply concerned with the course of that carnage. And yet the tragic melancholy of those independent but lonely ladies, those out-of season resorts, those baths with their scratched enamel, and the little treats for supper – above all the cold, calculating greed – have secured for George Joseph Smith a permanent place among the monsters of crime.

CHAPTER SEVENTEEN

THE ERRANT KNIGHT

The Great War was fought to secure the liberty of small nations. For Conan Doyle, as for many people of Irish blood, that cause was ironically crossed by Britain's treatment of Ireland. In the years before the war the political conflict in Ireland nearly brought the country to the verge of revolution and civil war. He feared a conflict between the fifteenth century in the South and the seventeenth century in the North, with the twentieth century in London looking on. But the conflict might not have been confined to Ireland only.

Conan Doyle, an Imperialist at heart, had come out in favour of Home Rule for Ireland in 1911, and this was granted in 1914. The act received the royal assent in the ominous first weeks of September; but was suspended for the term of the war, which at that time, of course, everyone thought would be 'over by Christmas'. But by now mere self-government was not enough for a minority of Irishmen: on the extreme Republican right and extreme Socialist left. They wanted the appearance and substance of complete independence; and were prepared to die to bring it to the majority.

On 21 April 1916, a stranger was arrested in a prehistoric fort near Banna Strand in County Kerry on the west Coast of Ireland. He could give the local police no account of himself, though his muddy clothes were stained with brine. The police suspected he

197

was Sir Roger Casement and that he had landed on a special mission from Germany to bring assistance for an intended republican *coup d'état*. Within hours the prisoner was on his way to England, to a cell in the Tower of London and a capital charge of treason. Casement had been involved in trying to land rifles for the Republican movement, but these had never come ashore. In Dublin the Easter Rising went ahead, beginning the fight for Irish independence.

Sir Roger was an old friend of Conan Doyle's, and the writer was stunned by the former British diplomat's arrest. He had come to know Casement through his involvement with Edmund Dene Morel, who was leading a passionate campaign for reform of the Congo Free State (now the Democratic Republic of Congo), from where, in 1903, Casement had reported to the British Foreign Office on the atrocities committed by the exploiting Belgian colonists. The Congo Free State was the private domain of Leopold II, King of the Belgians. It has been suggested since that Casement's original reports were exaggerated, arising partly from the over-emotional nature of his personal relations with the Congolese. Conan Doyle, who was connected with Congo Reform Association from 1909 to 1913, taking advantage of Casement's papers and notes, wrote a brisk, biting attack on Belgian rule in a pamphlet *The Crime of the Congo* (1909). But the horrors of the Congo are not quite crime as we mean it in this book.

Casement, meanwhile, had moved on to South America, where as British Consul General in Rio de Janeiro he began an investigation into atrocities committed against the Putamayo Indians by companies cashing in on the rubber boom. These inquiries, prompted by the treatment of black labourers from the British West Indies, covered the years 1909–12. While he was there, Casement was in correspondence with Conan Doyle, largely over political matters, but also providing background material for Doyle's new novel, *The Lost World*; in which the character of

Lord John Roxton is based in part on Casement. While Casement was in England on leave, Conan Doyle took him to see the stage adaptation of *The Speckled Band*.

In August 1913 Casement was honoured by King George V with a knighthood, which he later claimed he had been reluctant to accept, and retired from the diplomatic service.

As Sir Roger Casement, he returned to live in Ireland and his letters to Conan Doyle became increasingly concerned with the injustices in Ireland, and her right to freedom. He persuaded Conan Doyle to support the movement for Home Rule, but then the war came. By now their friendship had cooled, Casement embracing the extreme minority view that war with Germany provided Ireland's opportunity to separate from Britain, and Conan Doyle expressing the more general view of the day that Ireland would have to play her part in the war once it had begun.

Casement went to America, and then on to Germany. His statements became (in Conan Doyle's opinion at least) more outrageous. He attempted to raise among the Irish-born prisoners of war in Germany an Irish Brigade to fight the British in Ireland, or in the Middle East in an attack on Egypt. But he was soundly repulsed by the Irish prisoners. As soon as news of Casement's arrival in Berlin reached London at the end of November 1914, Conan Doyle wrote to *The Times* it was inconceivable to anyone who knew Casement that he should be 'in full possession of his faculties and a traitor to the country that has employed and honoured him'.

A key factor in all of this, as Conan Doyle knew, was the armed resistance by the Ulster Volunteers to Home Rule for Ireland. They had even imported arms from Germany in 1914, with the help of British Conservative politicians such as Edward Carson and Frederick E. Smith. Conan Doyle in New York in May 1914 had spoken to the press about his fears of an insurrection in Ulster and of civil war in Ireland. The Great War had since brought Smith into the government as Attorney-General. The Irish National Volunteers raised to support Home Rule had rallied to the cause, save for a small wing which brought about the attempted *coup d'état* at Easter 1916. It was to them that Casement now gave his allegiance.

Casement had come over to Ireland in a submarine accompanied by a ship bearing arms for the Rising. But as the ship had been scuttled with a loss of the arms on board, Casement landed with the hope of postponing the planned rebellion. He was arrested too soon to get his message for the leaders in Dublin through to the local Republicans. He was quickly moved to England.

Now he was imprisoned in London, and being prosecuted by his political enemy F.E. Smith as a traitor to the King. The irony of this was not lost on Casement, his Irish lawyers, or on Conan Doyle. But no advantage could be made of it at his trial. Smith managed to convince the jury that the man who had laboured so long abroad for the cause of justice was indeed a traitor to the King. Casement was convicted and under a medieval act was sentenced to hang. His appeal was dismissed, and F.E. Smith, as Attorney-General, refused leave for an appeal to the House of Lords.

Conan Doyle had followed these events with dismay. Clement King Shorter, the editor and publisher who was married to the Irish poet Dora Sigerson, was trying to organize a reprieve for Casement. He approached Sir Arthur, who wrote a petition which Shorter amended. Conan Doyle collected a list of distinguished names in British public life, science, religion, and the arts to sign the petition which he then sent to the Prime Minister, Herbert Asquith.

It had been foreseen that the trial of such an eminent man as Sir Roger Casement, with all his well-connected friends in Britain, Ireland and America, would present a problem. The government, or rather the Attorney-General F.E. Smith, had earlier sought a way out of this impasse.

In Casement's Ebury Street lodgings the police had discovered in 1914 a trunk containing letters and papers, including a series of journals for the years 1903 and 1910, and a cash ledger for 1911. These were the notorious 'Black Diaries' which detailed, among many other things, the private homosexual life of Roger Casement.

Some pages from the first diary for 1903 were shown to a group of British and American journalists in May 1916. The diaries were then typed up. (These proceedings suggested to some fervent Irish nationalists that the sexual passages in the diaries – which are in fact numerous and continuous – had been forged by the British secret service.) A set of copies were given to Casement's solicitor, George Gavan Duffy. He did not look at them, and Casement's counsel refused even to consider them. The copies were handed back to the prosecution on the opening day of the trial. It is clear that F.E. Smith hoped that the defence would plead guilty but insane, and in this way the British government would be saved the embarrassment of hanging an Irish hero Great Britain had knighted.

The diaries as a whole were shown to others, among them Sir Arthur Conan Doyle. Many prominent people, such as John Redmond, the leader of the Irish Party, were influenced against Casement by what they were told or saw of the diaries.

Conan Doyle as a writer chose to limit the nature of the subjects he dealt with; Conan Doyle as a doctor, however, had seen many aspects of life. He was not impressed with the contents of the diaries, and he chose to disregard them. The charge of treason which Casement faced was far more serious that any accusation of sexual aberration. (Male homosexuality was then a criminal offence under the *Offences Against the Person Act* of 1865.)

For Conan Doyle, Casement's homosexuality (if it could even be proved) was evidence of a mental imbalance which should certainly be enough to prevent his execution. Casement, he thought, was both physically and mentally ill from all those long years in the tropics.

Casement now seems to have viewed Conan Doyle with disdain. In his diaries he refers to Doyle in inverted commas as 'my friend', and he was outraged that in the opening passage of his petition and in newspaper interviews Conan Doyle should have suggested he was mentally disturbed.

Conan Doyle campaigned hard to gain justice for Roger Casement. It is not true, however, that he donated £700 to Casement's defence fund, as H. Montgomery Hyde suggests. Conan Doyle subscribed no money to the defence, nor did he visit Casement in prison. (The reference to 'Doyle' in the private list of those who subscribed to the defence funds drawn up by his solicitor Gavan Duffy refers to his American lawyer, Michael Francis Doyle, who had brought some $5,000 with him from America, some of which he was paid by Casement as his fee. The £700 represents the residue paid into the defence fund. This American money had come from the Fenian John Devoy, who was swiftly reimbursed by the German government through agents in Washington. (Casement's defence was, ironically, largely paid for by the German Imperial government.)

Casement was convicted. A reprieve was refused and he was hanged on 3 August 1916. Conan Doyle felt 'shame and disgust' at the gloating reaction of some newspapers to Casement's death sentence. To Conan Doyle, as a convinced Imperialist, this was a mistake. Casement's conviction and his death would be exploited by every enemy of England 'from Dublin to San Francisco'. It was not in the interest of the Empire that he be made a martyr: that was what Casement 'very earnestly' desired.

In supporting a reprieve for Casement after the trial went against him, Conan Doyle was moving against the tide of popular feeling in Britain. (Popular feeling in Ireland was something else again.) He showed great courage in this, as indeed he always showed courage in doing what he thought was right – and damn the consequences. He shared this very Irish characteristic with Roger Casement himself. Conan Doyle later supported Sir Horace Plunkett, the progressive Unionist, in his campaign for a Dublin seat in 1918, but quickly tired of the bitter, violent nature of Irish politics, then moving towards outright war with Britain, and eventually to a divisive and damaging civil war, not now between North and South, but between the Free State and the Republicans in the South alone, between Right and Left.

Conan Doyle had Sherlock Holmes in his wartime service to the Crown penetrate an Irish-American revolutionary group and work under cover in rural Ireland in the little town of Skibbereen, to explore the nefarious connections between German militarism and Irish rebellion. (Basil Thompson, through whom the Casement diaries came to public attention, describes in his memoirs the comic reality of such espionage.) This was Conan Doyle's oblique way of commenting on the unhappy background to the death of Roger Casement.

This disappointment grew throughout the Great War as, touched by so many useless deaths, some very near to him, Conan Doyle turned away from the call of politics to begin his crusade for spiritualism. He still believed in justice, but his experiences during the Casement affair had left him disillusioned with the blind passion of politics.

For it was in 1916 that Conan Doyle publicly announced his formal adherence to spiritualism. He long been interested in psychic matters. As long ago as the mid-1880s in his Southsea days he had attended seances with a circles of friends including General Drayson. The second of the three Southsea Notebooks (in the first of which the birth of Sherlock Holmes is recorded) covering the years 1885 to 1888, contains an account of ten seances, lists books on occult and spiritualist themes, animal magnetism, hypnosis, and the eccentric opinions of the General. Conan Doyle's Catholicism had hardly survived his schooldays. He refused his family advice to build his medical practice in Southsea on the basis of a Catholic connection; though this did not prevent him joining a Masonic Lodge, and doubtless making use of that connection.

He had joined the Society for Psychical Research in 1893, and had even taken part in investigations. One haunting at Charmouth was always mentioned by him. Yet he maintained the same rational approach to such little-known phenomena. He was as rational-minded as his great detective. Soon after the death of his first wife, he even joined the Rationalist Press Association. He was a member of that vigorously secularist society from 1908 to 1916, as Nicolas Walter, the secretary of the Association, pointed out in a public controversy with Anthony Burgess. These were also significant years for his amateur detective work.

He himself felt that when he embraced spiritualism he brought to this new cause the same spirit of inquiry. Many of his friends and critics would have disagreed with him. From 1916 onwards his interest in crime and detection was hemmed about with psychic beliefs. Had he lost his good sense? Or was he merely opening new doors of perception? Was his gullible foolishness over the photographs of the Cottingley fairy photographs merely the minor aberration of a great mind, or a symptom that he was now beyond the reach of reason?

This was and remains a matter of controversy. The Jesuit Fr Hubert Thurston, who had known Conan Doyle from their Stonyhurst days, wrote sharply – from an orthodox Catholic perspective – about Conan Doyle's beliefs, introducing some very personal comments from his private knowledge of other members of Doyle's extended family who remained Catholic. Others, like the stage magician Houdini, were more circumspect. But the spiritualist beliefs that dominated the last fourteen years of his life still dismay many who remained devotees of Sherlock Holmes. Another old school friend, the *Punch* cartoonist Bernard Partridge, published a caricature of Sherlock Holmes chained to the leg of a Conan Doyle whose head is enveloped in a cloud of psychic nonsense. It brilliantly summed up what the majority of Doyle's readers thought.

There can be little doubt that Conan Doyle's reputation and standing sank in the eyes of many influential people. *The Land of Mist*, published in 1926, brought the hero of *The Lost World*, Professor Challenger, back for adventures in the spirit world that appalled most admirers of Conan Doyle's earlier work, especially the Sherlock Holmes stories. How strange that Conan Doyle, who all his life had opposed intolerance, should towards the end his life have been himself the victim of religious prejudice, from some of the highest in the land.

But in those last years there were also many who were helped by his still active interest in crime. Not only in England, but in the further reaches of the Empire, beginning in faraway Australia.

CHAPTER EIGHTEEN

NED KELLY AND FISHER'S GHOST: CRIME IN AUSTRALASIA

For Sherlock Holmes, the Antipodes provided an exotic colonial background for crimes which took place in the more peaceful surroundings of the Mother Country.

In 'The Boscombe Valley Mystery', written in 1891, the seeds of an English murder were planted in the gold rush days of the early 1860s around Ballarat. Conan Doyle seems to have drawn his inspiration for the story from the career of Henry Beresford Garrett, one of a gang who robbed the Bank of Victoria at Ballarat in October 1854 and stole £14,300. Garrett, who had planned the robbery, escaped with his share to England, where he lived quietly for some time before being arrested and sent back to Victoria. This parallels the story of Black Jack of Ballarat, as related by Conan Doyle, very closely.

We have seen the contempt in which Conan Doyle held Fergus Hume's novel *The Mystery of a Hansom Cab* (1887). But the huge popularity then enjoyed by Rolf Boldrewood's *Robbery Under Arms* (1888), a book of literary excellence and social insight which Conan Doyle had also read, ensured that Australia would always be assured of a place in the chronicles of crime.

That novel deals with bushrangers. Conan Doyle had also been impressed by the somewhat specious aura of romance surrounding the figure of Ned Kelly, hanged in November 1880 at Melbourne for murder and outlawry. In 1890 Conan Doyle recommended the Irish bandit's use of body armour to the British Army, a theme he was still pursuing during the Great War. 'When Ned Kelly, the bushranger walked unhurt before the rifles of the police clad in his own hand-made armour,' Conan Doyle wrote in a 1915 letter to *The Times*, 'he was an object lesson to the world.' If, however, he had consulted F.A. Hare's *The Last of the Bushrangers* (1892), Conan Doyle would have learnt that Kelly found it very difficult to move in his armour, and that the police had captured him alive by the simple expedient of shooting at his unprotected legs. Indeed had it not been for the weight of his armour, Ned Kelly might well have escaped.

Among the many letters which Conan Doyle received while that first series of Sherlock Holmes stories was appearing in 1892 was one concerning a celebrated poisoning case in New Zealand, which it was suggested he might be able to make use of in some fictional way.

This was Timaru *cause célèbre* of 1886, in which Thomas Hall was charged with poisoning his wife with antimony in order to collect the insurance and her inheritance to support his floundering business. Mrs Hall's unusual condition after her child was born had alerted her doctor, who sent samples of her food and water to be tested. Hall had also foolishly bought a book, *Taylor on Poisons*, from a local bookseller a short time before: even today it still falls open at the section on antimony. (Alfred Swaine Taylor was the pioneer of forensic toxicology who gave expert testimony at the trials of Dr Palmer in 1856 and Dr Smethurst in 1859.) Hall was convicted and sent to prison for life; the nurse who attended his wife and with whom he had been having an affair, was acquitted. In a sensational development the body of Hall's father-in-law, whom he had attended assiduously throughout his last illness, was exhumed. He too had been poisoned with antimony. Hall was tried for this second murder and sentenced to hang. On appeal it was ruled that evidence of the earlier conviction, suggesting he was an habitual antimony poisoner, should not have been admitted, and so his conviction was quashed. Thomas Hall was transferred to Auckland to serve his life sentence.

This affair, the most famous poisoning case in Australasia, created great interest among criminologists all over the world. Not the least interesting part was the working of the New Zealand Appeal Court, which was an established fact long before Great Britain sought to provide a measure of protection for victims of miscarriages of justice. Though the extraordinary nature of the evidence interested Conan Doyle, he found (as so often in the case of real-life crimes) that there was no direct way in which he could use the material. The callous, cold-blooded nature of Thomas Hall would not transfer easily to his kind of fiction; indeed, for some time he even tried to suppress his story 'The Cardboard Box' (published first in January 1893) because of its shocking elements, including a severed ear found in a postal packet.

Conan Doyle had one very special connection with Australia. His sister Connie married in the summer of 1893 the writer E.W. Hornung, who had lived in Australia as a young man. Best known as the creator of *Raffles the Amateur Cracksman* and his friend Bunny, the criminal counterparts of Holmes and Watson, much of Hornung's early work dealt with crime and cunning in the gold fields of Victoria. Stingaree, a Raffles-like character operating in Australia, was a creation of 1905.

The opportunity for Conan Doyle to visit Australia did not arise until after the Great War. This long trip, from September 1920 until February 1921, was his first mission abroad to spread the new gospel of spiritualism. Alas, on this excursion he was not concerned with Ned Kelly, the bushrangers, or even with the Tichborne claimant. When crime did attract his attention it was in a psychic context – as at one of his lectures when an hysterical woman in the audience accused him of being Jack the Ripper.

Among the classic criminous tales of Australia was one which has passed into popular folklore: the curious story of Fisher's Ghost, which dated from 1826 – quite early in Australia's short history. A new edition of a version by John Lang had been reissued in 1920, bringing it again to wide attention. This was a tale which had all the elements that now appealed to Conan Doyle.

The case occurred in Campbelltown, just outside Sydney in New South Wales. In October of the year 1826, a young farmer named Frederick Fisher disappeared from his farm. An ex-convict himself, Fisher had hired as charge-hand another ticket-of-leave man, George Worrall. At first nobody commented on Fisher's absence, but a neighbour named Farley who was owed money became persistent until Worrall at last confided that Fisher had gone back to England. Farley was not particularly pleased to learn this, but when Worrall offered to write to Fisher reminding him of the debt, Farley seemed at least temporarily satisfied.

The next time Farley passed the Fisher farm he was astonished to see the figure of Fred Fisher sitting on the paddock fence whittling a piece of wood. He called out to him and received a cold blank stare. Offended, Farley jumped off his horse, intending to have the matter of the bad debt out with him. But before he reached the paddock fence, the farmer took his eyes off Fisher just for a moment.

When he reached the fence Fisher had vanished. There were no wood chips, no footprints, no sign that anyone had been there at all.

A black tracker was brought in by the police, and by the paddock fence he claimed to have found blood, white man's blood. Then following a faint trail across the paddock, an hour later at a point a mile from the house, the tracker pointed to a spot in the ditch. The police started digging and three feet down they found the still identifiable body of Fred Fisher. He had been dead for some months.

George Worrall was put on trial in Sydney, and Farley gave evidence about what he had seen. He remained convinced that the figure of Fred Fisher had been sitting on the fence that afternoon, and soon legend had it that Fisher's ghost had pointed out the spot where he had been struck down by Worrall. The court did not concern itself with superstition; besides there was enough evidence against the prisoner without invoking the shade of Fred Fisher. Worrall was hanged on 11 February 1827, after making an eleventh-hour confession, according to report in the *Sydney Gazette* the next day.*

On his travels around Australasia Conan Doyle was told of more recent incidents which he duly set down in his published account of the trip. In Auckland, New Zealand, in 1920, Conan Doyle had a conversation with what he described as 'a curious type of psychic'. He claimed to be a psychometrist who did not need a material object to be put in rapport with his subject.

> This gentleman, Mr Pearman, was a builder by trade, a heavy, rather uneducated man with the misty eye of a seer. He told me that if he had desired to turn his powers upon anything he had only to sit in a dim room and concentrate his thought upon the matter, without any material nexus. For example, a murder had been done in Western Australia. The police asked his help. Using his power, he saw the man, a stranger, and yet he *knew* that it was the man, descending the Swan River in a boat. He saw him mix with the dockmen in Fremantle. Then he saw him return to Perth. Finally, he saw him take train on the Trans-continental Railway. The police at once acted, and intercepted the man, who was duly convicted and hanged.

* The record of the trial has not survived, but despite the efforts of sceptics there is little doubt about the essential facts, which were detailed as early as 1835, long before Lang wrote his semi-fictional version.

This was one of several cases which this man told Conan Doyle, and his stories he thought carried conviction with them, 'All this, although psychic, has, of course, nothing to do with spiritualism, but is an extension of the normal, though undefined, powers of the human mind and soul.'

Near the end of his trip, in Sydney during the first weeks of February 1921, Conan Doyle called on another well-known medium, Mrs Foster Turner. This gifted, middle-aged sensitive was one of the leading spiritualists in Australia. She specialized in a species of medical diagnosis, a form of clairvoyance according to Conan Doyle, and had applied her talents to detective work.

> Mrs Foster Turner's gift of psychometry is one which will be freely used by the community when we become more civilised and less ignorant. As an example of how it works, some years ago a Melbourne man named Cutler disappeared, and there was a considerable debate about his fate. His wife, without giving a name, brought Cutler's boot to Mrs Turner. She placed it near her forehead and at once got *en rapport* with the missing man. She described how he left his home, how he kissed his wife good-bye, all the succession of his movements during the morning, and finally how he had fallen or jumped over a bridge into the river, where he had been caught under some snag. A search at the place named revealed the dead body. If this case be compared with that of Mr Fox [sic], one can clearly see that the same law underlies each. But what an ally for our C.I.D.

The case to which Conan Doyle refers here was an early triumph for a celebrated society medium named Von Bourg.

Early in December 1900 a London stockbroker, Mr P.L. Foxwell, left his home at Thames Ditton to go into his firm in the city. He never returned home. The police were called in, and after a time they concluded that he had gone to America, to begin a new life there under an assumed name.

But this official solution failed to satisfy his family and friends, who thought there was no reason for him to take such a strange step. For some weeks the matter remained a mystery. Then a lady called on Mr Von Bourg. She wanted him to use his crystal ball for her. She was a complete stranger to him and did not give her name.

'I remember the first thing I saw was the body of a man floating in the river.' She asked for more details and he told her how the man was dressed. Then he invited her to look into the crystal ball and she too saw the vision. 'That is my husband,' she exclaimed, and told him she was Mrs Foxwell.

Other visions now came, of their house, of Thames Ditton, of the river and its banks, and of the spot where the body was to be found. 'That spot,' said the medium, now speaking as a clairvoyant, 'is a mile from your house. But not yet will the body be found. It will be recovered on January 31st, about five o'clock in the evening and I "see" another picture, which looks as though the man was struck on the head.'

Events turned out as predicted by Mr Von Bourg. The body was recovered on the afternoon of 31st, and the doctor who examined the corpse found a bruise on the back of the head. (The inquest on Mr Foxwell was reported in *The Times* on 6 February 1901.) In those circles interested in the occult the Foxwell case caused a sensation and the fame of Mr Von Bourg soon spread. For Conan Doyle this was to remain one of the most remarkable cases of its kind on record.

This 1921 trip coincided with the death of Conan Doyle's mother at the age of 83. What was more, he docked in Marseilles just in time to attend the funeral of Willie Hornung at St Jean-de-Luz, where he had died on 22 March 1921. For Doyle the loss of his mother was an important one, but the tragedy of Hornung's passing at only fifty-five cut him off finally from the literary period to which he belonged – the late Victorian and Edwardian. Conan Doyle's future would now be less with literature – although his best books were by no means all written – but with the cause of spiritualism. What interest he retained in crime and detection would be coloured by his dedication to that cause. Ned Kelly had lost out to Fisher's Ghost.

CHAPTER NINETEEN

NEW LIGHT ON OLD CRIMES

In 1919 Conan Doyle gave a talk to his fellow members of the Crimes Club on 'Crime and Clairvoyance'. Since October 1916 spiritualism had become the dominating force in his life, and would remain so until his death. Though the exact text of what he said has not survived, the material of the talk will have been reused in articles he later wrote for *The Strand* and other magazines and newspapers. Conan Doyle's talk was (like all Crimes Club contributions) a private one, but the substance of what he had to say formed the basis of an article, 'The Uncharted Coast', in *The Strand* early in 1920, which was later incorporated as a chapter into his last book, in 1930, *The Edge of the Unknown*.

For the last fifteen years of his life psychic matters would take precedence over everything else, even his creative writing. Many of his admirers were to feel this was a sad fate for a novelist. But the novelist himself was never happier. For Conan Doyle the certainty of life beyond the grave had become a matter of religious conviction.

Inevitably his views on crime were affected by his new beliefs.

Sherlock Holmes relied on his rational intelligence. 'This Agency stands flat-footed upon the ground, and there it must remain. The world is big enough for us. No ghosts need apply,' he

214

told Watson.* Now Conan Doyle was suggesting to his friends and admirers that detection could and should be aided by the almost unknown powers of the mind, assisted by the spirits in the world beyond. Where his readers hoped for ever more tales of Sherlock Holmes, Conan Doyle wished only to promote his new philosophy.

His interest in this area was not new. Conan Doyle heard a spiritualist speaker while he was living in Birmingham in 1880. While he was in Southsea he was a member of a group interested in psychical research, which included the notorious Major-General Alfred Wilkes Drayson.† Conan Doyle even published an account of his own experiences in *Light*, the leading spiritualist paper of the day, on 2 July 1887. Though he came in contact with such luminaries of the movement as Frederic W. Myres, Prof. William Fletcher Barrett, Henry Sidgwick and Edmund Gurney, it was not actually until November 1893 (significantly, three weeks after the death of his father) that Conan Doyle became a member of the Society for Psychical Research.

'About this time I had an interesting experience, for I was one of three delegates sent by the Psychical Society to sit up in a haunted house. It was one of those poltergeist cases, where noises and foolish tricks had gone on for years.'

This was at Charmouth in Devon, and even though the case was not interesting enough to merit a record in the Society's journal, for Conan Doyle it presented an immediate encounter

---

* In 'The Sussex Vampire' (*The Strand*, January 1924), a story which seems, however, to have been drafted long before 1916.

† Though many students of Conan Doyle do not seem to realize it, Major-General Drayson was an intellectual eccentric of the ripest kind. Spiritualism was only one of his interests. He held curious views about the language spoken by Jesus Christ, and thought that the globe was ever-expanding. He also had a range of astronomical theories. Critical accounts of him can be found in Martin Gardner's *Fads and Fallacies in the Name of Science* and Augustus De Morgan's *Budget of Paradoxes*.

with the unexplored frontier between life and death. The phenomena they witnessed that night could, he thought, be traced back to a dead child and its unhappy end.

The modern spiritualist movement began at Hydesville in New York State with what had amounted to a murder investigation. Early in 1848 the Fox household was beset by strange rapping noises. On 31 March 1848, the 'spirit' began to respond through the medium of Kate Fox, one of the daughters of the house. A new era, either of religious advance or of vain credulity, depending on your point of view, had begun.

For Conan Doyle the Hydesville case was a crucial one. The entity seemed well informed about the Fox family and their neighbours. The noises (it was alleged) even persisted when Mrs Fox and her daughters were sent elsewhere.

On that vital night in March 1848 an informed local committee plied the unseen intelligence with questions. As Conan Doyle recounts it:

> According to its own account he was a spirit, he had been injured in that house, he rapped out the name of a former occupant who had injured him, he was thirty-one years old at the time of his death, which was five years before, he had been murdered for money, he had been buried in the cellar ten feet deep.

A neighbour named Duesler called over the letters of the alphabet and received the name of the victim – Charles B. Rosna.

At once the cellar was investigated. Noises seemed to come from one spot, but excavations got nowhere as the water level was struck a foot or so down. But this was not the end of the matter.

When the summer came, a new hole was dug in the cellar by David Fox, the young son of the family, who had arrived in the house only after the disturbances began. He and some of the neighbours (whose names are recorded) did the work and, as Conan Doyle notes, his account can be found in Eliab Capron's *Modern Spiritualism* (1855). The testimony was later confirmed by Robert Dale Owen, author of *Footfalls on the Boundary of Another World* (1860).

> They passed a plank five feet down, and below it came upon some crockery, charcoal and quicklime, under which was some human hair, several bones, and part of a human skull. Clearer evidence of murder and its concealment could hardly be asked for.

After this discovery, a young girl named Lucretia Palmer came forward and said that while she had been a servant to Mr and Mrs B—, the previous householders, a pedlar had come to stay one night, and when she returned after being sent away for three days he had disappeared.

This 'murdered pedlar' has passed into the mythology of spiritualism. The case would undoubtedly be more impressive if a conviction had been driven home, or if the bones had been found during the first dig (and not after an interval of several months in which time interested parties could have 'salted' the cellar). But nevertheless Conan Doyle was not alone in his conviction that the resources of spiritualism could cast some light on historical mysteries and murders.

The cases he adduced for his audience were all curious enough. The first in time was the celebrated disappearance of Owen Parfitt from Shepton Mallet on 6 June 1769. An old soldier, Parfitt was sitting on a chair outside his cottage one minute, half an hour later all that could be found of him was his shawl. He had totally vanished. Too old and ill to have just walked away, it was believed by his neighbours that the Devil had carried Owen Parfitt away. In 1813 it was thought that the mystery had been solved when bones were found in a garden nearby, but the mystery only deepened when they turned out to be those of a girl.

Evidence on the case was collected in the following year by a local lawyer. 'No psychic explanation can be accepted in any case until all reasonable natural solutions have been exhausted,' Conan Doyle observed. He himself suspected that blackmail and revenge lay behind the old man's disappearance, but he had no suggestion how it was done: 'It is a freakish, insoluble borderland case, and there we must leave it.'

Conan Doyle turned then to a real murder, the even more celebrated 'Mystery of the Red Barn', which was where Maria Marten was murdered in 1827, her lover William Corder eventually hanging for the crime. Conan Doyle believed that Corder did kill the girl – a fact not accepted by all students of the case. For him the mystery focused entirely on how the crime was discovered.

Corder (according to the traditional view of the case) lured Maria to the Red Barn with promises of marriage and killed her. He then announced that they had indeed married and had moved away to live on the Isle of Wight, supporting this deceit by sending letters to Maria's family apparently from the Isle of Wight but postmarked from London. All went well for a time.

The matter might have been overlooked [writes Conan Doyle] had it not been for the unusual action of an obscure natural law which had certainly never been allowed for in Corder's calculations.

Mrs Marten, the girl's mother, dreamed upon three nights running that her daughter had been murdered. This in itself might count for little, since it may only have reflected her vague fears and distrust. The dreams, however, were absolutely definite. She saw in them the Red Barn, and even the very spot in which the remains had been deposited. The latter detail

218

is of great importance, since it disposes of the idea that the incident could have arisen from the girl having told her mother that she had an assignation there. The dreams occurred in March, 1828, ten months after the crime, but it was the middle of April before the wife was able to persuade her husband to act upon such evidence. At last she broke down his very natural scruples, and permission was given to examine the barn, now cleared of its contents. The woman pointed to the spot and the man dug. A piece of shawl was immediately exposed, and eighteen inches below it the body itself was discovered, the horrified searchers staggering in a frenzy out of the ill-omened barn. The dress, the teeth and some small details were enough to establish the identification.

Corder was traced, tried and hanged. Here at least Conan Doyle felt was a clear-cut case of psychic intervention. It might have been a case of telepathy, but Doyle was inclined to believe there had been a genuine communication from the dead girl to her mother. Even telepathy postulated a phenomenon considered impossible until the publication of Frederic Myers's studies later in the century.

What Conan Doyle does not mention, what indeed he may not have known, is that such a dream leading to the discovery of a corpse was featured in an early gothic novel by Clara Reeve, *The Old English Baron* (1777), one of the very few books in the Marten household. This has led some recent writers, more cynical than kind, to suppose that Mrs Marten was not without some real knowledge of the murder, that she was in fact Corder's mistress, and had exposed him only after he had in turn deserted her.

Another dream case which Conan Doyle advanced may be more authentic. On 8 February 1840, Edmund Norway, the Chief Officer of the ship *Orient*, then off the island of St Helena in the South Atlantic, dreamed between 10 p.m. and 4 a.m. that he saw his brother Nevill being attacked by two men in Cornwall. It was a vivid and detailed dream, which revealed the incident as happening on a familiar road, which seemed somehow reversed. The dream was related to Norway's fellow officers and written down.

The murder had actually occurred; and the confession of one of the killers, hanged at Bodmin on 13 April, bore out the details of the dream. Norway had been thinking of his brother and was planning to write to him. St Helena and Cornwall are on the same longitude, roughly, so the time of the dream and the murder corresponded at least in a geographical sense.

Doyle suggested that this was a case of 'travelling clairvoyance', in which the spirit could leave the body and observe events at a great distance. It seemed to him an example of 'normal but unexplored powers of the human organism', and not an intervention by the spirit of the murdered man.

Conan Doyle's next case was drawn from Utah, the setting so long ago of the second part of *A Study in Scarlet*. It took place in 1901. A man named Mortensen owed a great deal of money to a company, of which the secretary was a Mr Hay. Mortensen enticed Hay to his house one evening, and he was never seen again. Mortensen later claimed that he had repaid the money to Hay, received a receipt and then watched him depart with the cash in glass jars.

When the sheriff arrived next day with Mr Sharp, Hay's father-in-law, the old man asked where Mortensen had last seen Hay.

'Here,' he replied, indicating a spot outside the door.

'If that is the last place you saw him,' said the old man, 'then that is where you killed him.'

'How do you know he is dead?' asked Mortensen.

'I have had a vision,' said Sharp, 'and the proof is that within 24 hours, and within one mile of the spot where you are standing, his dead body will be dug up from the field.'

It was December and there was snow on the ground. The next day a neighbour followed up a trail of bloodstains which led to a hasty grave in which lay the dead body of Hay, a bullet through his head.

'A rude and elementary affair,' commented Conan Doyle, quite in style of Sherlock Holmes. How could Mortensen have hoped to get away with it? He was duly tried, convicted and shot – 'the law of Utah giving the criminal the choice as to the fashion of his death'.

For Conan Doyle the interest of the case was in the psychic aspect revealed by the old man's vision. It might have been a bluff, but if so 'it involved a very extraordinary coincidence'. It also bears a striking parallel to the Australian case of Fisher's ghost, in which the dead man returns to wreak vengeance on his killer.

The next case in Doyle's talk was truly extraordinary, 'in fact, it is final in its clear proof of psychic action, though the exact degree may be open to discussion'.

Certainly it was a dream which had consequences in high places. Early in May 1812 a Cornish banker and mining engineer named John Williams, of Scorrier House, Redruth, had a vivid and repeated dream in which he found himself in the lobby of the House of Commons, with which he was quite familiar.

A small man, dressed in a blue coat and white waistcoat, entered; and immediately I saw a person, whom I had observed on my first entrance, dressed in a snuff-coloured coat and yellow buttons, take a pistol from under his coat and present it at the little man above mentioned.

The pistol was discharged, and the ball entered under the left breast of the person at whom it was directed. I saw the blood issue from the place where the ball had struck him; his countenance instantly altered, and he fell to the ground. Upon inquiry who the sufferer might be, I was informed that he was the Chancellor. I understood him to be Mr [Spencer] Perceval, who was Chancellor of the Exchequer [and Prime Minister]. I further saw the murderer laid hold of by several gentlemen in the room.

Disturbed by this dream, Williams related it to his wife and some of his friends. He was anxious about whether he should go at once to London to warn Mr Perceval, but his friends suggested he would only be making a fool of himself.

On 13 May one of Williams's sons returned home with the startling news that Spencer Perceval had been shot in the lobby of the House of Commons – exactly as in his father's vision. A little later, on a visit to London, John Williams saw a print of the assassination in which all the details of costume and action were as he had dreamed.

It seemed in some way that those who had visions of events were always powerless to prevent them coming to pass, but perhaps in the detection of crimes psychic aid might be invoked. Conan Doyle did not press on into this area with his audience at the Crimes Club, but it was an aspect of his new beliefs that absorbed his attention more and more.

The famous medium Von Bourg, whose talents as a crystal-gazer Conan Doyle had admired in the recovery of the body of Mr Foxwell from the Thames in 1900, was involved with one of the most outstanding cases of Edwardian times, the death of Mary Money, whose body was found on the track in Merstham Tunnel on the London to Brighton railway line in September 1905. Had she been murdered or had she killed herself? was the matter of the mystery.

This was an affair which had engaged the minds of many of the writers and lawyers involved in 'Our Society', notably John Churton Collins. However, by 1919 Conan Doyle would have been more concerned with the occult aspect of the case.

At the end of September 1905 the journalist F.A.H. Eyles, then working for the *Pall Mall Gazette* newspaper, took Von Bourg to the house of Mary Money's relatives. The medium brought with him the very crystal in which he had seen the location of Mr Foxwell's corpse five years before. He sat in a corner of the room, in an armchair, half bending over the crystal. He was asked by Eyles if he saw anything.

'Yes I can, but before I say what it is I want to see if the friends can see it too.' The young relatives of the victim had never looked into a crystal before. Now bending over the shoulder of the medium they stared into its milky depths.

'I see nothing,' a young man said.

'You must give yourself a little time,' Eyles suggested.

He looked again. Then of a sudden he exclaimed in tones of swift and certain conviction, 'Yes I do see something. I see a train moving through a tunnel and in one of the carriages a man and a woman.' He called over the woman and she too was able to see the same vision. They gave the journalist a vivid narrative of what they saw: the struggle in the train, the man's hand on the woman's shoulder, the woman thrust out of the carriage onto the line.

This was remarkable, Eyles later wrote, for it was only a week since Miss Money had been found and the police were still pursuing a suicide theory, and the medical evidence to support injuries sustained inside the train had not been revealed.

But there was more: the train emerging from the tunnel, a brilliant light from a signal box, the man alighting at a station and riding off on a bicycle, and returning later to gaze into the tunnel. The clairvoyant thought the bright light from the box meant a great light would be thrown on the case by someone in it: this was the signal man at Purley Oaks, who gave evidence at the inquest of seeing a man and woman struggling in the carriage. (Churton Collins spent part of a night in the signal box to establish just how much could be seen from that height of the inside of a passing carriage.)

'That there was a struggle, as Miss Money's relatives saw it re-enacted in Mr Von Bourg's crystal, was confirmed therefore by the signal man's story and supported by the doctor's evidence, and, in so far as it concerned one aspect of the mystery, it afforded an important clue and indicated a motive for the murder,' Eyles concluded. That same evening (30 September 1905) he described the seance in the *Pall Mall Gazette*. But these revelations – whatever their source – did not bring the killer of Mary Money to justice, and her death remained a mystery.

Churton Collins took a commonsense view of crime and detection. Conan Doyle had few doubts about the use of psychics like Von Bourg.

The police, he was to discover, were officially sceptical about the value of psychic science to detection. Aside from the historical cases, Conan Doyle had some personal experiences and encounters in the 1920s, especially on his worldwide travels preaching the cause of spiritualism, which reinforced his own views.

Psychic insights could also throw light not only on the mysteries of the past, but also on those of the present. Conan Doyle wrote up the account of the Langham Hotel mystery and the case of the Vanished Dane (both discussed in earlier chapters) in the 1920s. At that late date he still retained an interested in mysterious disappearances. On his return from one of his missionary trips, in the autumn of 1921, he was himself involved in a case where psychic detection was involved and tested.

On 15 September a seventeen-year-old schoolboy named Oscar Gray disappeared from Liverpool Street railway station in London. He arrived on 15 September 1921 on Platform 7 at the station, where he was to be met at 11.42 by a family friend before going on to stay with school friends before returning to Rugby. The plan was that he would take himself and his baggage to Victoria Station, from where he was to catch a train to Edenbridge to his school friend's home. While the family friend was finding out about his luggage, Oscar vanished. The friend left the baggage unclaimed.

Scotland Yard was called into the case a few days later. Oscar was distinguishable by a scar that ran up in front of his right ear into the hair, but his fate was a complete mystery. Conan Doyle was then consulted. But he too found this a true mystery, to which the key was missing.

His worried parents in appealing to Conan Doyle for help expected, no doubt, access to the Sherlock Holmes faculties for which Doyle was famous. Naturally, given his new mood, Conan Doyle contacted two experienced clairvoyants and let them have the use of a coat which had belonged to the boy. The clairvoyants had been able to confirm that young Oscar was alive, but where he was they could not say. 'The results were by no means perfect,' he later wrote in a letter to the *Daily Express*, 'but I am sure that Mr and Mrs Gray found consolation in them, and in some ways they were accurate.'

Then in October a sailor travelling by train to Tunbridge Wells overheard a party of soldiers talking about a young lad who had joined their barracks at Crowborough, quite near Conan Doyle's home former home at Windlesham. From the newspaper reports, which had included the offer of a £100 reward, he thought they might be talking about Gray. He reported his suspicions to the police at Tunbridge Wells. The district police inspector in the Sussex division was sent over on 16 October to the camp, and found Oscar Gray there.

In turned out that the boy had enrolled in the Royal Corps of Signals on 16 September, the day after he had vanished from Liverpool Street Station. He gave his name as Wilcox. A few days later he was sent down to the camp in Sussex. He was seeking a life of adventure, rather than a return to boring school. Here was a story very typical of the multitudes of annual disappearances, but in which Conan Doyle's intervention, alas, came to nothing. It was, notes Richard Lancelyn Green, 'a rather unimpressive example of the power of psychometry'.

Despite his growing concern with the psychic, Conan Doyle did not abandon his interest in the wider fields of criminology, blending the two sides of his character on his extensive travels during the 1920s.

CHAPTER TWENTY

CONAN DOYLE AND
THE MOTOR-BANDIT

On his way back from the Australasian tour Doyle and his party landed at Marseilles in March 1921, and travelled north to visit the battlefields of the Great War along the border with Germany and Belgium. On the way, they passed through Lyons and Conan Doyle took the opportunity of visiting the celebrated crime laboratory run there by Edmond Locard, the most celebrated forensic scientist of the day.

Long an admirer of Conan Doyle's stories, Locard never tired of pointing out how important the ideas of Sherlock Holmes were for the modern policeman. Indeed, a room in the institute was named after Conan Doyle.

The top floor of a building behind the Palais de Justice in the city centre had been given over by Locard to a Black Museum recording his cases since 1910. This exhibition was full of interest for any criminologist, for since that date Locard had been involved in one way or another in most celebrated French crimes. His services as a consultant were in continual demand – from abroad as well, so that crimes in South America and elsewhere were also on display. Weapons, clues, photographs, all lined the walls in cabinets and cases. It was very impressive.

Suddenly Conan Doyle paused before one of the portraits of 'criminal types'.

'But that is Jules, my former chauffeur!' he exclaimed.

Dr Locard was taken aback.

'No, you must be mistaken, Sir Arthur,' he said. 'That is Jules Bonnot, the motor-bandit.'

Jules Bonnot: from the years before the Great War, even Conan Doyle recalled this anarchist whose name had been a byword for terrorism. And this man had been his driver!

Conan Doyle was an early and enthusiastic motorist. He had bought his first car in 1903 – 'a fine little 10 horse power Wolseley with seats for five' – and greatly enjoyed driving, even though he was nearly killed in a serious accident in 1904 when he was pinned under his overturned car.

His greatest feat as driver was to take part (with his wife) in Prince Henry's Race from Homburg to Bremerhaven, then from Southampton around England and Scotland to finish in London. This was in July 1911, and Doyle was driving a Dietrich-Lorraine. The British team won, which, as the Germans were much disliked, pleased everyone. (German culture did not appeal to many British people at this time; Doyle himself, though he spoke German, felt a closer association with the France through his family connections and visited France many times, as the stamps in his surviving passport reveal.)

Doyle may have enjoyed driving, but the mechanics of car maintenance were beyond him, and so he employed a chauffeur to deal with that aspect of the car. The best known of these, in the coming years, was William Latter. But there were others. So it was, that for a short period in late autumn of 1910 or winter of 1911, he employed a detached but talented young Frenchman.

Quite how long Jules Bonnot worked for Conan Doyle is not clear. It must have been a matter of weeks rather than months. There is a photograph, taken before November 1910, of Bonnot at the wheel of a car belonging to Harry Ashton-Wolfe, the Paris-based criminologist and assistant to the celebrated Dr Bertillon, who was a close friend of Conan Doyle's in the late twenties. Bonnot seems to driven for Ashton-Wolfe in France, to judge by the background in the photograph. Ashton-Wolfe was also an associate of Edmond Locard's in Lyons a little later.

Could there be some mix-up in Locard's memory between the two English criminologists? This seems very unlikely, given Locard's tremendous admiration for Conan Doyle, and Ashton-Wolfe's friendship with him. They both dedicated books to Conan Doyle, and refer to him very often. And in any case, the celebrated American novelist Irving Wallace, who had written long articles on both Dr Bell and on Locard, confirmed for me by letter that Dr Locard told him the story of Conan Doyle's visit in 1949, confirming the conversation over the photograph.* At that time Wallace was a freelance journalist living in Europe. I doubt if he was confused either. The story is also recorded in Thomas Bernard's well-documented French biography of Bonnot and his gang – though he suggests the year was 1925.

Much of Bonnot's short life is obscure, despite the researches of enthusiastic anarchist historians in France. His death, however, was far from obscure.

Bonnot is thought to have returned to Lyons early in 1911, with a new conception for attacking the corrupt bourgeois society from which all ills derived. Since 1883 anarchists had been terrifying Europe and America with bombings and assassinations – the 'propaganda of the deed' espoused by the more radical among them. Bonnot planned to give this creed a new twist. In Lyons he ran an auto repair shop in the window of which he displayed, with a macabre sense of humour, a set of burglar's tools.

* In a letter Irving Wallace sent to me (12 January 1985) he says: 'I wish I could help you more on Doyle and Bonnot, but I can't, because my source was Locard himself and it came orally.'

Till now he and his friends had only stolen cars. Now he saw that the car itself, that distinctive mark of wealth and social standing, could be used as a means rather than an end. New York City, in 1903, he may have recalled, had been shocked by the motorized gangs of Paul Kelly and Monk Eastman, who had fought it out in running gunfights. Now, Bonnot realized, the car also liberated the criminal, giving him a mobility denied to the police and the ordinary citizen.

He and his gang began their new career of crime on 19 April 1911, when they robbed a safe using an oxyacetylene cutter. This, and a series of small-scale crimes, brought them to the attention of the police. Fame in the widest sense came a year later.

On 26 March 1912, near Villeneuve-Saint-George in the Senart Forest fifteen miles from Paris – where the Lyons Courier had been robbed in 1796 – a new motor-car was seized by bandits and the chauffeur shot. The band took the car to Chantilly, where they held up a branch bank, shooting two clerks. Overtaken at Asnières on the Seine, they escaped their pursuers by train.

The sensational nature of this crime shocked the whole nation. This was the very first time in history that a motor car had been used in a bank robbery. But this was only the beginning of an extraordinary crime spree that held the amazed attention not only of France in the end but the whole world. The Bonnot gang's exploits were now being reported everywhere. The Paris region was terroriszed. The police seemed powerless. Day after day there were more raids, more speculations. But it could not last.

On 26 April at Choisy-le-Roi, to the south-east of Paris, a garage was surrounded by the police at 8.30. A shoot-out followed, in which one of the gang, Dubois, was killed and Jules Bonnot fatally wounded. 'Swine, oh you swine,' he cursed as they took him away to die in hospital. On 14 May at Nogent-sur-Marne, Garnier and Vallet, the survivors of the gang, were cornered in a villa, which was bombed out by soldiers assisting the police. Vallet was shot dead on sight.

Bonnot, as the leader of the gang, has entered into the criminal folklore of France. Hence Dr Locard's great surprise to learn that he had once driven the great Conan Doyle. The great author might easily have been murdered; a shocking thought for the criminologist.

One of Locard's colleagues had written a thesis on the medico-legal aspects of Conan Doyle's writings for the Lyons medical faculty as far back as 1906. Dr Locard himself published in 1924 a book *Policiers de roman et de laboratoire*, one of a long series of publications. This book included two essays which must have been inspired by Conan Doyle's visit. One dealt with Edgar Allan Poe as a detective and was published in a French review in July 1921. The same journal in February 1922 carried an article on the methods of Sherlock Holmes himself.

Having analysed three of the short stories, Locard extracted from the whole series all the details of detective method as applied by Sherlock Holmes, pointing out how advanced some of his ideas had been. One of Holmes' publications had been entitled 'Upon the Distinction between the Ashes of Various Tobaccos, an Enumeration of 140 Forms of Cigar, Cigarette and Pipe Tobacco.' Locard followed this hint and actually published a long learned paper on the significance of the ashes left at the scene of a crime.

Again, Sherlock Holmes had emphasized the significance of the dust found on a person's clothes. Dr Locard had solved problems by applying the same technique.

He was only too delighted to be called the Sherlock Holmes of France, and delighted also to recall the visit Conan Doyle had made to his laboratory, and how Conan Doyle had shivered on hearing the details of the criminal career of Jules Bonnot.

'Actually shivered,' Dr Locard told Irving Wallace. 'It was quite a coincidence. That is why I always say that I caught the man who might have abruptly ended Sherlock Holmes' career. Bonnot chauffeuring Sir Arthur Conan Doyle. The flesh creeps. Think how close we came to not having all we do have of Sherlock Holmes.'

CHAPTER TWENTY-ONE

THE STRANGE DEATH
OF THE GENERAL'S WIFE

Towards the end of 1921 Conan Doyle, in casting around for a plot for a new Sherlock Holmes story, investigated the circumstances of a crime which remains unsolved to this day, the mysterious murder in 1908 of the wife of Major-General Charles Luard at Ightham.

This Edwardian tragedy had electrified the counties of Kent and Sussex in 1908, soon after Conan Doyle and his family had moved into Windlesham, on the outskirts of Crowborough. It had also been discussed by no less an authority than Bernard Spilsbury at the Crimes Club, where that great forensic scientist would have dwelt at length on the gunshot evidence. Being by now one of the classic English murder mysteries it could not but have interested Conan Doyle.

But there was a personal connection as well. The vicar of St Peter's church, Ightham, was the Reverend B. T. Winnifrith, who was a friend of the Doyle family. His daughter Anna (later the well-known actress Anna Lee, Mrs Robert Nathan) was at school with Doyle's daughter Jean, and his sons Adrian and Denis had gone to a preparatory school run by Mr Winnifrith in his rectory. Conan Doyle made several visits in 1920 to his friend the rector, visits which Winnifrith recorded in the Ightham Tithe Book for that year. On those occasions the vicar showed Conan Doyle the parish diary in which his predecessor had recorded the distressing events of 1908. In due course the Tithe Book for 1921 recorded these conversations as well.

The murder was only too well remembered in the neighbourhood. Major-General Charles Edward Luard was sixty-nine, short but muscular, a brisk active man despite his age. His face was tanned by long years in the open air, his balding hair grey. He wore a heavy white moustache. Luard had been commissioned into the Royal Engineers at the age of nineteen had served at Woolwich, in Morocco, Gibraltar and Natal. He had retired in 1888, and had then returned to his childhood home at Ightham.

Caroline Luard was fifty-eight, a handsome woman, popular in the district, where the couple had lived for some thirty years. Their house, Ightham Knoll, was remote, remoter than it is today, when Kent is a mere dormitory for London. Their nearest neighbours were Horace Wilkinson and his wife, who lived half a mile away at Frankfield House, and whose land ran with their own.

At 2.30 on 24 August 1908, General Luard and his wife left their home to walk to the Wildernesse Golf Club at Godden Green. With them went Mrs Luard's dog, an Irish terrier named Scamp. Only the general and Scamp would return home from this ramble, leaving the terrible fate of his wife a mystery to this day.

They walked on that fine afternoon about half a mile along the main road to the village of Crown Point, turning off through Frankfield Park and up a bridle path to a wicket gate near St Lawrence's school.

As Mrs Luard did not care to go as far as the club, she proposed to turn off down a path that led to a summer house called the 'Casa', overlooking Casa Pond and the woods beyond. The Casa was a charming wooden building with a balcony along the front, from which Mrs Luard often admired the view.

It was agreed that Mrs Luard should make her own way home,

and the couple parted, the general setting off for the golf club. It was now about three o'clock. At 3.30 the steward at the club saw General Luard arrive. He had come to collect a set of golf clubs. This did not take him long, some ten minutes. Then he set out again on an alternative homeward route along the main road through Seal Chart Wood and Crown Point.

In Seal Chart Wood the local vicar, Rev. Arthur Cotton, caught up with Luard in his motor-car. He offered the general a lift, but though he put his golf clubs into the car, Luard walked on. The vicar, who was collecting a small party of ladies photographing in the woods, caught up with the general again at about 4.15 and this time he accepted the offered lift. He arrived home at 4.30.

Mrs Luard had not returned, which surprised the general as she had been expecting a guest for tea. General Luard did his best to entertain Mrs Stewart, and she left at five o'clock. Luard went part of the way with her to look for his wife, the dog following them. Mrs Stewart went on to another appointment, while the general turned aside to the Casa, which he reached at about 5.30.

The dog ran on ahead, and some way off Luard could hear it whining. But he could see nothing. When he reached the Casa the general found his wife lying face down on the verandah, the dog licking her face. At first he thought she had fainted; then he saw the blood.

Mrs Luard was dead.

Her hands were raised above her head, open, palms up. Four rings were later found to have been stolen from her fingers. Her dress had been torn, rather as if somebody had tried unsuccessfully to turn the body over and her purse was missing.

In a stricken state, the general plunged down the slope to the cottage occupied by Wickham, Horace Wilkinson's coachman. Mrs Wickham rushed out to find the general breathless, and quite distraught 'Dead. Shot . . . dead. Shot,' he moaned faintly.

Wickham fetched Harding the butler, and together they returned to find the general near collapse: 'Mrs Luard is dead in the Casa.'

The three men then hurried back to the Casa. Once, on the way, the general cried out 'The brutes! They've killed her.'

On the way the party collected Daniel Kettel and another labourer. Arriving at the verandah, General Luard fell on his knees clasping his wife's hand, Harding sent for a doctor and the police. Scamp still whined and licked his mistress's face.

At the subsequent post mortem Drs Mansfield and Walker found two bullet wounds in Mrs Luard's head; one of which had entered from below into the left eye. There was a bruise on the head – made when she fell on to the cement floor, Dr Walker thought, though Dr Mansfield felt it might have been made by a bludgeon. A second bullet had entered the skull by the right ear, and further investigation revealed a third which had been fired into the floor of the Casa. The rings had been pulled off Mrs Luard's hand after she was killed.

It was quickly established by the police that shots had been heard by workers in the area of the summer house at 3.15. This gave the general a complete alibi, as he had been seen a mile and a half away at 3.20. The police carefully checked all the distances to confirm times. Luard could not have arrived at the golf club at 3.30 if he had fired the shots at 3.15. Who could have killed Caroline Luard? A tramp or a hop-picker down from London were suggested, with robbery of the purse and rings as the motive. A description of these items was circulated, and though they were very distinctive none were ever traced.

Rumours about strangers in the neighbourhood were followed up. Reverend Cotton, for instance, had seen a tramp in the wood at about the time of the shooting. But tramps, or even labourers, do not carry expensive revolvers around with them. A torn-up note is said to have been found at the scene, which was, it seems, pasted together, but not presented as evidence. Was the theft of the rings a mere cover for something more personal?

Did Mrs Luard meet someone at the Casa? Someone she could not, or would not, bring to the house; someone she did not want her husband to meet.

If the notion of a romantic liaison seems out of the question, what else could have brought Caroline Luard to the Casa on an assignation?

In 1950 in a memorandum to the Gowers Committee on Capital Punishment, C.H. Norman made an astonishing revelation. He had attended as official shorthand writer under the Criminal Appeal Act the 1910 trial of John Alexander Dickman, who was accused of murdering and robbing a cashier named Nisbet of £370 on a train from Newcastle. The evidence against Dickman was not conclusive, and five of the jurors in the case had signed a petition for reprieve. Despite the protests, Dickman was hanged.

In 1914 the Dickman trial transcript was edited for the *Notable British Trials* series by Sir Sidney Rowan Hamilton. This edition came to Norman's attention only in 1939, and he then wrote to Hamilton (by then a former Chief Justice of Bermuda). From the judge, then living in Northern Ireland, Norman received the following remarkable reply:

All the same Dickman was justly [convicted], and it may interest you to know he was with little doubt the murderer of Mrs Luard, for he had forged a cheque she had sent him in response to an advert in *The Times* (I think) asking for help; she discovered it and wrote to him to meet her outside the General's and her house and her body was found there. He was absent from Newcastle those exact days. Tindal Atkinson [prosecuting counsel at the Dickman trial] knew this, but not being absolutely certain preferred not to cross-examine Dickman on it. I have seen repliques of the cheque.

Now having read in an account of the Luard case by Percy Savage, the police officer in charge of the investigation, that the murderer was unknown, Norman wrote again to Hamilton. He received a brief note, with the promise of a longer reply.

Norman was deeply disturbed by these discoveries. He claimed in his memorandum that Lord Coleridge, who had tried Dickman, Lord Alverstone, Mr Justice A.T. Lawrence, and Mr Justice Phillimore of the Court of Appeal were all friends of the Luards. Lord Alverstone, moreover, he added, had denounced those who had written poison-pen letters to the general after his wife's death. To Norman this suggested that Dickman was condemned as much for what he was thought to have done in the Luard matter, as for what it was claimed in court he had done in the Nisbet murder. Norman heard no more from Rowan Hamilton.

Were these legal friends of the Luards mistaken? Norman believed so, and indeed the notion does seem far-fetched.

These allegations by Norman have been disputed by some more recent writers, but given the closed world of the English judicial system, they may not be without foundation. Even if the Luard cheque had been forged, surely it would have come to light at the time. There is no evidence that it was known to the local police. As with all unsolved crimes there is no shortage of theories in the case of the Luard mystery.

Had Mrs Luard killed herself, and the gun been removed or stolen? Had she killed herself to implicate her husband in a charge of murdering her? Conan Doyle, despite the trend of his own short story 'The Problem of Thor Bridge', which repeats some of the circumstances of the Luard Case, thought that the killing was the result of a vendetta by some enemy made during the general's long service overseas. He thought of an Indian, and indeed there was some talk at the time of a dark stranger in the neighbourhood.

But all this smacked too much of *The Sign of Four* to be really convincing. In any case General Luard had not served in India, only in Europe and Africa.

Two curious points arose during the police investigation. One was the way in which Mrs Luard's glove had been removed, by pulling it back over itself – as a woman might take it off. This led to more local talk that the killer was a woman. Secondly, gossip went so far as to suggest that the general was having an affair – at sixty-nine! – and doubtless the presence of Mrs Stewart on that tragic afternoon inspired this loose talk. Inevitably rumour manifested itself in anonymous poison-pen letters pointing the accusing finger at the grief-stricken Charles Luard; letters so spiteful that they caused him to take his life under a railway train a little later.

The question of the anonymous letters, most of which were local, seems to have gone uninvestigated by the police. Doyle commented: 'It was those letters that focused attention on the general as a suspect, and it is likely that the murderer sent a number of them and played a part in starting the whispering campaign that drove the general to suicide.'

In 1967, after the murder had again received renewed local attention, several people still claimed that the culprit was the general. One man even said the general had a pistol of the calibre of the murder weapon, but that this had not come out at the inquest.

There was also a tale of love letters being found in a tiny drawer in Mrs Luard's bedroom. They had been signed simply ' J'. One single sheet carried the words, 'Goodbye my dear love. I die with you.'

These were not, however, Mrs Luard's letters, but those of a friend who had entrusted them to her after her young man was killed. Rumour, nevertheless, attached them to Mrs Luard.

The most remarkable piece of the 'new' evidence was the account of Mr Bill Seer, at the time of the murder a lad of seventeen. Seer was working in the woods with his father. They saw the general pass on his way to the golf club and ten minutes later heard shots – but not, they were sure, from a shotgun.

Then in the lane near his home, Bill Seer encountered a tall dark man who asked the way to the nearest railway station. 'I've just shot a woman,' the stranger said. Retracing his steps the boy was in time to see the body of Mrs Luard being taken up to Frankfield House. He tried to tell the police but he was shooed away as they thought him unlikely to have anything to say worth listening to.

Two years later *The News of the World* published an article which claimed that at the time of her death Mrs Luard was wearing rings one stone of which had come from an Oriental temple. The rings were never traced. Was the gem stone the motive? Was the 'dark man' an Oriental on an errand to retrieve them? Seer later learnt that the stranger had spent several days in the Ightham area prior to the murder. These echoes of *The Moonstone* smack more of fiction than real life.

For years Mr Seer had tried to get his evidence taken seriously. With so many local people convinced that the general had committed the murder, he thought his evidence cleared the old man. Many in the locality still think him guilty.

But with all these theories and counter-theories, the murder of Caroline Luard remains as much a mystery today as it was to Conan Doyle and his contemporaries.

Casting around for a story in 1921 Conan Doyle had suggested a competition for plots to the editor of *The Strand*. Greenhough-Smith did not care for this idea, and instead had drawn his attention to an incident in Germany in which a supposed murder turned out to be suicide though the gun was not found with the body.

The case was related by no less an authority than the great Hans Gross in his celebrated work *Criminal Investigation*, several English editions of which had already been published. A chip in the paint on the wooden rail of the bridge on which the body was found had attracted the notice of the police investigators. A search was made and a length of string was found with a large stone tied to one end of it; to the other was tied the missing gun. The victim had shot himself, and the gun had recoiled out of his hand and into the water, pulled by the weight of the stone. The case proved to be an insurance fraud.

Gross observed that 'it is common to find no weapon beside persons who have undoubtedly committed suicide. This is generally attributed to the theft of the weapon by those arriving first on the scene, the weapon used by a suicide usually being supposed to produce superstitious effects.'

This case provided Conan Doyle with the germ of the story he wished to write. Some of the circumstances of the Luard case, which he researched on those visits to the Winnifriths in 1921, inspired 'The Problem of Thor Bridge' which came out in *The Strand* in February and March 1922. Holmes solved that mystery with his usual ease, but the Luard case still defies solution.

CHAPTER TWENTY-TWO

DEATH BESIDE THE SEA

Almost since it was launched, Conan Doyle had been associated with the *Daily Express*, and was very friendly with its American-born managing editor, Ralph D. Blumenfeld. In April 1922 Blumenfeld appealed to Conan Doyle for his help in a case which had shocked the nation. Could the creator of Sherlock Holmes suggest a new approach to capturing the brutal murderer of Irene Wilkins?

The case had begun some months before. In the middle of December 1921 the following advertisement had appeared in the *Morning Post*, at that time the most conservative and respectable newspaper in the country.

> Lady Cook, 31, requires post in school. Experienced in school with forty boarders. Disengaged. Salary £65. Miss Irene Wilkins, 21 Thirlmere Road, Streatham, S.W.16.

Irene Wilkins was the daughter of a barrister, and nothing if not highly respectable herself. On the afternoon of 22 December, a reply to her advertisement came by telegram.

> Wilkins . . . Morning Post. Come immediately 4.30 train Waterloo, Bournmouth Central. Car will meet train. Expence no object. Urgent. Wood, Beech House.

242

Miss Wilkins, having packed her case in haste, duly caught the 4.30 train. The following morning a retired farm labourer on his regular morning stroll at 7.30 noticed some cows gathered around what looked like a bundle in a field. He climbed over the fence to investigate, and found the dead body of Irene Wilkins.

Although her dress had been pulled up, rape had been incomplete. She had died from shock and loss of blood due to severe blows to her head from a hammer or similar weapon. It had rained during the night, and as the ground under the body was dry, the police calculated that she had died before eight o'clock the evening – before when the rain had started.

Irene's umbrella was leaning against the fence, and a few feet away were the unmistakable tracks of a car fitted with Dunlop Magnum tyres.

The police at once began a laborious search of all the cars in Bournemouth and the surrounding area. They learned, too, that other telegrams had been sent from false addresses attempting to lure girls to Bournemouth. Miss Wilkins, according to several witnesses, had been met by a chauffeur-driven car at the station, but the descriptions of the driver were vague.

Nine days later, on 3 December, Miss Wilkins's small attaché case was found lying in a wood on the Branksome Tower estate, some miles outside Bournemouth. It looked as if it had been hurriedly disposed of.

In the course of the police inquiries a car was routinely checked which was fitted with three Dunlop Magnums and a worn Michelin tyre. The driver, a young man named Thomas Allaway, gave a good account of his movements at the time of Irene Wilkins's murder, which satisfied the police. The car clue seemed to lead nowhere.

But there were still the three telegrams: one to Irene Wilkins, and two inviting other young women to work in Bournemouth.

All included consistently misspelled words such as 'Bournmouth' and 'expence'. The telegrams were reproduced in facsimile in the press in case the handwriting would be recognized. It was not.

All the police inquiries led nowhere. Four months passed. Then Superintendent Garrett realized there was nothing for it but to begin all over again with a review of the evidence. Some 22,000 documents alone had been filed in connection with the case. Many of these were letters from cranks or from clairvoyants – Bournemouth with its retired middle-class population was the natural habitat of many mediums and spiritualists. In the shaded parlours of suburban Bournemouth the spirit of Irene Wilkins was now a popular feature of many seances.

At one series of seances given by Mrs Charlotte Starkey, an attempt was made to reconstruct the murder. The 'spirit of Irene' was contacted, and by means of clairvoyance Mrs Starkey discovered the identity of the murderer. Or so she later claimed.

Meanwhile, Superintendent Garrett was going through the files. Among the letters he was startled to find one from an engineer named Frank Humphris which opened up a new line of inquiry. Humphris had travelled down by train to Bournemouth from London and had noticed Irene Wilkins among the other passengers. He described her clothes in detail, and later was able to pick out the hat she had been wearing that day from a group of others.

Coincidentally, Mr Humphris designed cars. In the station car park he had noticed a grey limousine, a Mercedes of peculiar interest because it was a pre-war German model with an unusual bonnet. At the back was a special luggage rack, also of unusual design, which impressed Mr Humphris so much that he was interested to have one made. The expert eye of the designer also rested for a few critical moments on the driver of the car.

It was a windy evening and some of the papers were blown off the railway bookstall across the station yard. A man in a chauffeur's uniform put his foot on them to save some from scattering. Humphris gave him a hand to retrieve them. A few moments later the woman he identified as Irene Wilkins was being driven off in the Mercedes by the chauffeur.

As soon as he read about the murder, Humphris contacted the police and gave them his information. It had been ignored. On 4 January Frank Humphris again saw the grey touring car in Bournemouth. This time he noted down the registration number and sent it to the police; it was LK 7405.

Incredibly, the police interviewed the driver a few days later on 7 January, but the report was mislaid. So much 'information' was coming in about cars that they could not see the overwhelming importance of what they had been told.

A month later one of the clerks in Boscombe Post Office recognized the man who had sent one of the telegrams. This information too was ignored by the police. A few days later an official from the Post Office followed the same man to his home, having been tipped off by the clerk. Again, there was no follow-up.

The man was Thomas Allaway, who had already been questioned more than once. There was little against him, and it is likely that the general confusion would have allowed Allaway to slip through the police net, but he lost his nerve. Thomas Allaway absconded, taking with him the chequebook belonging to Mr Sutton, his employer, from which he forged a cheque. Sutton alerted the police. Now at last the pieces began to fall together. Superintendent Garrett was certain he had identified his man.

Naturally the newspapers were privy to more than they could publish. Blumenfeld, at the *Daily Express*, was aghast at the incompetence of the police in letting Allaway slip through their hands at almost the last moment. In April he sent the facsimiles of the telegrams to Conan Doyle along with a letter actually written by Allaway.

What did Conan Doyle think of the evidence?

Dear Blumenfeld,

I find it hard to think that the letter is in any hand but that which wrote the telegram. Could not a trap be laid in this way? The man naturally wants to get out of the country. He is a chauffeur. Suppose you put an advertisement in the *Express* and other papers 'Skilled chauffeur. A gentleman starting on an extended tour in Spain needs services of chauffeur. Steady man over 25 years – for four months. Apply by letter.' The replies would be very likely to contain one from him. All which are like his writing could be interviewed. He could fill up papers for a passport. Then you could see scratches, etc., on hands. Don't you think this is a possible line?

Readers will recognize in Doyle's advice as a 'consulting detective' in this case more than an echo of the ploy adopted by Sherlock Holmes himself in the story of 'Black Peter' written in 1904:

I argued that the man was probably in London, and that he would desire to leave the country for a time. I therefore spent some days in the East End, devised an Arctic expedition, put forward tempting terms for harpooners who would serve under Captain Basil – and behold the result.

Blumenfeld was delighted to fall in with Conan Doyle's scheme, and the advertisements were prepared. Meanwhile, local police had been watching the house in Reading where Allaway's wife May had gone after he had deserted her in Bournemouth. On April 28 Allaway was detained trying to enter the house, and on the following day Garrett went to Reading and arrested Allaway on a charge of forging his former employer's cheque. At the same time he asked Mrs Allaway if she had any letters written before the forgeries. She produced some written by her husband while he was with the British Army in Germany. They were, as Garrett had hoped, in the same hand as the telegram forms.

Thomas Henry Allaway was remanded for trial in July 1922. The case outlined by the police was complete. The evidence of Frank Humphris and Miss Alice Waters, one of the Post Office clerks who had identified Allaway, convinced the jury. A further detail was added by a Boscombe newsagent who recalled Allaway was in the habit of buying the *Morning Post*.

At his trial at the Winchester Assizes in August, Allaway attempted to establish an alibi, but it collapsed. The circumstantial evidence was too strong. One day after the murder, for instance, he had driven Mrs Sutton to tea with her sister, and had been required to wait some ninety minutes for her to return: the attaché case belonging to Irene Wilkins was found nearby.

The jury found Thomas Allaway guilty after an hour's deliberation. The sentence passed by Mr Justice Avory was secretly photographed, and is the only instance of a judge wearing the Black Cap being recorded by the camera. On 19 August 1922, after making a confession, Thomas Allaway was hanged at Winchester.

Conan Doyle followed the case to the end. Here, at least, he could have no doubts that the right man had been convicted, though his doubts about the justice of hanging remained.

Still, the most absorbing aspect of the case for Conan Doyle and many of his new friends was the one passed over almost in silence by the official reports. This was the 'detective work' of Mrs Charlotte Starkey in reconstructing the case. Her achievement was the subject of a small book, *The Spirit of Irene Speaks*, published locally by her friend, William Tyler, and though it entered the folklore of spiritualism, the general public were unaware of it.

About this time *Punch* published a Bernard Partridge cartoon of a frustrated Sherlock Holmes shackled to an unworldly Conan Doyle, with his head in the clouds. It was perhaps an apt comment on this aspect of the Allaway case.

CHAPTER TWENTY-THREE

THE CROWBOROUGH
CHICKEN FARM MURDER

An attraction of Conan Doyle's home at Crowborough in Sussex was its distance from London. There he could lead a quiet rural life, pleasing himself, and above all free from the demands of public life. Indeed, many of the villagers thought him a rather remote figure. Crime rarely intruded on his rural peace.

Once there was a burglary at the village inn, not more than a stone's throw from Windlesham. Conan Doyle and the village constable – doubtless much like Constable Anderson in 'The Lion's Mane', 'a . . . man of the slow, solid Sussex breed; a breed which covers much good sense under a heavy silent exterior' – investigated. The policeman, with no theories at all, seized the culprit soon enough, 'while I had got no farther than that he was a left-handed man with nails in his boots'. The rough-and-ready had triumphed over Conan Doyle's laboured, quasi-scientific methods.

But crimes in Crowborough were not always so trivial, as events over the Christmas season of 1924 showed.

The arrest in May 1924 of Patrick Mahon, and his subsequent trial for the murder of his mistress, Emily Kaye, on the Crumbles, at Eastbourne, had shocked Sussex. The dismemberment of the body was *Grand Guignol* of the bloodiest kind and dismayed the nation. Mahon had made just too many mistakes to have got away with it. Or so one resident of Crowborough evidently thought.

In January 1925 it became known that a girl from Kensal Rise in West London, who had planned to visit her fiancé in Crowborough, had disappeared. Slowly a new mystery was unravelled, involving a chicken farmer named Thorne.

In the limited social circle around Crowborough Norman Thorne was a familiar figure. Conan Doyle's chauffeur, William Latter, knew Thorne and liked him. Thorne was a member of the Band of Hope, a religious temperance society, and popular at local dances. A nice ordinary lad, but not very business-like and in financial difficulties with his Wesley Chicken Farm, which in name at least sounded like a respectable Methodist firm.

His other problems were his girls. He was engaged to the missing secretary, who was called Elsie Cameron, but was also walking out with a local girl, Bessie Coldicott. Elsie was an hysterical personality and in desperation had brought emotional pressure to bear on Norman which included a fictitious pregnancy.

Elsie had visited Norman at his Blackness chicken farm before, so when she set out on 5 December to visit Crowborough again her parents were not put out. But days passed and there was no word from her. Elsie's parents telegraphed Thorne; he replied that she had never arrived. Eventually the police were informed and a notice about her disappearance circulated.

At once the press was alerted, and that same evening Trevor Allen arrived at the chicken farm as the herald of a much larger Fleet Street contingent that descended on Crowborough in due course. For days Thorne bore patiently with their questioning. It was all a mystery to him. 'Perhaps,' he suggested 'they think I killed her with that' – indicating an Indian club – 'and buried her there'– pointing to a spot in one of the hen runs.

Eventually the police, having built up a picture of Elsie Cameron's movements that brought her to the threshold of the

Thorne small-holding, detained him on 14 January and asked him to make a statement. A more intensive search was now begun of the land and the hen runs. Digging started the next day, and at 8.30 a.m. in the morning, searchers uncovered Elsie Cameron's attaché case. At 11 p.m. that night, acting on Thorne's statement, they dug up the Leghorn run and found the parts of Elsie's body. She had been cut in three.

The discovery caused a sensation. In a statement to the police which later became the basis of his defence, Thorne admitted that Elsie had visited him at his hut. She had insisted on their marriage. Soon. He had refused. He had, he claimed, left her alone preparing for bed while he went out to meet his new girlfriend and her mother at the railway station. When Norman Thorne returned to the hut he found that Elsie had hanged herself from a beam. He cut her down, and thought of sending for a doctor. Then, fatally, he changed his mind. Getting his wood saw, he cut her body up by the light of the fire and buried the remains in one of the hen runs.

The decomposing remains of Elsie Cameron were examined by Sir Bernard Spilsbury, who had been knighted only the year before. If any one person epitomized the changes in forensic science since 1880 it was Spilsbury. He was then at the pinnacle of his career. The great pathologist found many bruises on Elsie's body, but when he came to examine her neck he found no marks consistent with hanging, only the natural folds of the neck. He was now so certain of his own opinions that he neglected to prepare any histological slides to support his contention. In the event his theory was supported by the police who found no evidence of a rope having been run over the beam in the roof of Thorne's hut. In Spilsbury's opinion Thorne had beaten Elsie, probably with the Indian club he had so proudly displayed, and she had died of shock.

The defence also consulted its own experts: Dr Robert Bronte, an Irish surgeon, who had worked as an official pathologist for the Irish Free State, and David Nabarro of the Great Ormond Street Hospital. At Norman Thorne's insistence they had exhumed Elsie's body – it was now three months since she had died – and re-examined the neck tissue for rope marks.

According to their studies there were bruises which were consistent with hanging. The other body bruises, they contended, had been caused when Thorne cut down the dying girl and dragged her over the floor to the bed.

Spilsbury now belatedly prepared slides to support his position. He claimed that examination at such a late date, with the body drained of blood, was almost useless. Bronte and Nabarro, he haughtily alleged, had mistaken remains of cutaneous glands for effusions of blood.

The trial centred around this medical evidence. Spilsbury had been over-confident in not preparing slides on his first examination, but he could yet have been right in dismissing the claims of the defence. There remained, however, a strong doubt.

The judge in his summing up rather imprudently advised the jury that Spilsbury's was the best opinion to be had, prompting Thorne's lawyer to respond: 'We can all admire attainment, take off our hats to ability, acknowledge the high position that a man has won in his sphere. But it is a long way to go if you have to say that, when a man says something, there can be no room for error.'

The jury clearly agreed with Mr Justice Finlay and found Norman Thorne guilty. He was sentenced to hang. *The Law Journal* commented afterwards that 'Thorne is entitled to feel that he has been condemned by a tribunal which was not capable of forming a first hand judgement, but which followed the man with the biggest name.'

Local opinion was shocked by the Thorne affair. William Latter, though he told Doyle that he liked Thorne, had no doubt he was guilty. What weighed with his neighbours, as it had with the jury, was Thorne's brutal mutilation of the body to hide the death. Why would he have done that if he were not guilty?

But thinking a man guilty is not to prove him guilty. Had Thorne's guilt been proved beyond a reasonable doubt? Conan Doyle thought not. He visited the scene of the crime, the sordid hut among the hen runs in which Norman Thorne had lived, in which he had entertained, and in which Elsie Cameron had met her end. He was prepared to lend his weight to those anxious to obtain a reprieve for the condemned man. Two days before Thorne was to hang Conan Doyle was interviewed by the *Morning Post*.

'I think that there is just one chance in a hundred that Thorne was not guilty of murder, and as long as there is one, I do not think he ought to be hanged. The evidence is strong, but it is circumstantial. Personally, I am against capital punishment except in very extreme cases, and to justify it I think the evidence should be stronger than it was in this case.'

The Home Secretary was obviously unmoved, and Norman Thorne was hanged, still protesting his innocence, but buoyed up by his renewed religious faith. The case, however, was not forgotten. In her edition of the trial for the *Notable British Trials* series, Helena Normanton refought the medical controversy, emphasizing the possibility of Thorne's innocence. Much later, Spilsbury's biographers, while admitting that Conan Doyle had no axe to grind, dismissed Bronte's views as unreasonable compared with their great man's.

The doubt, which should have acquitted Thorne, nevertheless remained.

CHAPTER TWENTY-FOUR

THE CASE OF THE MISSING LADY

'This is decidedly a Sherlock Holmes case. Even you cannot have failed to notice the similarity between it and the disappearance of Lady Frances Carfax.'

Agatha Christie: *Partners in Crime* (1929)

On 3 December 1926 Agatha Christie disappeared from her Berkshire home in mysterious, not to say sinister, circumstances.

A new and final series of *Sherlock Holmes* stories was then running in *The Strand* – the December issue already on sale carried 'The Adventure of the Lion's Mane', narrated by Holmes himself. With Holmes in the air – his return had been welcomed by an admiring leader in *The Times* – it was inevitable that Conan Doyle should have become involved in the mystery of the missing novelist.

The circumstances surrounding her disappearance were, and still are, confused. In June 1926 Mrs Christie had published *The Murder of Roger Ackroyd*, her astonishing *tour de force* that marked a milestone, and a controversial milestone at that, in the history of detective fiction. She was already recognized as a leading writer in her field; but this was her first book for her new and permanent publishers William Collins and, moreover, the first of her books to sell really well. Having become a public figure of a special kind, her disappearance six months later became at once headline news in newspapers across Britain.

A mystery in 1926, the affair remains a mystery still, the last unsolved 'Christie for Christmas' puzzle, as her semi-annual, seasonal publications were once billed. Even an otherwise frank official biography only casts confusion over what really happened. Her authorized biographer, Janet Morgan, though she devotes two chapters to the incident, seems to have worked largely from secondary or late sources. She fails to mention Conan Doyle's involvement at all. In her own autobiography Agatha Christie never mentions the affair.

Despite the success of her novel, 1926 had been an unhappy year for Agatha Christie. Indeed she had not really been happy for several years. A holiday that summer with her sister had been fun, but on coming home she was faced with her mother's illness and subsequent death. The heartrending tedium of clearing out the collections of a lifetime in the family home had depressed her still further. A nervous breakdown was frequently invoked by the newspapers to account for her disappearance.

Her new novel, *The Mystery of the Blue Train*, was proving difficult to complete and is not among her best. She accepted the suggestion of her new publisher that she draw together three stories about her Belgian detective Hercule Poirot, already published in the *Sketch* magazine, to make a sort of novel to be called *The Big Four* to appear in the first weeks of the New Year. But she had to be helped with this by her brother-in-law. She felt that she was at a personal and professional crisis point.

The root cause of her unhappiness was the breakdown of her marriage to Archie Christie, a charming but ineffectual war hero, since moving to a new house near Sunningdale, which they had called Styles, after the house visited by murder in her first published novel. She felt over the next eight months she had become a golf widow, as more and more of Archie's time was spent on the famous local golf links.

Then, on her daughter's birthday, 5 August, Agatha learnt that Archie had fallen in love with a girl named Nancy Neele, whom she also knew. He wanted to arrange a divorce and to marry Nancy. Agatha would not consent to this, on religious and social grounds, and so for months their marriage existed in an outwardly respectable way, but in private they lived quite separately.

On the morning of Friday, 3 December, the Christies had a row. Colonel Christie left the house with a packed bag to spend the weekend with their friends Madge and Sam James at Hurstmore, near Godalming in Surrey. Nancy Neele (who then lived in Croxley Green) was to be there, and the party was to announce their 'engagement'. Archie was pressing Agatha hard on the matter of the divorce, and this deeply upset her. She still hoped to be able to save her marriage somehow.

Agatha spent the afternoon having tea with Archie's mother, Mrs William Hemsley in Dorking. Archie's behaviour must have been the one and only topic of conversation over the cucumber sandwiches. Asked why she was not wearing her wedding ring, she had a moment of hysteria before kissing her daughter's head. On her way home by car, Agatha would have had to pass the Silent Pool at Newland's Cross, between Dorking and Guilford, on the A25 road.

That evening her secretary, Miss Charlotte Fisher, had gone up to London to dine and dance with a friend. After dinner she rang Agatha. All seemed to be well. But when Miss Fisher returned from town she learnt from the staff that Mrs Christie had driven off in her car at sometime near ten o'clock. Her daughter Rosalind had been left asleep in the house. Miss Fisher rang Archie, who is said to have left his dinner party in a hurry, probably in an effort to head off Agatha from blundering into the James's house and making a scene.

Next morning the Berkshire police arrived at Styles. Mrs Christie's grey bull-nosed Morris Cowley two-seater had been found abandoned on a slope above a pond near Newlands Cross, the very place she had passed on her way home the previous afternoon.* The car was in neutral gear, and the lights had been left on, causing the battery to run down. Inside were a fur coat and other items which easily identified the owner as Mrs Agatha Christie. The car had been found by gypsies, and then by a local man who had called the police.

Witnesses spoke of seeing a woman who answered Agatha's description, but these accounts were not very reliable, with the exception perhaps of a man who had helped try to start the car at 6.20 a.m. Of Mrs Christie there was no sign. She had vanished completely.

The sensation was immense, and the London newspapers all sent special correspondents down to report from the scene. Curious sightseers, including Dorothy L. Sayers, followed them. There was a division of police responsibility; the car lay in Surrey, but the Berkshire police held the letters Agatha had left behind at Styles. These, they hinted, gave rise to serious worries that she might be dead. The text of the letters was never released; and they are not now available, though the daughter of the Surrey officer in charge of the case, Inspector Kenward, told Gwen Robyns (the author of a controversial biography of Christie never published in the UK) that the letter he received was open to a sinister interpretation. But as Archie Christie told a friend in the city of London that the police suspected he had murdered his wife, their startling content can be guessed at. He had destroyed the letter left for him without showing it to the police, which some thought suspicious.

It was at this point that Conan Doyle entered the case. When he was knighted at the time of the Boer War, in 1902, Conan Doyle had been appointed Deputy-Lieutenant of Surrey. He had re-signed this position of honour in 1921, as part of the process of breaking his connections with the Establishment that accompa-

---

* Or what the press called the Silent Pool; Jared Cade claims the car was actually found slight further west.

nied his new espousal of spiritualism. As the days dragged on bringing no solution to the case, it was reasonable that the Chief Constable of Surrey should ask his advice. Certainly Conan Doyle seems to have had the assistance of both the police and of Colonel Christie.

However, it was not the spirit of Sherlock Holmes that was called upon to preside over his inquiry. Conan Doyle obtained from the police one of Mrs Christie's gloves. He took this at once to his friend Horace Leaf, a well-known medium and psychometrist. Conan Doyle gave Leaf no other information at all about the glove. This was on Sunday, 12 December, when Mrs Christie had been missing for eight days.

Horace Leaf at once got the name Agatha. 'There is trouble connected with this article. The person who owns it is half-dazed and half-purposeful. She is not dead as many think. She is alive. You will hear of her, I think, next Wednesday.' That same evening Conan Doyle sent a report of this session to Colonel Christie.

What a contrast to Conan Doyle's earlier detective work is this resort to the psychic. Horace Leaf had told him more, however: 'There was a good deal about the character and motives which was outside my knowledge,' he later wrote. Here, perhaps, he was being discreet about a fellow writer's private life.

Sure enough, it all turned out as Horace Leaf had predicted. On Wednesday morning the papers were full of the news that Mrs Christie was alive and well. She had been found living under a false name in a hotel in Harrogate, the Yorkshire spa. The circumstances of her discovery were as extraordinary as her disappearance.

While the police were searching the Downs with tracker dogs and spotter planes and thousands of volunteers, and the press was frantically finding daily twists to keep the story alive, the object of their interest was many, many miles away.

On Saturday, 4 December, a pleasant well-dressed lady checked into the Hydro Hotel in Harrogate. She signed the register as Teresa Neele, and said she was from South Africa. She lived quietly, taking tea in a local tearoom, shopping, sight-seeing, and in the evening joining the other guests in the lounge. She did not escape the notice of the staff, some of whom thought she resembled the missing novelist whose pictures filled the popular papers. (A small witness to all of this was the young Patrick White, future Nobel laureate, who was staying in the hotel with his family.)

Eventually the police were notified by the owners, and they set a watch on her for two days. The *Daily News* had offered a reward of £100, and eventually received a phone call from one of the staff at the hotel. This was on Monday, 13 December. Sidney Campion (later a barrister and artist) was sent north at once, and Ritchie Calder followed on a later train to help him. The reporters approached the lady in the hotel lobby – she answered to the name of Mrs Christie. Calder recalled in 1976: 'When asked how she got there she said she did not know and was suffering from amnesia. She eventually retreated to her room with many questions unanswered.'

By now Colonel Christie had arrived, and was waiting quietly in the hall with the local police inspector. At seven o'clock Agatha came downstairs. 'Fancy,' she said to a hotel friend, 'my brother has just arrived.' They went in and sat by the fire the dining-room. Not together, but apart. After their talk, Archie Christie talked to the pressmen, who by now had flooded into the hotel. He announced that Agatha was suffering from a complete loss of memory. The next morning the Christies left the hotel by a rear door, being caught in flight by an astute photographer from the *Daily Mirror*.

The press was not pleased at this rather tame outcome of the affair. There were hard questions asked in the papers and in Parliament about the costs of the searches. These were estimated to have amounted to £10,000, though the Home Secretary would admit only to the sum of £25.

Mrs Christie went to stay with her sister, and her doctors issued statements about her health. It was claimed that she had lost three years out of her life, that she had not known Archie or that she had a daughter, nor could she say how she had got to Harrogate. No further explanations were provided by the novelist or her family. What had happened to Agatha Christie?

The clue lies in what Conan Doyle, reporting Horace Leaf's psychic impression, called the 'character and motives' of Mrs Christie. It was certainly not a publicity stunt. Though she had a new book, *The Big Four,* already on its way to the shops, she hated personal publicity.

However, the literary journalist Eric Hiscock, who worked at that time with William Collins (indeed it was he who had suggested to the firm that they should acquire Agatha Christie after reading her first novel) had a strange recollection he reported after her death in 1976. 'I know that on the morning after she disappeared [4 December] Sir Godfrey Collins told me I was not to talk to the press about her disappearance. 'She is in Harrogate, resting'.'

Indeed at the time it was reported in *The Times* that Mrs Christie had told her brother-in-law in a letter posted in London the day after she left home that she had not been well and was going to stay at a spa in North Yorkshire. Naturally the police followed this up, but could not find her registered under her own name anywhere in the county. They were not looking for a Mrs Neele. Yet Collins had known, it seems, exactly where she was.

Nor were her publishers the only ones in contact with her. From Harrogate, the leading London store, Harrod's of Knightsbridge, received a query by letter about a ring left for alteration by Mrs Christie. If it was ready they were to send it on to 'Mrs Teresa Neele' at Harrogate. She also placed an advertisement in *The Times* asking friends and relations of Teresa Neele, arrived from South Africa, to communicate with Box 703.

These facts suggest that Mrs Christie was not suffering from amnesia, despite the claims of her family, doctors and official biographer. She knew who she was and where she was. Certainly she had been under great emotional strain, and this may have disturbed her judgement. But the devious mind that created more than eighty cunning plots should not be forgotten.

Another crime writer, Edgar Wallace, writing in the *Daily Mail* before Mrs Christie was found, saw her disappearance as 'a typical case of 'mental reprisal' on somebody who had hurt her. To put it vulgarly her first intention seems to have been to 'spite' an unknown person who would be disturbed by her disappearance. He did not suspect foul play, nor suicide, 'from the fact that she deliberately created an atmosphere of suicide by the abandonment of her car'. He concluded that if 'Agatha Christie is not dead of shock or exposure within a limited radius of the place where her car was found, she must be alive and in full possession of her faculties, probably in London. It is impossible to lose your memory and find your way to a determined destination.'

Later he added: 'If she had intended suicide and if her body had been found in the Silent Pool, say, I have no doubt from what I know of the police attitude, that Colonel Christie would have been held, on circumstantial evidence.'

Was this her revenge, to have Archie arrested, and then in a great demonstration of her love and need for him, to rescue him from a murder trial, perhaps at the last moment? It begins to sound like one of her own plots, but then that is basically what it was. What she had not foreseen was the bizarre and over-heated nature of the interest which the press would take in the matter, or that she would be traced so easily.

Eventually, from close family sources, Jared Cade in 1998 learnt something of the truth. After carefully arranging the car and its contents at Newlands Cross, Agatha walked to nearby West Clandon Station and caught a train to London. (But what, one asks, of the local man who had seen a woman at the car at 6.20 a.m.?) She stayed the night with her sister-in-law Mrs Nan Kon, who provided her with clothes and money. First thing the next morning she took a train north from Kings Cross. In about four hours she would have reached Yorkshire and begun the charade at Harrogate. When her husband arrived at the Hydro she confessed all this, and he was very surprised at Mrs Kon, who had claimed to be as shocked as anyone at the 'disappearance'. The cover-up of amnesia and a fugue began.

The press was right after all: it was a plot. And maybe there was something too in the later talk of a publicity stunt. When Agatha disappeared Collins already had her new book in hand and were printing and distributing copies. *The Big Four* was published in January 1927, only a couple of weeks after the return of Mrs Christie; it sold some 8,500 copies, 3,000 more than her previous book. But other Christie books were appearing as reprints at this time, some four books altogether, which had been arranged for before her disappearance. Mrs Christie was news, and it did not damage sales at all.

The Mystery of the Blue Train, that had caused her so much trouble, was eventually completed, and was published in March 1928; it sold 7,000 copies. The publicity was still paying off. *The Seven Dials Mystery* early in 1929 went on to sell 8,000 copies. Though it could be argued that she had gained from it, Agatha Christie deeply resented the press intrusion, which she seems not to have anticipated, perhaps feeling that the private affair of a middle-class couple was not the business of the public at large.

Mrs Christie was eventually forced to make a public statement about her disappearance when it was referred to in the High Court by counsel for the *Daily Express* defending a libel action by the explorer Mitchell-Hedges as a 'foolish hoax on the police'.

Counsel for Mrs Christie, who asked to be heard by the court, denied this, but did not go much further in explaining frankly what had happened. She eventually told her story to the *Daily Mail*, but it was account filled with discrepancies. This was in February 1928; in April she divorced Archie Christie. He had provided the usual evidence of adultery with a young woman that had to be created for the divorce court in those days. Mrs Christie, a devout Anglican, believing herself to be now in a state of sin, never took Communion again, until after Archie died. In a sense the affair of the missing eleven days was brought to mind every time she went to Church.

Conan Doyle drew other conclusions from the affair, as he wrote in a letter to the editor of the *Morning Post* about his own investigation:

> The Christie case has offered an excellent example of the uses of psychometry as an aid to the detective. It is, it must be admitted, a power which is elusive and uncertain, but occasionally it is remarkable in its efficiency. It is often used by the French and German police, but if it is ever employed by our own it must be *sub rosa*, for it is difficult for them to call upon the very powers which the law compels them to persecute.

Conan Doyle was very proud, it would seem, of what he saw as the accurate forecast provided by Horace Leaf, though reluctant to reveal those curious details of 'character and motive' which would interest us now. 'The only error was that he had an impression of water, though whether the idea of a Hydro was at the bottom of this feeling is at least arguable.'

Agatha Christie cannot have been pleased to discover Conan Doyle's connection with the affair. She owed him a great deal: after all Poirot and Hastings are modelled directly on Holmes and Watson; her use of detail owes much to Doyle; and both had written books on and about Dartmoor. A couple of years later in her Tommy and Tuppence Beresford book *Partners in Crime*, published in 1929, she had her subtle revenge. The diverting adventures in detection collected in that book are meant as parodies of other detective writers of the day. The parody of Conan Doyle, first published in *The Sketch* in October 1924, is called 'The Case of the Missing Lady', and guys his earlier story 'The Disappearance of Lady Frances Carfax' published in December 1911 and collected in *His Last Bow* (1917), by giving it a farcical twist.

The missing lady of the title is tracked down staying under a false name at a health clinic where she is losing weight before she gets married! The partners are disappointed at this outcome. 'And you will oblige me,' Tommy Beresford sedately instructs Tuppence, his wife and partner in detection, 'by not placing this case upon your records. It has absolutely no distinctive features.'

Agatha Christie, it seems, by reprinting the story, had the last laugh on Sir Arthur Conan Doyle.

CHAPTER TWENTY-FIVE

THE ZOO PARK MURDER

Conan Doyle and his family spent the winter of 1928–9 in South and East Africa. He hoped his health would benefit by the warmer climate, an escape from the cold and damp at home. As he had many engagements to speak about spiritualism, the schedule proved hectic enough, but nevertheless he also found the time to take an interest in local crime.

'There is not much real crime in South Africa, either in the Union or in Rhodesia,' he writes in *Our African Winter*, 'though there is a very great deal of artificial crime depending upon the diamond monopoly and upon the laws relating to the natives.' In Johannesburg, on 15 January 1929, Conan Doyle went out with police commander Colonel Quirke and his Chief Constable to witness some of the typical calls upon the police. That was interesting enough, but soon he was absorbed in one of the few real mysteries in the history of South African crime. This was the brutal murder of Irene Frances Kanthack on 24 November 1927, a case still unsolved when Doyle arrived in South Africa. 'Few South African crimes,' wrote veteran reporter Benjamin Bennett later on, 'are today recalled more vividly or with greater sense of horror. About few has there been more controversy and lack of accurate information.'

Conan Doyle by his direct intervention only added to the controversy. But first, the facts of the case.

Irene Kanthack was the eighteen-year-old daughter of a civil engineer who had formerly been Director of Irrigation for the Union of South Africa. The family lived at 35 Oxford Road, Forest Town, an exclusive area in the suburbs of Johannesburg beside the Zoo Park. Irene was a first-year student of biology at the University of Witwatersrand. She arrived home from her lectures on Thursday, 24 November, in time for tea with her mother. She changed her dress, and said she was taking the dog, a black Cairn terrier, for a walk. She often did this, and usually followed a fixed route: going past the War Memorial, around the west side of the Zoo, and out onto the Parkview Golf Course. She left the house between 4.30 and 4.45.

At 6.15 Irene was seen at the back of the Zoo by Constable Johannes Bezuidenhout, who was on point duty at the Saxonwald plantation. (This area has since been built over.) She was then on her way home. A rainstorm was threatening.

'You'd better hurry up, Miss, or you'll get wet,' he called out to her, but the girl seemed absorbed in her thoughts, swinging her stick, with the dog at her heels. She went along Upper Park Drive towards her home and out of the policeman's sight.

Five minutes later a white tourer car passed, going in the same direction as the girl, its side screens up against the impending rain.

It was nearly half an hour later when the storm finally broke, and Bezuidenhout and his colleague Constable van Tonder sought shelter. They looked out over the rain-washed neighbourhood, which now seemed empty of people. These tropical storms are very fierce, and the sheets of rain obscure the view completely. No cars passed. The two officers waited for the rain to stop before going off-duty. Nearby a murder was being committed.

When Mr Kanthack arrived home at 5.30 he was told that Irene was out for her walk. Though the storm loomed, he was not concerned about his daughter until her dog came whimpering back to the house an hour later. As there was no sign of Irene,

Kanthack reported her missing to the Parkview police post and arranged for an appeal to be broadcast from the Johannesburg radio station.

This appeal alerted police chief Colonel Trigger, who at once arranged a search party. By seven o'clock there were already searchers in the area, but nothing was found. Police dogs were used the next day to no avail. Every spare policeman was drafted in on the Saturday morning and light aircraft were sent up from Pretoria to survey the area from the air; the zoo lake was dragged; Pathfinders and Boy Scouts were detailed to scour the local woodlands.

One of the Scouts searching an area of the park to the south of the War Memorial – Irene's route home – kicked over a heap of leaves and debris. Pulling aside a branch he found the body of Irene Kanthack.

The boy blew his whistle to summon the policeman in charge of his group, who was none other than Johannes Bezuidenhout. He at once recognized the girl as the one who had passed him on the road before the storm. Tracker dogs were brought in immediately, but the trail had gone cold.

From traces at the scene, police investigators were able to establish that Irene had been killed about fifteen feet from where she was found. It seemed that she had been intercepted opposite the gate leading into the zoo. She had tried to run away towards Lower Park Drive. A broken piece of her stick was found at one spot, and another piece a hundred yards away, where it seemed she was attacked a second time. Once again she escaped, down towards the path leading to the Memorial, no doubt hoping that someone might be there to help her.

She was stunned by a blow from a wooden peg, and carried into the plantation. When she came to she must have resisted, as there were signs of a fierce struggle. Irene's attacker now stabbed her, cutting her finger, the blade entering her body under the sternum and biting deep into the flesh. Realizing that she was dead or dying, the attacker carried her to the spot where she was found. Rape rather than robbery had motivated the attack. Her wristwatch, in classic detective story style, was broken. The hands stood still at 6.35.

Investigating officers at once suspected a native, and indeed one was arrested. But this was a case which would not be solved so easily. The suspect was soon released without charge. Public reaction was hysterical – girls were not allowed out of the house; fathers bought guns; the fear that underlies South African life rose to the surface. The police were criticized in the press and at public meetings. White virginity was threatened.

Public interest centred on the white tourer seen on the evening of the murder, though the driver never came forward. An expensive car of that kind was unlikely to be owned by a native. However, the police were still convinced that the culprit had to be a native.

There had been a curious incident reported from Hyde Park some miles away, where a native was boasting that he had murdered 'a person', and he was said to have a scar on his chest. Colonel Trigger assigned detectives to check this lead, but although several more natives were routinely detained, nothing concrete emerged that would help the investigation.

A white woman claimed she had been attacked by a native near the same spot some months before, but again nothing came of this line of inquiry. The woman's description seemed similar to the Hyde Park boaster – but at that date, all natives looked alike to some eyes in South Africa.

Colonel Trigger stubbornly refused to change his mind, even when it was suggested that he should be looking for a European, possibly the driver of the white car. Trigger's answer was that the body was hidden in the same way natives hid the game they killed. A reconstruction was arranged for the benefit of the Minister of

Justice, Mr Teelman Roos, and he and Detective Head Constable H. Gottlieb Boys agreed that a native was a more likely culprit than a nebulous European.

As always in sensational cases, offers of help came from the public and from spiritualists. A well-known Pretoria spiritualist arrived to cover the scene, and he provided a reconstruction of the crime quite at variance to the police version. He said Irene Kanthack had been murdered on the east side of the lake and carried by car to the place the body was found. As this contradicted all the physical evidence, the police were confident in dismissing the theory.

Yet another spiritualist summoned up the spirit of Irene for Detective H.W. Atkinson (later a well-known private detective). Through the medium, 'Irene' said that she had been walking past the zoo with her dog when she was accosted by two men. 'I was frightened and must have fainted because I don't remember anything else till I woke up where I am now. I was quite surprised to find my throat had been cut.'

According to Atkinson, the medium then related that the murderer wore no tie or collar, but overalls like a painter wears when working. He was, in fact, an unskilled worker at the zoo. 'He was one of the men who poisoned the lion cubs at the zoo a few months ago.'

Atkinson called at the home of one of the suspects in the earlier poisoning case and found he left on the weekend of the murder. Again the details related by the medium were so different from what they had established that the police were not inclined to follow up this lead either. Indeed, it may not even have been reported to Colonel Trigger.

There the case looked like ending, another addition to the unsolved list.

Then in the summer of 1929 there was a sensational development. A young painter was arrested in Rhodesia and brought back to Johannesburg for trial. Though he appeared in court as 'Mr Brown' and has so far remained unnamed in the accounts I have seen of the murder, his name was in fact Vermaak. It was alleged by a former girlfriend of his that she had evidence that Vermaak was responsible for the murder. Her evidence consisted of a set of rather racy letters, padded out with some circumstantial evidence. The painter was brought up before the magistrate, Mr C.W. Lawrence, when an adjournment was allowed over Vermaak's protests. At the second hearing a week later, the case against him collapsed. The magistrate dismissed the charge after hearing the Crown case, and said he was sending the papers to the Attorney-General with a view to having the girlfriend prosecuted.

Vermaak had been arrested in June 1929. By this time Conan Doyle had left the country and was writing his impressions of the case in *Our African Winter*, to which he added a final footnote mentioning the Vermaak arrest. His involvement with the case was, however, more complicated than appears from his own account.

Miss Kanthack's murder, he wrote, was an 'unsolved mystery of first-class importance . . . I refused to discuss this, though I was asked to give an opinion in the local press, as it was a painful matter to revive.' One of the policemen on the case recalls, nevertheless, that the press brought Conan Doyle into the case whenever they could. Now back in England Conan Doyle felt he could be a little more forthcoming about the case.

There was one feature of the crime which struck me as particularly remarkable, and that was the time. The poor girl was seen approaching the fatal grove at 6.15 – at 6.30 her little dog arrived home in a bedraggled condition – at 6.35 her wristwatch had been shattered by a blow, and a little after 7 the alarm had been given, and there were searchers in the wood who failed to see the concealed body, or to trace it with dogs the next day.

270

This is so remarkable that a persistent rumour got about that she had been abducted in a car, and then brought back the next day and laid in the wood. This is quite inadmissible. It certainly was not so. The body was hid within a very few yards of the place where the poor girl had been slain, and had certainly never been anywhere else. That being so, we are presented with a curious problem. In a space of time which could hardly have been more than twenty minutes the criminal had been able to drag the body across, and then cover it with such skill that for three days it lay hid, though Boy Scouts and others were hunting every yard of the wood. I would venture to draw two deductions from this. The first is that in all probability there were at least two criminals, since from what I saw of the undergrowth I should not think it possible for one man to have collected sufficient boughs and foliage to have covered the body in time. It is a pity that it rained heavily, for those boughs were certainly stained with finger-prints before they were washed off. My second deduction would be that the criminals were probably Europeans or men of some brain power, who lived at a distance, and wanted time for getting away. A native living in a hut within a few hours journey would naturally have made off and left the body. But if the man had a long motor or train journey before he would be in safety, it would mean everything to him to hide the body so that there should be no general search and alarm before he got outside the danger zone. Those are the two points which struck me, but one is arguing from very insufficient data.

According to Detective Theo Zeederburg the crime absorbed Conan Doyle during his time in Johannesburg. 'However, the famous British writer's methods were fairly unorthodox and we detectives sometimes had to smile at his flights of the imagination and far-fetched theories. The man who could solve murder

271

mysteries so easily on paper, was bogged down in the reality of the murder in the plantation.'

Here, I think, we hear the authentic voice of Lestrade and his colleagues at Scotland Yard. Was Conan Doyle really that out of his depth?

The murder had been of great interest to the spiritualist circles in which Conan Doyle moved in South Africa. But also, on his arrival in Johannesburg early in 1929, he was approached by Mr Stephen Black. Black was a well-known figure, a playwright, actor, former crime reporter and maverick political journalist, who had once worked for the *Daily Mail* in London. He delighted in the inconvenient exposure of corruption and bribery, much to the disquiet of the local government in Johannesburg. It was he who brought Conan Doyle out to Saxonwald to see the site of the murder, and together they attempted to solve the mystery.

Black, like many others in the city, at first thought that a native had committed the murder; then he changed his mind, and felt that the police should search out a European to whom specific clues pointed. Conan Doyle also had certain information which he believed would have enabled Sherlock Holmes to have solved the crime. But the police did not care for Black, and to them Conan Doyle was a mere romancer. (The account that follows is based on information in letters Stephen Black wrote to the detective H.W. Atkinson in October 1929, which were seen by Benjamin Bennett. Black, ruined by libel actions, died of liver cancer in August 1931. No material relating to the Kanthack case now seems to survive among Stephen Black's papers, so I understand from his biographer Professor Stephen Gray.)

On Conan Doyle's behalf Black made extensive inquiries. He interviewed dozens of people who claimed to have clues or information, cross-questioning them with all his skills, and asking them to set out their facts in affidavits. After any sensational crime there are, as the police know only too well, numerous 'witnesses' who are really wasting police time, but one of Black's leads seemed especially interesting to Conan Doyle.

On the day after the Kanthack murder (the Friday), a European living in the Saxonia Buildings, on Diagonal Street near the offices of *The Star* newspaper, was seen by the janitor washing out a bloodstained garment in the bathroom.

The janitor had his suspicions aroused, and opened one of the letters that arrived while the man was out. It was a warning from a woman in Vrededorp claiming that the police intended to exhume Miss Kanthack's body and that some hair from her attacker would be found in her hand. After the first letter the man had stayed in his flat.

The janitor took the letter to the police at Marshall Square, the Scotland Yard of Johannesburg. He handed it in and waited a quarter of an hour, was then told it was 'alright', and went home. That was the last he heard of the letter.

When the police did nothing, the clue was brought to the attention of Conan Doyle. He and Black went around to the Saxonia Buildings, where they were allowed to inspect the room recently vacated by the 'suspect', and Conan Doyle was shocked to find the walls covered with pornographic pictures. According to Stephen Black, these were 'indecent drawings, more or less life size, drawings copied from pornographic Continental papers and in some cases reproducing the French text, a language the 'artist' obviously did not know.' (Black himself had lived for a time near Nice.)

Conan Doyle arranged to pay the rent on the room for a month, hoping he would be able to persuade the C.I.D. to come and photograph the weird interior, and use their facilities to follow up what seemed to him a promising clue. Conan Doyle believed that if this man was kept under police observation, his habits, relations with women and even the company he kept might lead to something concrete and eventually connect him with the Zoo Park murder.

Working on the theory that this was not the first crime the suspect had committed, Conan Doyle discovered that when the man in question had been living at Kroonstad (ninety-six miles south-west of the city) a woman there had disappeared in mysterious circumstances. Conan Doyle applied for permission to excavate near a group of willows at Kroonstad, where he thought the body was buried. The police were more than just sceptical, they were incredulous. Though this is not confirmed by my sources, I suspect that this 'information' may have come from a spiritualist.

The police at Marshall Square refused to help Conan Doyle. They were not going to follow up the letter. The room in the Saxonia Buildings was not thought to hold the key to the Kanthack case. That the body of another victim lay under the willows was not accepted. Discouraged by this non-co-operation of the police – and not for the first time in his life – Conan Doyle gave up any further efforts to assist in the solution of the case in the manner of Sherlock Holmes.

After Conan Doyle left the country, Vermaak was arrested, and once again the papers were full of the story. Stephen Black was furious. He was now editing a weekly scandal sheet called *The Sjambok*, and as he explained in a later issue, he was astonished that the police had not made use of the 'valuable facts' in his possession. It seemed that they had made few inquiries about Vermaak.

'We are assured by the Police that every movement and action of Vermaak, immediately before and after the Kanthack murder, had been checked and verified. They knew all about him.

'Yet they did not know that he had, at the time of the murder, been living in the Saxonia Buildings . . .'

It was Vermaak the painter, he alleged, who had decorated the notorious room. 'Yes, the Police did not know where Vermaak lived at the time of the infamous murders with which he was to all appearances, unjustly charged.'

Black made a direct connection between Vermaak and the man who had received the warning letters and who had painted the room in the Saxonia Buildings. No official inspection of the pictures had been made, 'though unofficially, many have done so, because the Saxonia Building is a favourite hunting ground of police officers.'

Despite all the efforts of Conan Doyle and Stephen Black, the Kanthack case was shelved. Certainly rumours about the case were later current in police circles: that the suspect had killed again and had been hanged, and that he had been a workman at the zoo. Considering all the small points of the evidence it would seem that Conan Doyle and his friend were on the right track, that the crime was committed by two men, both associated with the Saxonia Buildings, and that Vermaak was indeed one of the culprits. But the police, intent it seems on finding a native killer, were not prepared to consider evidence relating to a white murderer. When they did, the case was rushed at, and the evidence found could not be taken to court.

For Conan Doyle it was a familiar story. It meant, too, that Irene Kanthack's parents never had the satisfaction of seeing their daughter's killer, black or white, convicted.

CHAPTER TWENTY-SIX

A PECULIAR DEATH AT UMTALI

During the last stages of their African trip Conan Doyle and his family stayed briefly in Salisbury, where he was also to lecture. They arrived there on 29 January. Their hosts, Judge McIlwaine and wife Sophia, were Irish, and fellow spiritualists. Robert McIlwaine (later Sir Robert), a distinguished figure in the public life of the colony, was then a judge of the Rhodesian High Court. He related to Conan Doyle a very extraordinary crime which had recently before him on the bench, 'which presented some features which seem to me unique, and which would have rejoiced the heart of my old friend Churton Collins, who was a connoisseur in such matters'.

His colleague from the early days of the Crimes Club had been dead some twenty years, but it was a relaxation for Conan Doyle to turn away on this trip from the controversies of spiritualism and the social problems of South Africa to 'the fascinating subject of criminology'.

In Umtali, a small town near the Mozambique border in what was then Rhodesia (it is now Mutare in Zimbabwe), there stopped shortly before an Englishman named Job Winter, a travelling salesman for Mabie Todd Ltd of London, the long-established firm which manufactured the Swan Pen, 'the pen of the British

Empire'. He was putting in a short wait until the steamer should arrive at Beira (the important port on the coast of the neighbouring Portuguese colony of Mozambique) which would take him on to India, where his business lay.

Job Winter was staying at the Royal Hotel, and there seemed to be nothing outwardly odd about him. He was a friendly, harmless sort of man, forty-four years of age, with a wife and family in England. He was a respectable senior salesman, born in Berkshire, who had started out life as a stationer's apprentice.

The same small town was home to Miss Mary Knipe, a recent arrival from Cape Town, who was employed at Meikle's, the local stores. Forty-three years of age, she was possessed of no physical attractions and no particular qualities, save that she was remarkably strong, almost as muscular as a man. She also had lodgings at the Royal Hotel.

This middle-aged pair never met until 5 November 1928, and on the evening of 6 November they went for a short walk in the Umtali Park, a large, ill-lighted place furnished with only the occasional seat. The woman was of good character, the man sober, they were new acquaintances; it did not seem a promising prelude to a most dramatic sequel. What happened within the next hour was a problem which vexed South African opinion for months and intrigued Conan Doyle.

It was after eight o'clock when the couple entered the park, and sat down on a bench near the tennis courts. It chanced that another couple, a Portuguese named Louis Lambeiro and an Irish girl, Miss Hannah O'Mahoney, sat courting on another bench not far off. However, it was too dark for either couple to be aware of the other. At 8.45 a hooter blew which gave the exact time. Shortly afterwards the Irish girl swore that she heard the sound of a quarrel, a confused noise, with a woman's and a man's voice mingled. This lasted for some time, followed by a few minutes silence. Then from the same direction came four distinct screams.

277

Miss O'Mahoney, who appears to have been both brave and truthful, implored her companion to go and investigate, but he refused, and at the subsequent inquiry declared that he had heard nothing – a claim which was so manifestly false that there was talk of a prosecution for perjury. Silence followed the screams, but after an interval Hannah O'Mahoney heard a man's voice calling for help three times in English. This would have been shortly after nine o'clock. About 9.15 she saw three natives pass, though there was nothing remarkable about their behaviour. Shortly afterwards the couple left the park, having made no further inquiry into what they had heard.

Several other people had heard the cries and were less timorous. They were at a greater distance, however, occupants of the houses which surrounded the park, and it was some time before they reached the spot.

The first to arrive was a Mr Kirkland. It was just after nine that he heard the cries, which seems to fit with the evidence from Miss O'Mahoney. Rushing through the park, he came upon the body of a woman, Miss Knipe it transpired, lying huddled across the path, quite dead though bleeding from many wounds. There was no sign that rape had been attempted. Kirkland was carrying an electric torch, and as he flashed it round the scene he heard a voice in the dark say, 'Here I am. I am knocked out.' A man, who proved to be Job Winter, then rose from behind a tree twenty-five yards away, and tottered towards him. He had blood on his face and seemed to be dazed and delirious. He kept repeating, 'Who hit me? Who hit me?' He sat down on the grass as one exhausted. Presently other people began to arrive, including a police constable named Rowe and soon after, Dr Jackson. Winter was removed to hospital, and said on the way, 'Oh, doctor, don't take me to hospital. I have to catch my boat for India.' (He was due to sail on the SS *Khandalla* from Beira to Bombay the very next day.) Afterwards he said, 'You must have a madman running round loose here.'

Let us now take Winter's own account of what had occurred in Umtali Park. He said that Miss Knipe and he were sitting in perfect amity, the lady being on his left. He had a recollection of seeing a native pass within twelve feet of him, but remembered nothing more until he came to his senses lying on the ground near the bench. Staggering to his feet, he looked round for his companion, missed her, staggered some forty yards down the path and came across the body. (As it was pitch-dark it was remarkable that he staggered in the right direction.) He then collapsed again, and could recall no more until he found himself in the midst of the group of people who had been attracted to the scene of the crime.

As to his injuries, they were most certainly not self-inflicted. His left jaw was cracked, and according to the medical evidence he had received three other severe blows, one of which cut him behind the ear, and one near the eye. A heavy, edged instrument seemed to have been used, so it could hardly have been a knife. The sharper end of the head of a hammer would be more probable. No weapon of any kind was found near the seat where the attack took place, or on the person of the other protagonist.

Now let us take a look at the murdered woman's injuries. Her hands and forearms were cut to pieces in defending herself against the repeated stabs of a knife. In addition there were numerous cuts on the body, one of which had penetrated the lung, a second the stomach, and another in the back of the left shoulder. Death had been due to loss of blood.

There is one other point which deserves attention. There was a native hut sixty-four yards from the scene of the crime. Two native women occupied it at the time, and gave evidence to the effect that after the hooter blew (at 8.45) they heard a woman's voice raised as if in a quarrel, and that after this came the screams. This tale of a quarrel is confirmed by the evidence of the Irish girl, and it is difficult to fit it in with the idea of a sudden stealthy attack.

Such was the case as Conan Doyle received it from Judge McIlwaine, and as he himself recorded it. Further details are to be gleaned from the Rhodesian newspapers of the day.

At the inquest evidence was given regarding the scene in the park by the first eyewitnesses. Constable Rowe (who had been called on the telephone by the manger of the Masonic hotel) arrived at 9.15. A group of people were already there when he arrived: Mr Stokes, Mr Kirkland, Mr Glassen and Miss Kingsford Smith.

The body of Miss Knipe was lying on her back in the centre of the path. Her clothes were saturated with blood and she was bleeding from the mouth. On the right side of the path was Mr Winter, to whom Miss Kingsford Smith was attending. The policeman noted the cut on the left side of his head, the bruise on his ear, a cut on his cheek and a black eye, all on the left side.

'Who hit me?' was the first thing Winter said. He appeared more or less dazed, and repeated himself two or three times.

The policeman asked him if he knew who had struck him. 'No.' Had he been struck from behind. 'Yes.' Asked his name, Winter made no reply. Then he asked 'Where is the little woman?' and said something about being knocked out. He had nothing in his hands.

Rowe went back forty yards to a seat pointed out by Kirkland. Here there was a pool of blood, and under the seat a small handkerchief which he later handed over to Detective Bond. The grass border was much disturbed in front of the seat, as if there had been a struggle. The trail of blood led away from this in an irregular way, as if someone had been staggering. There was no sign of a weapon.

The next day Winter himself gave evidence. He was, he said, anxious to clear up the dreadful affair. He related how he had met Miss Knipe by joining the party she was with at the hotel and watching the fireworks – 5 November being, of course, Guy

Fawkes night. The next day he had called at Meikle's stores to inquire about business there and had talked with Miss Knipe. He arranged to meet her after work and they had walked back to the hotel where they dined, sharing a bottle of wine between them. (During the day he had drunk six whiskies.)

Winter wished to avoid the men in the hotel bar (the British distaste for rough Colonials, doubtless), so they walked to the park. Having tried one seat, they moved on to another. It was a secluded area, and while they sat on the bench Winter talked of his Indian experiences, the beat between Karachi and Lahore. Then he remembered nothing more.

Earlier he had seen a native, but nobody else. When he regained consciousness, Miss Knipe was not there. He saw lights and heard voices in the park and went towards them; then he saw the body, stopped, recognized Miss Knipe, then fainted again. Job Winter could recall nothing more of what had happened, nor could he supply a motive for the attack. It must have been, he thought, the work of a native. He agreed he had made a statement to the police the following day, and that he had said to a policeman on the way to the hospital: 'You're not going to make a case out of this are you?'

The evidence of further witnesses was then heard. On the fourth day the inquest was brought to an end, and Winter was arrested and charged with the murder of Miss Knipe. The police *were* going to make a case out of it.

The preliminary hearing before the Umtali magistrates opened on 3 December. Winter's jaw was shown by x-rays to have been seriously fractured, and he would need to go into hospital. Evidence was also heard concerning the bloodstains on Winter's clothes and shoes; and on tests done to ascertain where in the park the stains had been picked up. Having been remanded by the magistrates Winter was committed for trial at the Central Criminal Court in Salisbury. However, on 26 December 1928, it was officially announced that the Attorney-General, having considered the case fully, declined to prosecute.

Such was the mysterious affair in Umtali Park. Inspector Bond, who had handled the case, seemed to Conan Doyle to have acted in a very intelligent way. He searched everywhere for a weapon, but found none – a most fundamental point. He noted the earth in front of the seat showed signs of disturbance, but could find none at the back or sides. He traced drops of blood with two small pools of blood along the path to the point where the body was found, about forty yards in all. Miss Knipe had evidently backed away down the path screaming, while the assailant had showered blows upon her, most of which were caught upon her arms. She may have fallen at the two points where the pools of blood were. There was no indication of robbery.

'These are the essential facts, so far as known,' Doyle concluded. Conan Doyle thought the dismissal of the case very wise:

In the absence of motive, weapon, and evidence there could be no case for the prosecution. And yet what a perfect mystery the whole affair seems – more remarkable, I think, than any which a romancer could invent. What possible theory would cover the facts? And why should he assault her? And where was the weapon? Is it possible that in spite of her age she had a jealous admirer who assaulted Winter, and then when she had turned upon him – hence the sound of quarrelling – made a murderous attack upon her. This is most unlikely, for there was no record of such an admirer. Or was there some homicidal maniac – native for choice – who might have attacked them? There was, it seems, an attack not entirely dissimilar some months before by a native. But would Winter have no recollection of it? And how came his injuries upon the left side of his head when the lady was seated to the left of him? It is to be remembered that blows upon the head sometimes remove the memory of events which led up to the blow, even to the extent of some minutes. That shadowy native, who Winter says he saw, may have emerged and struck blows which left no trace in the memory. I confess that without further evidence I should be loath to give an opinion. One conceivable theory is that the attack was not meant for the prosaic and middle-aged couple, but that in the dark the assailant chose the wrong people. It is even possible that the Portuguese and the Irish girl were the real objects of the vindictive hatred of some jealous rival. It is far-fetched, but within the bounds of possibility.

Winter was released and left Rhodesia, passing out of public knowledge. Miss Knipe's strange death itself would now be quite forgotten had it not been for the fortuitous interest of Conan Doyle, who devoted seven pages to the case in his travel book about Africa, more than to many of his spiritualist lectures on that trip.

Perhaps in his heart of hearts Conan Doyle really found murder mysteries more interesting than the secrets of the world to come.

CHAPTER TWENTY-SEVEN

THE COBBLER AND
THE FISH-PEDLAR

In Kenya, on the last stage of his trip through Africa in 1929, Conan Doyle was 'agreeably occupied in reading Upton Sinclair's *Boston*'. This was a massive 'modern historical novel' dealing in fine detail with the case of Sacco and Vanzetti, the Italian-born anarchists who had been executed by the Commonwealth of Massachusetts in 1927.

It was a case which had aroused, and still arouses, worldwide interest. Protests followed upon the executions, and many doubts still surround the case. That there should remain any doubts at all, after long and diligent investigations by both lawyers and historians, is more than enough ground for believing that the pair were put to death unfairly. So, at least, Governor Michael S. Dukakis of Massachusetts finally decided in 1977, when he pardoned them.

It was one case about which Conan Doyle had no doubts either. 'I look upon Sinclair as one of the greatest novelists in the world, the Zola of America, and his power of detail and marshalling of facts leaves me amazed. I think he has become almost monomaniacal in his reaction against our settled law and order, but his high, unselfish soul shines through it all.'

This was written when Sinclair was at a low ebb in his literary fortunes. He was then publishing his novels himself, owing to the difficulties he had encountered with established publishers. Even today his reputation is still eclipsed: 'mere socialist propaganda' is the clichéd view. And yet Conan Doyle's parallel with Zola was exact. Both wrote as a means to an end. And though the Frenchman is undoubtedly the greater writer, the American socialist Upton Sinclair has many virtues.

Boston was a long and complicated book. The case of Sacco and Vanzetti was even longer and more complicated. By the time Sinclair wrote, hysteria had distorted many of the facts.

On Christmas Eve 1919, four men, apparently foreigners, attempted to rob the payroll truck of the White Shoe Co., at Bridgewater, Massachusetts. The guards in the truck put up a spirited defence, and after a heavy exchange of gunshots the bandits escaped and were never traced.

Some months later, on 15 April 1920, a gang robbed the payroll office of Slater and Morrill's shoe factory at South Braintree. The cashier Frederick A. Parmenter and his guard Alessandro Berardelli were shot dead in the affray.

Again, no immediate trace could be found of the gang. And it was not until 5 May that Nicola Sacco, a shoemaker, and Bartolomeo Vanzetti, a fish-pedlar, were arrested, quite by chance, while visiting the home of a suspect in the crimes whose car the police were curious about. They were actually arrested on a street-car. Sacco was found to be armed with a pistol. Both were unable to explain themselves. By the following day the police were convinced, as is the way of the police, that they had found their men.

That at least was the liberal view at the time, and indeed the manner in which the two Italians were treated aroused great concern.

In June 1920 Vanzetti was convicted of the first Bridgewater robbery. He was identified by five eye-witnesses, though his alibi that he was peddling eels on Christmas Eve was supported by 16 fellow Italians. If the State case had been stronger this evidence might not have been totally satisfactory – these witnesses, as Conan Doyle tartly observed, were supposed by the prosecution to be in a conspiracy to shield the prisoner.

'Late in the proceedings the defence had the idea to approach the wholesale eel merchants. Seven years had elapsed, but by some miracle the dusty old invoice had been preserved and it was shown that on the day before they actually forwarded a barrel of eels to Vanzetti. Surely that alone should be enough for any reasonable man.'

Vanzetti, however, was convicted and sentenced to 15 years in the state penitentiary.

There then followed the trial of Sacco *and* Vanzetti for the second robbery and the murders at Slater and Morrill's in South Braintree. Here again there was confused eyewitness testimony. But there was also material evidence, in the shape of Nicola Sacco's .32 Colt Automatic handgun, the one he was carrying the night he was arrested. Ballistics evidence showed that the fatal bullet that struck Berardelli had been fired from this gun. More recent tests, done in 1961, have confirmed this. But the defence argued then, as partisans of Sacco argue now, that there was some dark work about the bullets, and that these had been switched. The bullet tested came from the gun, but not from the guard's body.

The prosecution case was a confused one, but such was the aroused state of feeling against the 'anarchists', that they carried the day. The testimony of Sacco and Vanzetti, defending their philosophical views, did not make them attractive figures to the conservative jury. Even if the eye-witnesses were wrong, there remained the evidence of the gun. Sacco and Vanzetti were electrocuted on 23 August 1927. As the foreman of the jury commented at the time, 'Damn them, they ought to hang anyway.'

On 31 October 1928, just as the first edition of *Boston* was ready, there appeared in *Outlook*, an old-established New York weekly magazine, the true story of the Bridgewater crime. It was a detailed confession by Frank Silva, one of those who had been involved. The raid had been the work of a regular gang, and Sacco and Vanzetti had nothing to do with it. The man identified as Vanzetti was in fact a professional criminal named Doggy Bruno, who also wore a moustache, and was named by Silva as the 'shot-gun bandit'.

'It is impossible to read the facts,' Conan Doyle observed, 'without realizing that the two Italians were executed not as murderers but as anarchists. On the other hand it might be fairly be argued that because an anarchist is a man admittedly out to destroy the State, the State has an equal right to destroy him. Even if this were so, however, it should not be done under the pretence that the man is an ordinary vulgar criminal. Far from this being the case, Vanzetti was a man of such rare and exalted character, in spite of his extreme social views, that one thinks of St Francis of Assisi as one reads his utterances. His personality is likely to grow into a legend.'

Conan Doyle felt that the evidence had become so complex that the public were not in a position to see the true proportions of the pleas for and against. He was impressed with such things as the American Express lading bill for Vanzetti's eels, which seemed to demonstrate that his claim to have been selling fish at the time of the raid was true; the then Governor of Massachusetts, Alvan T. Fuller, was not. If he had doubts at all, he stifled them. For Conan Doyle, fresh from Upton Sinclair's vivid presentation of the evidence, there could be no doubts. 'If half of what he says is true – and it is well documented – then Sacco and Vanzetti, the two anarchists, were undoubtedly put to death unjustly by the State of Massachusetts.' More recently, that state, by pardoning the two men, has come round to this view itself. But in the 1920s things were very different, as Conan Doyle observed.

'Police procedure and judicial procedure and the whole criminal administration of the United States would seem now to be amongst the worst in the world, and torture is often as much a part of the system as it was in medieval Italy, though disguised under a specious name. We have little right to criticize, for the shame of Glasgow over the Slater-Trench scandal is quite as great as that of any American frame-up; but two blacks do not make a white, and if one has protested against the one, one may be allowed to do so against the other.'

Sacco and Vanzetti, whatever their political activities may have been, played no part in the crimes with which they were charged – that at least was the public stance of their defenders, such as Upton Sinclair.

Yet by 1952, on the basis of what they had been told by the leading Italian anarchist Carlo Tresca before his assassination, and what they had not been told by others, Upton Sinclair and the defence lawyer Fred Moore had come to believe that though Vanzetti was innocent, Sacco (who had been armed when he was arrested) had indeed been involved in the murders at South Braintree. To the end the saintly Vanzetti pleaded his innocence; Sacco proclaimed his abiding belief in the philosophy of anarchism. The contrast of attitude is suggestive.

Despite their posthumous pardons, the controversy over the lives and deaths of the Cobbler and the poor Fish-Pedlar, which so perplexed Conan Doyle, endures to this day.

EPILOGUE

THE FILES ARE CLOSED

The case of Sacco and Vanzetti was almost the last criminal affair in which Conan Doyle took an interest and certainly on which he commented at length in print.

Conan Doyle had differed with the journalist and thriller writer Edgar Wallace over the disappearance of Agatha Christie. Wallace thought the explanation of that mystery lay in Mrs Christie's mental state. Doyle, of course, had recourse to a psychometrist. In the autumn of 1928, they clashed again more publicly in a debate that raged over several weeks in a Sunday newspaper.

In the middle of August Conan Doyle was reported as claiming that a clairvoyant would be part of 'the well-equipped police-station of the future'. This claim was soon picked up by other papers.

Wallace, described in the headline of an article on 25 August as 'a great criminologist' – which was surely an exaggeration – opened the debate, claiming he was unimpressed by disembodied spirits, which he referred to as 'aerial bloodhounds' as detectives. He said mediums were no use in a murder hunt. Conan Doyle replied a week later, recounting some murder mysteries he claimed mediums did solve. He mentioned, too, his own intervention in the Agatha Christie case.

A second article by Wallace said that mediums simply could not solve mysteries. This was countered again by Conan Doyle. Towards the end the discussion became a little heated and over-personal. It is unlikely that the readers of *Lloyd's Sunday News* were left much enlightened by this debate, which was far from being a meeting of minds.

After his return to Europe in the summer of 1929, Conan Doyle made one more missionary journey, travelling through Holland and the Scandinavian countries, Norway, Sweden and Denmark, to lecture on spiritualism. This trip seems, however, to have been devoid of criminal interest. An earlier visit planned for 1925 had been cancelled after warnings from the spirit world. But the 1929 visit was ill-starred nevertheless. When he reached Stockholm in November, Conan Doyle was taken ill with *angina pectoris* and was ordered to return to England and rest; something he found hard to do.

Back in England he was nearly as active as ever. In March 1930 he resigned from the Society for Psychical Research in a welter of controversial publicity over the critical attitude of the society towards a series of seances in Italy. Then in July he travelled up to London to join a delegation calling on the Home Secretary to protest about the difficulties suffered by 'genuine mediums' under the witchcraft acts from the time of James I, which the police were then using as a convenient device for prosecuting frauds.* Controversy over this misuse of the law had been going on for some years. This was to be his last, painful, protest on behalf of those he felt were being unjustly treated. A week later he was dead.

In the preface to *The Case Book of Sherlock Holmes*, published in 1927, Conan Doyle had provided a summary of the great detective's career: 'He began his adventures in the very heart of the later Victorian Era, carried it through the all-too-short reign of Edward, and has managed to hold his own little niche even in these feverish days.'

These were words which might have described their author. Now

---

* Especially 5 Geo. IV c.83 (section iv) which said that those 'professing to tell fortunes, or using any subtle Craft . . . to deceive and imposes on any of His Majesty's Subjects', were 'rogues and vagabonds' and liable to up to three months in prison with hard labour.

Conan Doyle himself was dead. And so too was Sherlock Holmes, long retired to the Sussex Downs near Eastbourne to keep bees, who died (in the words of Vincent Starrett, the eminent American Sherlockian) 'in the presence of his creator' on 7 July 1930.

Hearing this sad news, many of his readers must have recalled another passage in that preface:

> One likes to think there is some fantastic limbo for the children of the imagination, some strange impossible place where Scott's heroes still may strut, Dickens' delightful Cockneys still raise a laugh, and Thackeray's worldlings continue to carry on their reprehensible careers. Perhaps in some humble corner of such a Valhalla, Sherlock Holmes and his Watson may for a time find a place, while some more astute sleuth with some even less astute comrade may fill the stage which they have vacated.

Doyle was buried in the grounds of his Sussex home. On the simple final memorial his family cut the words:

Steel True
Blade Straight
ARTHUR CONAN DOYLE,
Knight
PATRIOT, PHYSICIAN & MAN OF LETTERS
22 MAY, 1859–7 JULY, 1930

– a just summary of his own chivalrous career.*

---

* After Windlesham was put up for sale in July 1955 his remains were re-interred in All Saints' churchyard, Minstead, near Bignell Wood, where he had bought a house in 1925. There they are to this day, near a great oak tree which has been struck by lightning, not once or twice, but *three* times, leading some villagers to think such a dabbler in the forbidden as Conan Doyle should never have been buried there.

All his life Conan Doyle had been prepared to use his great talents as a writer and detective to serve the ends of justice, never shirking the burden, ignoring the abuse. It was a fitting epitaph for a great man.

He crusaded to the very end. Carl Sifakis reports that, shortly before his death, Conan Doyle interested himself in the case of a young woman who was tried and convicted of defrauding several large stores by uttering forged cheques. She claimed she was quite innocent of the offences. Despite his ill-health, Conan Doyle had begun an investigation of the matter when he died. Some six months later another woman was arrested and confessed to the crimes for which the first woman had been convicted.

Sir Arthur Conan Doyle, a detective to equal his own Sherlock Holmes, had been proved right again in his instincts about an injustice.

As Sir Basil Thomson, the former Assistant Chief Commissioner of Scotland Yard, wrote, 'Sir Arthur Conan Doyle would have made an outstanding detective had he devoted himself to crime detection rather than authorship. There was much of Holmes in Doyle.' And that too was a fitting epitaph from one detective to another.

(This mysterious poem, written in the 1890s, seemingly describes a murder on the wild moors of northern England: *for Conan Doyle this is the moment where detection begins.*)

A Tragedy

Who's that walking on the moorland?
  Who's that moving on the hill?
They are passing 'mid the bracken,
But the shadows grow and blacken
  And I cannot see them clearly on the hill.

Who's that calling on the moorland?
  Who's that crying on the hill?
Was it bird or was it human,
Was it child, or man, or woman,
  Who was calling so sadly on the hill?

Who's that running on the moorland?
  Who's that flying on the hill?
He is there – and there again,
But you cannot see him plain,
  For the shadow lies so darkly on the hill.

What's that lying in the heather?
  What's that lurking on the hill?
My horse will go no nearer,
And I cannot see it clearer,
  But there's something that is lying on the hill.

Arthur Conan Doyle

ACKNOWLEDGEMENTS

For their help in various ways I am deeply grateful to the following individuals and institutions:

Robert Allen Photography; Atlanta-Fulton Public Library; the Marquess of Anglesey; Peter E. Blau; Ruskin Bond; Manuscripts Department (Herbert Gladstone Papers), British Library; Undine Concannon, archivist Madame Tussaud's; DM Prints; Owen Dudley Edwards; Tony Farmar; the late Andrew Fayle; General Assembly Library, New Zealand House of Representatives; Prof. Stephen Gray; Dr. Derham Groves, University of Melbourne; Hampshire Central Library, Portsmouth; Michael Harley; the late Dr. Bernard Heuvelmans; the late Cameron Hollyer; Humanities Research Center, University of Texas at Austin; Kendal Library, Cumbria; Records Office, Law Society; Janice McNabb; Metropolitan Libraries, Toronto; Mitchell Library, Glasgow; Manuscripts Department (Casement Papers), National Library of Ireland; New York Public Library; Pembroke Public Library, Dublin; Chris Redmond; Rosenbach Museum and Library, Philadelphia; Library, Royal Dublin Society; the late John Bennett Shaw; Rev G.F. Smith, Great Wyrley; Staffordshire County Record Office; South African Library, Cape Town; Trinity College Libraries, Dublin; Madame Tussaud's Ltd.; Bill Waddell, curator Black Museum, New Scotland Yard; the late Irving Wallace; Richard Whittington-Egan; John Winnifrith; Cecilia Zeiss.

Like everyone else who writes on Conan Doyle these days I am indebted to the bibliographical researches of John Michael Gibson and the late Richard Lancelyn Green. The fine biography by Owen Dudley Edwards shows just what we can still learn about Conan Doyle.

Among the many other debts incurred while writing and revising this book, I would especially like to mention again the late Dame Jean Conan Doyle (Lady Bromet), Sir Arthur's youngest child, for her gracious interest, and to express the hope that it may lead readers on to explore further her father's widely varied writings. Lady Bromet and I were later associated in an attempt to vindicate Sir Arthur from the extraordinary charge levelled by an American academic of being the malicious culprit behind the notorious Piltdown Man hoax – but that affair, like the Giant Rat of Sumatra, is 'a tale for which the world is not yet ready'.

Also thanks are due to Gerry Long, National Library of Ireland; the librarian and staff of Trinity College Library, Dublin; in particular Geraldine Ryan; Thierry Joanis; Jean-Paul Crauser; Christopher Roden; Mr X; Jane Webber, Law Society Library; Trevor McFarlane, Cheslyn Hay Local History Society; and Gordon Weaver.

I have not been able to contact all those who previously helped me with the first edition, some, as the Sherlockians say, having passed 'over the Reichenbach Falls'.

I am grateful for the all care that my literary agent, Sara Menguc, takes of all my professional life. Brian Lane, the crime writer, and Catherine Cooke, curator of the Sherlock Holmes Collection at Marylebone Library, originally read the manuscript and have enabled me to correct some errors; I have not always agreed with their views, however, so the misapprehensions and mistakes that remain must be laid to my account.

The dedication is an expression of an even more special research friendship, which dated back nearly forty years by the time of my friend's death. He gave me much help with the French sources for this book. As a friend and admirer of his fellow Belgian, Georges Simenon, detective fiction, indeed detection in all its forms, was most congenial to him, and he also assisted me with a projected book on the history of the private detective, as yet incomplete.

ILLUSTRATION CREDITS

The author and publishers are grateful to the following for their kind permission to reproduce photographs in their control:

The Country Record Office, Stafford and Peter Rogers (Photographic) Ltd. for George Edalji's father, the Rev Shapurji Edalji; one of the horses slashed in the Edalji affair; Wyrley Vicarage; part of one of the mysterious letters giving details of the animal mutilations; police searching for clues in a field. Topham Picture Source for the *Daily Mirror* headline on the discovery of the missing Agatha Christie; the portraits of Sacco and Vanzetti; the demonstration in the Sacco and Vanzetti case.

All the other illustrations are from the author's own collection.

NOTES AND SOURCES

General

Until very recently mystery surrounded some aspects of Conan Doyle's legacy. When he died he left his papers to his wife, Lady Jean Conan Doyle, who sorted and arranged what he held at the time of his death. In turn the papers passed to Adrian and other members of the family. They were used by John Dickson Carr and by Pierre Nordon for their books in 1949 and 1964. Adrian also sold over the years some small batches of papers. For instance, the Harry Ransom Library in Austin, Texas, acquired Conan Doyle's spiritualist papers.

After Adrian's death Conan Doyle's heirs fell to bickering about the division and disposal of his papers. Dame Jean, Sir Arthur's youngest daughter, willed her share of them to the British Library, where she hoped they would all go, so creating a single centre for the study of Conan Doyle's life and literary work. But other family members had different ideas, and after a long-drawn-out dispute, during which the papers were inaccessible, they were eventually sold at auction by Christie's of London in May 2004 for a large sum, albeit much less than had been hoped for, as many lots were left unsold. The papers were scattered to institutions and collectors around the world, so making the writing of biographical studies (such as this one) a more difficult task.

Nor was the veil of mystery that hangs over the career of Conan Doyle completely lifted. About this time the leading Doyle scholar, Richard Lancelyn Green, to whom anyone writing about Arthur Conan Doyle is greatly to be indebted, was found dead in bed, strangled by a shoe lace, surrounded by stuffed toys. The flat was filled with his Doyle rarities, but none had been stolen.

Was it murder, as some of his friends thought, or was it a bizarre accident resulting from some perverse sexual game? Eventually the local coroner recorded an open verdict, despite all the gossip about murder. But there is little doubt that the detective instinct in Conan Doyle would have been aroused by the mysterious circumstances.

Green's magnificent collection was left in his will to Portsmouth Library, thus placing at the front of Conan Doyle research the Hampshire town where Jack Hawkins died in 1885, where Sherlock Holmes was created in 1886, and where this book opened. It was an altogether appropriate ending. (David Grann, 'Mysterious Circumstances: The strange death of a Sherlock Holmes fanatic', *New Yorker*, 13 December 2004, pp. 58-73.)

Biographical and literary details for all the chapters have been drawn from the following biographical, critical and historical works.

Arnold, Armin and Josef Schmidt: *Reclams Kriminalromanführer* (Stuttgart: Philipp Reclam jun., 1978).
Baden-Powell, Robert: *Scouting for Boys* [1908], ed. Elleke Boehmer (Oxford: OUP, 2004).
Baring-Gould, William S.: *Sherlock Holmes. A Biography of the World's First Consulting Detective* (London: Rupert Hart-Davis, 1962).
Carr, John Dickson: *The Life of Sir Arthur Conan Doyle* (London: John Murray, 1949; Pan Books ed., 1953).
Christie's of London: *The Conan Doyle Collection* (London: Christie's, 2004).
Doyle, Adrian: *The True Conan Doyle* (London: John Murray, 1945).

Doyle, Arthur Conan: *Memories and Adventures* (London: Hodder & Stoughton, 1924; rev. ed., London: John Murray, 1930; with a foreword by R. L. Green, London: OUP, 1989).

———————— *Letters to the Press: the Unknown Conan Doyle*, ed. John Michael Gibson and Richard Lancelyn Green (London: Secker and Warburg, 1986).

Edwards, Owen Dudley: *The Quest for Sherlock Holmes* (Edinburgh: Mainstream, 1983).

Green, Richard Lancelyn ed.: *The Uncollected Sherlock Holmes* (London: Penguin Books, 1983).

———————— *Letters to Sherlock Holmes* (London: Penguin, 1985).

Gibson, J.M. and Green, R.L.: *A Bibliography of A. Conan Doyle* (Oxford: OUP, 1983; new ed. London: Hudson House, 2000).

Griffiths, Arthur: *Mysteries of Police and Crime* [1898] (London: Cassell, 1904.)

Hall, Trevor H.: *Sherlock Holmes and His Creator* (London: Duckworth, 1978).

Harrison, Michael: *The World of Sherlock Holmes* (London: Frederick Muller, 1973).

Higham, Charles: *The Adventures of Arthur Conan Doyle* (London: Hamish Hamilton, 1976).

Keating, H. R. F.: *Sherlock Holmes: The Man and His World* (London: Thames & Hudson, 1979).

King, Daniel P.: Conan Doyle and the Holmes: The pursuit of Justice', *The Criminologist* (London), vol. 9. no 31, winter 1974, pp. 37–45.

Klinefelter, Walter: *Ex Libris A. Conan Doyle* (Chicago: Black Cat Press, 1938).

Lambert, Gavin: *The Dangerous Edge* (London: Barrie & Jenkins, 1975), pp. 31–34.

Lamond, John: *Arthur Conan Doyle* (London: John Murray, 1931).

Locard, Edmond: *Policiers de roman et de laboratoire* (Paris: Payot, 1924).

Nordon, Pierre: ed.: *Sir Arthur Conan Doyle Centenary Record 1859–1959* (London: John Murray, 1959).

———————— *Sir Arthur Conan Doyle, l'homme et l'oeuvre* (Paris: Didier, 1964).

———————— *Conan Doyle* (London: John Murray, 1966).

Orel, Harold ed. *Sir Arthur Conan Doyle. Interviews and Recollections* (New York: St. Martin's Press, 1991).

Pearsall, Ronald. *Conan Doyle. A Biographical Solution* (London: Weidenfeld and Nicolson, 1977).

Pearson, Hesketh: *Conan Doyle: His Life and Art* (London: Methuen, 1943).

Redmond, Donald A.: *Sherlock Holmes: A Study in Sources* (Kingston, Ont.: McGill-Queens University Press, 1983).

Stashower, Daniel: *Teller of Tales: The Life of Arthur Conan Doyle* (London: Allen Lane, 2000).

Stone, Harry: *The Casebook of Sherlock Doyle* (Romford: Ian Henry Publications, 1991).

Thorwald, Jurgen: *The Century of the Detective: The Marks of Cain* (London: Thames & Hudson, 1965).

——————— *The Century of the Detective: Dead Men Tell Tales* (London: Thames & Hudson, 1966).

Tracy, Jack: *The Encyclopedia of Sherlockiana* (New York: Doubleday, 1977).

Ch.1: A Detective Calls

Brend, William A.: *A Handbook of Medical Jurisprudence and Toxicology*, 5th ed. revised (London: Charles Griffin and Co., 1924).

Doyle, Arthur Conan: *The Stark Munro Letters* (London: Longmans, Green & Co., 1895).

Garrod, Alfred Baring: *The Essentials of Materia Medica and Therapuetics* [1855], 6th ed.(London: Longmans, Green & Co., 1877). Doyle's copy is in the Harry Ransom Library, Austin, Texas.

Gerald, Michael: *The Poisonous Pen of Agatha Christie* (Austin, Texas: University of Texas Press, 1993).

Hampshire Telegraph, 'Marriages', 8 August 1885; also *The Times* (London), Tuesday, Aug 11, 1885.

Jack, William R: *Wheeler's Handbook of Medicine* [1894] 8th ed. (Edinburgh: E & S Livingstone, 1927).

Mann, J. Dixon: *Forensic Medicine and Toxicology* [1891] 2nd ed. Revised and enlarged (London: Charles Griffin and Company, 1898).

Milne, Alexander: *Manual of Materia Medica and Therapeutics* [1864] 2nd ed. (Edinburgh: Livingstone, 1869).

A New Pictorial and Descriptive Guide to Southsea and Portsmouth (London: Ward, Lock and Co, 1907).

Pepper, William, ed.: *A System of Practical Medicine by American Authors*, vol. I (London: Sampson, Low and Marston, 1886). Information on chronic cerebral meningitis and its contemporary treatment.

Stavert, Geoffrey. *A Study in Southsea. The Unrevealed Life of Doctor Arthur Conan Doyle* (Portsmouth: Milestone, 1986).

Taylor, Alfred Swaine: *On Poisons in Relation to Medical Jurisprudence and Medicine* [1848], 3rd ed. (London: J and A Churchill, 1875).

Ch.2: Dr Doyle and Mr Holmes

Bell, Dr. Joseph. 'Adventures of Sherlock Holmes,' preface to *A Study in Scarlet* (London: Ward, Lock, [1893]. This appeared first in the *Bookman*, vol.3, pp. 79–81, December 1892.

Brook, Peter, essay on 'The Musgrave Ritual' in *Reading for the Plot* (New York: Random House, 1985).

Carr, John Dickson: *The Life of Sir Arthur Conan Doyle* (London: Pan Books ed., 1953).

Chabon, Michael, 'Inventing Sherlock Holmes,' *New York Review*, February 10, pp. 17–22, and February 12, pp. 14–17, 2005.

Doyle, Adrian: *The True Conan Doyle* (London: John Murray, 1945).

Doyle, A. Conan: 'South Sea Notebooks' MSS, vol.1, 1885–8, pp. 55/26; now in the private collection of Dr. Constantine Rossakis.

———————— 'The Recollections of Captain Wilkie', *Chamber's Journal* (Edinburgh), 26 January 1895.

———————— 'Gelseminum as a Poison', *British Medical Journal* (London), 20 September 1878; reprinted in *Letters to the Press*, ed. J. M. Gibson and R.L. Green (London: Secker & Warburg, 1986), pp. 13–14.

———————— *The Uncollected Sherlock Holmes*, ed. R.L. Green (London: Penguin, 1983).

Doyle, Lady Jean Conan: 'Conan Doyle was Sherlock Holmes', *Pearson's Magazine* (London), December 1934.

Jones, Dr. Harold Emery, *The Original of Sherlock Holmes* (Windsor: Gaby Goldscheider, 1980). This first appeared in *Collier's Weekly*, 9 January 1904.

Klinger, Leslie S., *The New Annotated Sherlock Homes*, 3 vols. (New York: W.W. Norton, 2004–05).

Lamond, John: *Arthur Conan Doyle: A Memoir*, with an epilogue by Lady Conan Doyle (London: John Murray, 1931).

Rosenberg, Samuel: *Naked is the Best Disguise* (Indianapolis: Bobbs, Merrill, 1974).

Wallace, Irving: 'The Incredible Dr. Bell', in *The Fabulous Originals* (London: Longman, Green, 1956). Originally appeared in *Saturday Review of Literature* (New York), vol.31, 1 May 1940, pp. 7–8, 28.

Ch.3: The Chamber of Horrors

Details of the contemporary catalogue and of the centenary dinner of Madame Tussaud's were supplied by the museum's archivist. The Vizetelly catalogue appears at the end of an edition of the *Plays of Beaumont and Fletcher* in the Mermaid Series, ed. J. St. Loe Strachey (London: Vizetelly, 1887).

Ashton-Wolfe, Harry: 'The debt of the police to detective fiction', *Illustrated London News*, 27 February 1932, p. 320.

Beavan, Colin: *Fingerprints. Murder and the Race to Uncover the Science of Identity* (London: Fourth Estate, 2002).

Burton, John Hill: *Narratives from Criminal Trials in Scotland* (London: Chapman & Hall, 1852).

Centenary Banquet of Madame Tussaud's (London, 1903).

Chadwick, Owen: *Victorian Miniature* (London: Hodder & Stoughton, 1960), pp. 103–120. On James Blomfield Rush.

Chapman, Pauline: *Madame Tussaud's Chamber of Horrors* (London: Constable, 1983).

Excoffon, A. *The Truth about the Lyons Mail being an authentic account given by one of the descendants of the murdered courier* (London: Greening & Co., 1903).

Gunn, Clement Bryce; ed. Rutherford Crockett: *Leaves from the Life of a Country Doctor* (Edinburgh: Moray Press, 1935).

Doyle, Charles Altamont: *The Doyle Diary*, ed. Michael Baker (London: Paddington Press, 1978).

Hall, Trevor H.: 'The Origin of Sherlock Holmes' and 'Conan Doyle and Spiritualism', in *Sherlock Holmes and His Creator* (London: Duckworth, 1978).

Hastings, Macdonald: *The Other Mr Churchill: A Lifetime of Shooting and Murder* (London: George G. Harrap, 1963), p. 52.

Jones, Harold: *The Original of Sherlock Holmes* (Windsor: Gaby Goldscheider, 1980).

Liebow, Ely: *Dr Joe Bell: Model for Sherlock Holmes* (Bowling Green, Ohio: Bowling Green University Popular Press, 1982).

Madame Tussaud and Sons' Catalogue (London, 1874).

McLevy, James: *The Casebook of a Victorian Detective*; ed. with introduction by George Scott-Moncrieff (Edinburgh: Canongate, 1975).

Messac, Regis: *Le 'detective novel' et l'influence de la Pensée scientifique* (Paris: H. Champion, 1929).

More, John ed.: *Trial of Alfred John Monson* (Edinburgh: Hodge and Son, 1908).

Oman, Charles: *The Lyons Mail* (London: Methuen, 1945).

Pemberton, Max: 'The Lyons Mail', in *Great Stories of Real Life* (London: Newnes, [1924]), pp. 17–30.

Queen, Ellery: *Queen's Quorum* (London: Victor Gollancz, 1953) On McGovan and Honeyman.

Richard Doyle and His Family. (London: Victoria and Albert Museum, 1983).

Rosenberg, Samuel: *Naked is the Best Disguise* (Indianapolis: Bobbs, Merrill, 1974; London: Arlington Books, 1975).

Roughead, William: 'The Arran Murder, 1889,' in *Twelve Scots Trials* (Edinburgh: William Green & Sons, 1913).

————— *Classic Crimes* (London: Cassell, 1951). On Dr Pritchard, The Arran Murder, The Ardlamont Mystery.

Saxby, Jessie M.E.: *Dr Joseph Bell: An Appreciation by an Old Friend* (Edinburgh: Oliphant, Anderson and Ferrier, 1913).

Smyth, Sir Sydney: *Mostly Murder* (London: George G. Harrap, 1959), ch. 2.

Starrett, Vincent: *The Private Life of Sherlock Holmes* (New York: Macmillan & Co., 1934; rev. ed. London: George Allan & Unwin, 1961).

Stewart, R. F.: '. . . And Always a Detective' (Newton Abbott: David & Charles, 1980), pp. 155–58. On McGovan and Honeyman.

Times (London), 'Obituary. Dr. Joseph Bell,' 5 October 1911, p. 9.

————————: 'Cinemas and 'Sherlock Holmes,' 6 May 1914, p.4.

303

——————————: 'Law report [trial of William Rea] 10 December 1895, p. 14.

Young, W.J.: 'Origins of Sherlock Holmes', *British Medical Journal* (London), 25 August 1934. George Hamilton's view.

Ch.4: By Every Post a Call for Help

I am indebted to the Research and Analysis Department of the Polish Interpress Agency for information and references on the De Bisping affair (February 1985); and to the writer Ruskin Bond, who lives in Mussoorie, for background information on the Garnett-Orme case from the Mussoorie end. (At some later date we still hope to collaborate on an account of mystery.)

Mysterious Letters

Carr, John Dickson: *The Life of Sir Arthur Conan Doyle* (London, Pan Books ed. 1953).

Doyle, A.C.: *Memories and Adventures* (London: Hodder & Stoughton, 1924).

Edwards, Owen Dudley: *The Quest for Sherlock Holmes* (Edinburgh: Mainstream, 1983).

Green, R.L. ed.: *Letters to Sherlock Holmes* (London: Penguin Books, 1985).

How, Harry: 'A Day with Dr Conan Doyle', *The Strand* (London), August 1892.

Nordon, Pierre ed.: *Sir Arthur Conan Doyle Centenary Record 1859-1959* (London: John Murray, 1959).

——————————— *Conan Doyle* (London: John Murray, 1966).

The Case of Mrs Castle

Doyle, A.C.: *Memories and Adventures* (London: Hodder & Stoughton, 1924).

Gibson, Michael and Green, Richard Lancelyn: 'The Case of Mrs Castle' in *The Unknown Conan Doyle: Letters to the Press* (Secker & Warburg, 1986), pp. 50, 352.

The Times (London): [Reports on the case of Mrs Castle], 14 October–7 November 1896.

Dreyfus Affair

Chapman, Guy: *The Dreyfus Affair* (London: Rupert Hart-Davis, 1955).

Christie-Murray, David: *Recollections* (London: John Long, 1909).

The Case of the Marquess's Jewels

Dew, Walter: *I Caught Crippen* (Edinburgh: Blackie and Son, 1938).

Higham, Charles: *The Adventures of Conan Doyle* (London: Hamish Hamilton, 1976), pp. 172–3.

Paget, Henry, 7th Marquess of Anglesey: personal communications (8 September 1985; 14 March 2006).

Reports of the Anglesey Jewels robbery in *The Times*, September–October 1901.

Saxon, John: 'The Mystery of the Stolen Jewels', in vol. II, *Great Stories from Real Life* (London: Newnes, [1924]), pp. 294–96.

Case of the Fugitive Fraudster

The letter referred to was in Lot. No. 29 in *The Conan Doyle Collection* (London: Christie's, 2004), 'Sherlock Holmes Plots and Ideas', pp. 48–49; it went unsold and remains with the heirs of Anna Doyle.

The Mysterious Death at Mussoorie

Resumé of reports in contemporary India papers in the India Office Library.

Times (London), 'End of Indian Will Case,' 14 October 1912, p. 5.

Wilson, Angus: *The Strange Ride of Rudyard Kipling* (London: Martin Secker & Warburg, 1977).

The Case of the Polish Prince

Okrêt, Leon: *Process Bispinga* (Warsaw, 1926).

Radziwill, Prince Michael: *One of the Radziwills* (London: John Murray, 1971), p. 23

Szenic, Stanislaw: *Pitaval Warszawksi* (Warsaw, 1958), vol.II, pp. 199–259.

Ch.5: Strange Studies from Life

Anon: 'The Walworth Murders,' *Annual Register 1860*, pp. 531–40. Youngman case.

Anon: 'The Derbyshire Murder,' *Annual Register 1863*, pp. 296–312. George Vincent Parker case.

Anon: 'The Stepney Murder', *Annual Register 1860*, pp. 541–64. Emsley Case.

Dovkants, Keith: 'The Baskerville Mystery: The riddle Holmes left unanswered', *London Standard*, 16 October 1986.

Doyle, A. Conan: *Strange Studies from Life* (New York and Copenhagen: Conan Doyle Society, 1963). First book publication; the essays appeared originally in *The Strand*, March, April and May 1901.

——————————— *Strange studies from life and other narratives: the complete true crime writings of Sir Arthur Conan Doyle*, selected and ed. by Jack Tracy; introduction by Peter Ruber; illustrated by Sidney Paget (Bloomington, Ind.: Gaslight Publications, 1988).

Evans, Peter: 'The Mystery of Baskerville', *Daily Express* (London), 16 March 1959.

Forster, John: *Studies in Black and Red* (London: Ward & Downey, limited, 1896).

The Hound of the Baskervilles

It has recently been alleged by Rodger Garrick-Steele, who now lives in Fletcher Robinson's old home in Devon, that Robinson was murdered by Conan Doyle, with the connivance of Mrs Robinson (with whom Conan Doyle was having an affair), for fear that Robinson would reveal to the world that he and not Doyle was the real author of *The Hound of the Baskervilles*, and that he had been cheated out of his just rewards by Doyle.

There is nothing credible, or creditable, in this farrago of nonsense. Further details can be found, if really wanted, in Garrick-Steele's book *The House of Baskerville* (Bloomington, Ind.: AuthorHouse, 2003).

Of far greater interest is Philip Weller's *The Hound of the Baskervilles: Hunting the Dartmoor Legend* (Tiverton: Devon Books/Halsgrove Direct, 2001), which contains the complete facts.

Ch.6: *The Mystery at Moat House Farm*

This chapter draws on articles by the American journalists Alan Hynd, Carl Sifakis, and Albert Ullmann for parts of the Conan Doyle content.

Hastings, Macdonald: *The Other Mr Churchill: A Lifetime of Shooting and Murder* (London: George G. Harrap, 1963).

Hynd, Alan: 'When Conan Doyle Played Sherlock Holmes', *Liberty* (Toronto), vol. 39, pp. 29, 40–41, February 1963.

Jesse, F. Tennyson ed.: *Trial of Samuel Herbert Dougal* (Edinburgh: Hodge & Co., 1928).

Sifakis, Carl: *The Catalogue of Crime* (New York: New American Library, 1979), p. 77.

Ullman, Albert: 'Greater than Sherlock Holmes', *True Detective Mysteries*, December 1939, pp. 38ff.

Wallace, Edgar: 'The Secret of Moat Farm,' in *Famous Crimes of Recent Times* (London: George Newnes, [1924]), pp. 69–86.

Ch.7: *The Club of Strange Crimes*

The crime writer and journalist Richard Whittington-Egan, a current member, kindly provided some background information of a general kind on *Our Society* (letter 9 February 1985), to which he can now add nothing more 'except that it still flourishes and is no longer an exclusively male bastion, which is a matter of regret to some of the more old-fashioned members, which includes myself' (email 16 March 2006).

Collins, John Churton: 'The Merstham Tunnel Mystery and Its Lessons', *National Review* (London), no. 274, December 1905, pp. 656–671.
——————— 'The Merstham and Crick Tunnel Mysteries: a Comparative Study', *National Review* (London), no. 277, March 1906, pp. 145–158.
——————— *Posthumous Essays* (London: J. M. Dent, 1912).
Collins, Laurence: *Life and Memoirs of John Churton Collins* (London: John Lane, 1912).
Griffiths, Major Arthur: *Mysteries of Police and Crime* 3 vols. (London: Cassell, 1898–1903).
Hall, Sir Edward Marshall: 'The Late H.B. Irving' in *Trial of the Wainwrights*, ed. H.B. Irving
Hornung, E.W.: 'The Criminologists Club', in *A Thief in the Night* (London: Chatto and Windus, 1905).
James, P.D. and Critchley, T.: *The Maul and the Pear Tree. The Ratcliffe Highway murders*, 1811 (London: Constable 1971; Faber, 2000).
Lambton, Arthur: 'The Crimes Club', *London Magazine*, March 1923.
——————— *My Story* (London: Hurst & Blackett, 1925).
——————— *The Salad Bowl* (London: Hurst & Blackett, 1928).
Le Queux, William: *The Crimes Club* (London: Eveleigh Nash & Grayson, 1927). A novel.
——————— *Things I Know* (London: Eveleigh Nash & Grayson, 1930).
Nash, James Eveleigh: *I Liked the Life I Lived* (London, 1941), pp. 162–66.
Oddie, S. Ingleby: *Inquest* (London: Hutchinson, 1938), pp. 43-57.
Parry, Sir Edward. 'The Mystery of the Merstham Tunnel', in *The Drama of the Law* (London: Ernest Benn, 1924).
Pemberton, Max: *Sixty Years Ago and After* (London: Hutchinson, 1936), pp. 238–46.
Warner, Sir Pelham: *Long Innings* (London: George G. Harrap, 1951), p. 191.

Ch.8: The Trail of Jack the Ripper

Details of Conan Doyle's visit to the Black Museum were provided by the then curator Mr Bill Waddell (letter 13 May 1985). These books are a mere fraction of those written about this notorious case. The volume by Stewart Evans and Keith Skinner is a good starting point for new readers.

Chat (Portsmouth): 'Whitechapel Murders', 23 November 1888, p. 7. Suggests that Doyle should call up the spirit of the latest victim and discover that way the identity of the Ripper.

Collins, Laurence: *Life and Memoirs of John Churton Collins* (London: John Lane, 1912).

Cornwell, Patricia: *Portrait of a Killer. Jack the Ripper Case Closed* (London: Little, Brown, 2002).

Cullen, Tom: *Autumn of Terror* (London: The Bodley Head, 1965).

Doyle, Adrian, quoted in Tom Cullen (1965).

Evans, Stewart and Paul Gainey: *Jack the Ripper: First American Serial Killer* (London: Arrow Books, 1996) Originally issued as *The Lodger* (London: Century, 1995).

Evans, Stewart and Keith Skinner: *The Ultimate Jack the Ripper Source Books* (Constable & Robinson, 2000).

Evening News (Portsmouth): ' 'Jack the Ripper.' How Sherlock Holmes Would Have Tracked Him', (Portsmouth), 4 July 1894, p. 4. Interview with Conan Doyle.

Griffiths, Arthur: *Mysteries of Police and Crime* (London: Cassell, 1898).

Lambton, Arthur: *The Salad Bowl* 2nd ed. (London Hurst and Blackett, 1928), p. 249.

McCormack, Donald: *The Identity of Jack the Ripper* (London, Jarrolds, 1959; new ed. London: Arrow Books, 1970).

Oddie, S. Ingleby: *Inquest* (London: Hutchinson, 1938), pp. 57–62.

Pemberton, Max: *Sixty Years Ago and After* (London: Hutchinson, 1936), pp. 244–46.

Tit-Bits (London), 'The Real Sherlock Holmes', 21 October 1911, vol. 61, p. 127. On Dr Bell's Jack the Ripper inquiries.

Whittington-Egan, Richard: *Casebook on Jack the Ripper* (London: Wildy and Sons, 1975).

Wilson, Colin and Odell, Robin: *Jack the Ripper* (London: Bantam, 1987), pp. 227–28. On Diosy.

Ch.9: The Persecution of George Edalji

Conan Doyle's own extensive file of papers relating to the Edalji case, 1906-1913, containing 425 letters, 2 notebooks, 10 photographs and related newspaper cuttings, was unsold at Christie's in May 2004 (Lot. No 54); and remains in the hands of the heirs of Anna Doyle.

The important collection of papers from the Edalji family, left in her by will by Maud Edalji to the Law Society in London, cannot now be found, so the librarian informs me. What became of this important archive is a mystery, though Sir Compton Mackenzie in correspondence in 1962 claimed they had been destroyed by an official of the Law Society to protect the reputation of some lawyers involved in the case.

Letters and papers, 1902-1904, collected by Sir Benjamin Stone, MP, concerning the trial of George Edalji are in the City Archives of the Birmingham Central Library; 370797 [IIR 89], ff. 163-168.

The Home Office Papers relating to the case are at the Public Record Office, Kew, London. Herbert Gladstone's secret memo on the Edalji affair is in the Herbert Gladstone Papers, British Library, add. ms. 46096 ff 96. I am grateful to Mr Michael Harley, to the staff of the Staffordshire County Record Office and Great Wyrley Library, and to Mr Trevor McFarlane of the Cheslyn Hay History Society for local information.

In 2005 Julian Barnes' novel *Arthur & George* (London: Jonathan Cape; New York: Random House, 2005), centred around the case, brought the Edalji scandal to the attention of readers around the world. However, being fiction, I have hesitated to read it for the purposes of revising this book; but this should not deter others. Barnes has admitted to interviewers that what he says about Edalji is nearly wholly fictional. See 'Case of the forgotten Victorian', an interview by Rebecca Wigod with Mr Barnes, *Vancouver Sun* (Saturday, 29 October 2005), which reports that 'Julian Barnes discovered little was known about George Edalji, so he made it up . . . The life of George Edalji had to be almost completely invented.'

A book by Michael Harley, *The Great Wyrley Mysteries: a Real Life Sherlock Holmes Adventure* announced in 1992 by Souvenir Press has not yet been published (March 2006); and I have been unable to discover why.

As this book goes to press, I have received from the author what will be the definitive book on the Edalji affair for some time to come: Gordon Weaver, *Conan Doyle and the Parson's Son: The George Edalji Case* (Cambridge: Vanguard Press, 2006).

Atkinson, G.A.: *'G.H. Darby' Captain of the Wyrley Gang*. Prefaces by Sir Arthur Conan Doyle and Captain A. G. Anson (Walsall, [March] 1914).

Buchan, John: 'On the Kirkcaple Shore', chapter I in *Prester John* (Edinburgh: Thomas Nelson, 1910).

Carr, J.D.: *The Life of Sir Arthur Conan Doyle* (London: Pan ed., 1953), pp. 183ff.

Clarke, Jerome. *Unexplained* (Detroit and London: Visible Ink Press/Gale Research, 1999).

Collins, John Churton: 'The Edalji Case', *National Review* (London), March 1907.

Cronin, A. J.: 'The Great Wyrley Mysteries' in *Great Unsolved Crimes* (London: Hutchinson, [1935]).

Davenport-Hines, Richard: 'Edalji, Shapurji (1841/2–1918), Church of England clergyman and victim of racial harassment,' *Oxford Dictionary of National Biography* (Oxford: OUP, 2004).

Doyle, A.C.: 'Stranger Than Fiction', *The Strand Magazine* (London), vol. 50 December 1915, pp. 12–517. The American letters sent by Sharp's brother (Conan Doyle's 'God-Satan').

———————— *Memories and Adventures* (London: Hodder & Stoughton, 1924).

———————— *The Story of Mr George Edalji*, ed. Richard and Molly Whittington-Egan (London; Grey House, 1985). Originally published in London by Blake & Co., 1907.

———————— 'The Strange Case of George Edalji', in *The Great Stories of Real Life*, ed. Max Pemberton (London, [1924]), vol. 1, pp. 30–40.

Doyle, Georgina: *Out of the Shadows: The Untold Story of Arthur Conan Doyle's First Family* (Ashcroft, BC, Canada: Calabash Press, 2005).

Edalji, George: *Railway Law for 'the Man in the Train'* (London: Wilson's Legal and Useful Books, 1901).

——————————— *The Case of Mr George Edalji: Memoranda and Papers* (London, 1907) Personal copy of Viscount Gladstone is in The British Library.

——————————— *Correspondence respecting the case of George Edalji*, etc. 1907 draft of the above. The personal copy of Viscount Gladstone is in The British Library.

——————————— 'My Own Story. The Narrative of Eighteen Years Persecution', *Pearson's Weekly* (London), 7 February–6 June 1907.

Edalji, Shapurji:'New Light on the Wyrley Gang Outrages,' *Daily Express* (London), 7 November 1934.

Edalji, Shapurji: 'A Strange Hoax' *The Times* (London), 16 August 1895.

——————————— *Correspondence between Rev. S. Edalji and the Home Secretary on the Case of George E. T. Edalji. [May] 1904.* (Printed by W. Henry Robinson, The Walsall Press).

——————————— *A Miscarriage of Justice: The Case of George Edalji: who was convicted on 23rd October 1903, and sentenced to seven years penal servitude on an unproved charge of horse maiming, by his father, Rev. S. Edalji, Vicar of Great Wyrley, Walsall* (London: United Press Association, 1905).

Fort, Charles: *The Books of Charles Fort* (New York: Henry Holt, 1941), pp. 349–667; 878–880.

Higham, Charles: *The Adventures of Arthur Conan Doyle* (London: Hamish Hamilton, 1976), pp. 199ff.

Hines, Stephen, ed.: *The True Crime Files of Sir Arthur Conan Doyle*, with an introduction by Steven Womack (New York: Berkley Prime Crime, 2001). This book deals *only* with the Edalji and Slater affairs.

Homes Office Papers Relating to the Case of George Edalji, Committee of Inquiry Reports Cd. 3503 (HMSO, 1907); microfiche edition, LXVII, pp. 403–410.

Juxon, John: *Lewis and Lewis* (London: Collins, 1983), pp. 297–300.

Lamond, John: *Arthur Conan Doyle* (London: Hodder & Stoughton, 1931), pp. 76ff.

Lester, Paul: *Sherlock Holmes in the Midlands* (Studley: Brewin Books, 1992).

Oldfield, Roger: *The Case of George Edalji* (Stafford: Stafford County Council Education Department, n.d.).

Rickard, Bob and Michell, John. *Unexplained Phenomena. A Rough Guide Special* (London: Rough Guides, 2000), pp. 146–149.

Sayers, Dorothy L.: 'Cross-Roads', Chapter XI in *Unnatural Death* (London: Ernest Benn Ltd., 1927), pp. 127–128.

The Times (London), 'Menacing Letters Charge. Labourer Sent to Penal Servitude,' 7 November 1934, p. 13, col. d.

——————————— 'Latest Wills [Miss Maud Evelyn Edalji, of Welwyn Garden City],' 27 March 1962, page 14, col. d.

Walters, John Cuming: *Knight of the Pen* (Manchester: Sherratt & Hughes, 1933).

Westminster Gazette, 'Vicar's Son Charged', 20 August 1903.

X, Mr: 'The Edalji Case Again', *Fortean Times* (London), no 21, pp. 8–9.

Ch.10: Stolen: The Irish Crown Jewels

A letter from Conan Doyle protesting about reports that he was involved in the investigation was included in the Conan Doyle Collection sale (Lot 116); other material was included in Lot 118; it was unsold and remains with the heirs of Anna Doyle.

Allen, Gregory: 'The Great Jewel Mystery,' *Garda Review* (Dublin), August 1976.

Bamford, Francis and Bankes, Viola: *Vicious Circle: The Case of the Missing Irish Crown Jewels* (London: Max Parrish, 1965).

Bay, Jens Christian: *The Mystery of the Irish Crown Jewels: A Critical Précis* (Cedar Rapids, Iowa: Torch Press, 1944).

Cafferky, John and Kevin Hannafin: *Scandal and Betrayal: Shackleton and the Irish Crown Jewels* (Cork: The Collins Press, 2002).

Christies of London: *The Conan Doyle Collection* (London: Christie's, 2004), Lots No. 116 and 118.

Deale, Kenneth E. L.: 'The Herald and the Safe', in *Memorable Irish Trials* (London: Brown, Watson, 1960).

Doyle, Arthur Conan: 'The Bruce-Partington Plans', *The Strand Magazine* (London), December 1908; *Colliers Weekly*, 18 December 1908.

Dungan, Myles: 'Theft of the Irish Crown Jewels', Supplement to the *Irish Times* (Dublin), 10 July 1982.

———————— *The Stealing of the Irish Crown Jewels: An Unsolved Crime* (Dublin: Town House, 2003).

Higham, Charles: *The Adventures of Conan Doyle* (London: Hamish Hamilton, 1976), pp. 204–207.

Hyde, Harford Montgomery: *Cases that Changed the Law* (London: William Heinemann, 1951).

The Leprachaun (Dublin), 'The Great Jewel Robbery. (By Our Sherlock Holmes)', August 1907, p. 53.

Magnus, Sir Philip: *King Edward the Seventh* (London: John Murray, 1964).

Perrin, Robert, *Jewels* (London: Routledge & Kegan Paul, 1977) fiction.

Thomas, Donald: *Honour Among Thieves* (London: Weidenfeld & Nicolson, 1991).

———————— *The Secret Cases of Sherlock Homes* (New York: Carroll & Graf, 1998) fiction.

Vice Regal Commission, *Minutes of Evidence*, Cd. 3936 (London: H.M.S.O., 1908).

Young, Filson: 'Sir Arthur Vicars' Case', *Saturday Review* (London), 12 July 1913.

Ch.11: The Langham Hotel Mystery

Christies: *Catalogue of Doyle Collection* (London: Christies, 2004), Lot no. 29 containing letters dealing with missing persons was unsold and remains with the heirs of Anna Doyle.

Begg, Paul: *Into This Air: People Who Disappear* (Newton Abbott: David & Charles, 1979).

Doyle, Arthur Conan: *Memories and Adventures* (London: Hodder and Stoughton 1924), pp. 110–13.

Churchill, Allen: *They Never Came Back* (Garden City, N.Y. Published for the Crime Club by Doubleday, 1960).

Doyle, Lady Jean Conan: 'The Trials of Marriage do not Exist', *Sunday Express* (London), 20 October 1929.

Fort, Charles: *The Books of Charles Fort* (New York: Henry Holt, 1941).

Higham, Charles: *The Adventures of Arthur Conan Doyle* (London: Hamish Hamilton, 1976), pp. 203–4.

Klinefelter, Walter: *Ex Libris Conan Doyle* (Chicago: Black Cat Press, 1938), p. 15.

Sanderson, Ivan T.: *Invisible Residents* (Cleveland: World Publishing Co., 1970), appendix A.

Ch.12: The Vanished Dane

Christies: *Catalogue of Doyle Collection* (London: Christies, 2004), Lot no. 29, containing Miss Paynter's three letters and two from an employee of the Danish East India Company in Copenhagen to Conan Doyle, was unsold and remains with the heirs of Anna Doyle. Doyle's letters are lost.

Carr, J.D.: *The Life of Sir Arthur Conan Doyle* (London: Pan ed., 1953), pp. 212–13.

Doyle, Arthur Conan: *Memories and Adventures* (London: Hodder & Stoughton, 1924), p. 132.

Nordon, Pierre ed.: *The Doyle Centenary* (London: John Murray, 1959), p. 69.
——————— *Conan Doyle* (London: John Murray, 1966), p. 116.

Ch.13: Was Crippen Innocent?

Birkenhead, Frederick E. Smith, Lord: *Famous Trials of History* (London: Hutchinson, 1926).

Bloom, Ursula: *The Girl Who Loved Crippen* (London: Hutchinson, 1955) Claims to be based on meetings with Ethel Le Neve.

Browne, Douglas G.: *Sir Travers Humphreys* (London: George G. Harrap, 1960).

Browne, Douglas G. and E. V. Tullett: *Bernard Spilsbury: His Life and Cases* (London: George G. Harrap, 1951; Penguin, 1955).

Carr, J.D.: *The Life of Sir Arthur Conan Doyle* (London, Pan ed., 1953), p. 202.

Cullen, Tom: *Crippen the Mild Murderer* (London: Bodley Head, 1972).

Dew, Walter: *I Caught Crippen* (Edinburgh: Blackie and Son, 1938).

Eddy, John Percy: *Scarlet and Ermine: Famous Trials as I saw them From Crippen to Podola* (London: William Kimber 1960).

Humphreys, Sir Travers: *A Book of Trials* (London: Heinemann, 1953).

Le Neve, Ethel: *Ethel Le Neve – Her story told by herself* (London, 1910).

Le Queux, William: 'Dr Crippen, Lover and Poisoner', in *Famous Crimes of Recent Times* (London: Newnes, [1924].), pp. 87–110.

Marjoribanks, Edward: *The Life of Sir Edward Marshall Hall* (London: Victor Gollancz, 1929).

————— *Famous Trials of Marshall Hall* (Harmondsworth: Penguin Books, 1950).

Nash, James Eveleigh: *I Liked the Life I Lived* (London: John Murray, 1941), p. 166.

Oddie, Samuel Ingleby: *Inquest* (London; Hutchinson, 1938).

Young, Filson ed.: *Trial of Hawley Harvey Crippen* (Edinburgh: William Hodge & Co., 1920).

————————— 'Dr Crippen', in *Famous Trials 10*, ed. James H. Hodge (Harmondsworth: Penguin, 1964).

Ch.14: The Case of Oscar Slater

Conan Doyle's own papers relating to the Oscar Slater affair, covering the years 1914–29, were bought (for £30,000) at Christie's in May 2004 (Lot. No 55) by the Mitchell Library in Glasgow.

(i) Murder in Queen's Terrace

Carr, John Dickson: *The Life of Sir Arthur Conan Doyle* (London: John Murray, 1949).

Hunt, Peter: *The Great Suspect* (London: Carroll & Nicholson, 1951).

Roughead, William: *Trial of Oscar Slater* (Edinburgh: William Hodge, 1910; 1915; revised ed., 1929).

—————————: 'The Slater Case', in *Classic Crimes* (London: Cassell, 1951).

—————————: 'Oscar Slater 1910-1929,' in *Famous Trials 10*, ed. James H. Hodge (London: Penguin Books, 1964).

Times (London) 'The Case of Oscar Slater,' 21 August 1912, p. 5.

(ii): *Why Miss Gilchrist Died*
I am grateful to the Mitchell Library in Glasgow for providing me with copies of newspaper articles relevant to the Slater case and the obituary of Dr Charteris.

Doyle Arthur Conan, *The Case of Oscar Slater* (London: Hodder & Stoughton, 1912).

——————: 'The Strange Case of Oscar Slater', *The Great Stories of Real Life*, ed. Max Pemberton (London: Newnes, [1924]).

Hines, Stephen, ed.: *The True Crime Files of Sir Arthur Conan Doyle*, with an introduction by Steven Womack (New York: Berkley Prime Crime, 2001). This deals *only* with the Edalji and Slater affairs.

House, Jack: *Square Mile of Murder* (Glasgow: Richard Drew Publishing, 1984).

Lamond, John: *Arthur Conan Doyle* (London: John Murray, 1931).

Park, William: *The Truth About Oscar Slater. With a Statement by Sir Arthur Conan Doyle* (London: The Psychic Press, 1927).

Roughead, William: *Knave's Looking Glass* (London: Cassell, 1935).

Toughill, Thomas, *Oscar Slater: The Mystery Solved* (Edinburgh: Canongate 1993).

Whittington-Egan, Richard: *The Oscar Slater Murder Story: New Light on a Classic Miscarriage of Justice* (Glasgow: Neil Wilson, 2001).

Ch.15: Into the Valley of Fear

Personal information about Williams Burns was provided by his own company, part of Baker Industries (now with Pinkerton's, its old rival, a part of Securitas Aktiebolag of Sweden); and by the Federal Bureau of Investigation, Washington DC.

Beavan, Colin: *Fingerprints: Murder and the Race to Uncover the Science of Identity* (London: Fourth Estate, 2001).

Burns, William John: *The Masked War* (New York, 1913; London: Hodder & Stoughton, 1914).

Dinnerstein, Leonard: *The Leo Frank Case* (New York and London: Columbia University Press, 1968).

—————— 'Leo Max Frank', in Coleman, Kenneth and Gurr, Charles Stephen, eds.: *Dictionary of Georgia Biography* (Athens, GA: University of Georgia Press, 1983).

Doyle Arthur Conan; *Western Wanderings* with an introduction by Christopher and Barbara Roden (Penyffordd, Wales: Conan Doyle Society; 1994).

———————— 'Western Wanderings', *Cornhill* (London), January–April 1915.

———————— 'The Last Resource', *The Strand* (London), December 1930.

———————— *Our American Adventure* (London: Hodder & Stoughton, 1923).

———————— *Our Second American Adventure* (London; Hodder & Stoughton, 1924).

Garrett, Franklin M.: *Atlanta and Environs* (Athens, GA, 1969), vol. 2. pp. 619–28.

Golden, Harry: *A Little Girl is Dead* (1965). Published in Britain as *The Lynching of Leo Frank* (London: Cassell, 1966).

Gowers, Rebecca: *The Swamp of Death: A True Tale of Victorian Lies and Murder* (London: Hamish Hamilton, 2004). Deals with the Blenheim Swamp murder.

Harlow, Alvin F.: 'William John Burns', in Stane, Harris E. ed.: *Dictionary of American Biography*, vol. xxi, Supplement One (New York, 1944).

Hertzberg, Steven: *Strangers within the Gate City: the Jews of Atlanta, 1845-1915* (Philadelphia: Jewish Publication Society of America, 1978).

Indianapolis Journal: 'Conan Doyle in Town', 16 October 1894.

Mackay, James: *Allan Pinkerton: The Eye Who Never Slept* (Edinburgh and London: Mainstream, 1996).

Pinkerton, Allan: *The Molly Maguires and the Detectives* [1877] (New York: Dover Books, 1973).

Redmond, Christopher : *Welcome to America, Mr Sherlock Holmes* (Toronto: Simon & Pierre, 1987).

Times (London). 'Corruption in California.' 1–3 January 1908.

———————— 'Sir A Conan Doyle in Sing Sing. Indictment of the New York prison.' 1 June 1914.

Tindall, George B.: *The Emergence of the New South 1913–1945* (Baton Rouge: Louisiana State University, 1867).

Ch.16: The Bluebeard of the Bath

Barker, Dudley: *Lord Darling's Famous Cases* (London: Hutchinson, 1936).

Bolitho, William: *Murder for Profit* (London: Jonathan Cape, 1929; new ed. London: Denis Dobson, 1953).

Browne, Douglas G. and Tullett, E.V.: *Bernard Spilsbury: His Life and Cases* (London: George G. Harrap, 1951).

Douthwaite, Louis C.: *Mass-Murder* (London: John Long, 1929).

Goodman, Jonathan: 'Also Known as Love', in *The Seaside Murders* (London: Alison & Busby, 1985).

Higham, Charles: *The Adventures of Arthur Conan Doyle* (London: Hamish Hamilton, 1976), p. 247.

Humphreys, Sir Travers: *A Book of Trials* (London: Heinemann, 1953).

Hynd, Alan: 'Bluebeard and the Armchair Sleuth', *Cosmopolitan* (New York), September 1940, p. 11.

———————— 'When Conan Doyle Played Sherlock Holmes', *Liberty* (Toronto), vol. 39. February 1963, pp. 29, 40–41.

Marjoribanks, Edward: *The Life of Sir Edward Marshall Hall* (London; Victor Gollancz, 1929).

Moiseiwitsch, Maurice: *Five Famous Trials* (London: Heinemann, 1962).

Neil, Arthur Fowler: *Forty Years of Man-Hunting* (London: Jarrolds, 1932), pp. 31–49.

Nordon, Pierre: *Conan Doyle* (London: John Murray, 1966), p. 116.

Sifakis, Carl: *A Catalogue of Crime* (New York; New American Library, 1979), p. 76.

Sims, George R.: *The Bluebeard of the Bath* (London: C. A. Pearson, 1915).

Ullman, Albert: 'Greater than Sherlock Holmes', *True Detective Mysteries* (New York), December 1939, pp. 40ff.

Watson, Eric R. ed.: *Trial of George Joseph Smith* (Notable British Trials) (Edinburgh: William Hodge & Co., 1922).

———————— 'George Joseph Smith,' in *Famous Trials II*, ed. Harry Hodge (London: Penguin Books, 1947).

Ch.17: The Errant Knight

The letters from Conan Doyle to Casement are in the Casement Papers in the National Library of Ireland, as are the trial papers of his solicitor George Gavan Duffy. The subscription list referred to is in the Casement Papers, mss. 10,763 (11). The British Library holds the Conan Doyle Casement Petition Papers, Add. MSS 63596. Three letters relating to Casement (Lot No. 58 in *The Conan Doyle Collection*) are in the hands (as of March 2006) of a dealer, Peter L. Stern, Boston MA.

The Roger Casement Affair

Doyle, A.C.: *A Petition to the Prime Minister* (1914).

Dudgeon, Jeffrey, *Roger Casement: The Black Diaries* (Belfast: The Belfast Press, 2004).

Gates, Peter Singleton: *The Black Diaries of Sir Roger Casement* (Paris: Olympia Press, 1959). This edition is based on the 1916 typescript.

Gwynn, Denis, *Traitor or Patriot: The Life and Death of Roger Casement* (London: Jonathan Cape, 1931).

Hyde, Harford Montgomery: *Trial of Sir Roger Casement* (London: William Hodge, 1960).

Inglis, Brian, *Roger Casement* (London: Hodder and Stoughton, 1973).

MacColl, René: *Roger Casement* (London: Hamish Hamilton, 1956).

McCormack, W. J.: *Roger Casement in Death, or Haunting the Free State* (Dublin: UCD Press, 2004).

Mitchell, Angus: *Sir Roger Casement's Heart of Darkness: The 1911 Documents* (Dublin: Irish Manuscripts Commission, 2004).

———————— *Roger Casement* (London: Haus, 2003).

Ó Síocháin, Séamus and O'Sullivan, Michael: *The Eyes of Another Race: Roger Casement's Congo Report and 1903 Diary* (Dublin: UCD Press, 2004).

Sawyer, Roger, *Roger Casement's Diaries: 1910 The Black and the White* (London: Pimlico, 1997).

Thomson, Sir Basil: *My Experiences at Scotland Yard* (New York: Doubleday, 1923).

———————— *The Scene Changes* (New York, 1939: Doubleday; London: Collins, 1939).

Tóibín, Colm, 'The Tragedy of Roger Casement', *New York Review of Books*, 27 May 2004, pp. 53–57.

Doyle and Spiritualism

Burgess, Anthony: 'Centenary of Sherlock Holmes', *Independent* (London), 10 January 1987.

Ernst, Bernard M. L. and Carrington, Hereward: *Houdini and Conan Doyle* (London: Hutchinson, 1933).

Jones, Kelvin I.: *Conan Doyle and the Spirits. The Spiritualist Career of Sir Arthur Conan Doyle* (Wellingborough: Aquarian Press, 1989).

Houdini, Harry: *A Magician among the Spirits* (New York: Harper & Brothers, 1924).

Stashower, Daniel: *Teller of Tales: The Life of Arthur Conan Doyle* (London: Allen Lane, 2000).

Thurston, Herbert S.J.: *Modern Spiritualism* (Sheed & Ward, 1928).

Walter, Nicolas: 'Doyle and Holmes', *Independent* (London) 14 January 1987. Doyle as member of the Rationalist Press Association.

Ch.18: Ned Kelly and Fisher's Ghost

Dr Derham Groves of Brunswick West, Victoria, now of the University of Melbourne, provided me with much information about Conan Doyle's itinerary in Australia.

Anderson, Johannes C.: *Jubilee History of South Canterbury* (Auckland and London, 1916), pp. 472–73. Hall poisoning case.

Clune, Frank: *The Kelly Hunters* (London: Angus & Robertson, 1954).

Collings, Rex ed.: *Classic Victorian and Edwardian Ghost Stories* (Ware: Wordsworth Classics, 1996).

Doyle, A. Conan: 'The Use of Armour' [letter on Ned Kelly], *The Times*, 27 July 1915, p. 7; reprinted in *Letters to the Press*, p. 222.

——————————— *The Wanderings of a Spiritualist* (London: Hodder & Stoughton, 1921).

Dyall, Valentine: 'The Silent Witness', in *Unsolved Mysteries* (London: Hutchinson, 1954), pp. 26–35; 241-242.

Hare, Francis A.: *The Last of the Bushrangers* (London: Hurst & Blackett, 1892).

Lang, John: *Botany Bay* (London: W. Tegg, 1859).

——————————— *Fisher's Ghost and Other Stories of the Early Days of Australia* (Melbourne: E.W. Cole, [1920?]).

Martin, Robert Montgomery: *History of the British Colonies* (London: J. Cochrane 1834-5), vol. 4.

Ned Kelly: Man and Myth, with an introduction by Colin F. Cave (Melbourne, 1968).

Sheehan, Jack R.: *Famous Murders in New Zealand* (Wellington, 1933).

Sydney Gazette: [Report of execution of George Worrall], 12 February 1823.

Taylor, Alfred Swaine: *On Poisons in Relation to Medical Jurisprudence and Medicine*, 3rd ed. (London: J and A Churchill, 1875).

Treadwell, C.A.L.: 'The Trial of Thomas Hall and Margaret Houston' in *Notable New Zealand Trials* (New Plymouth, 1936), pp. 147–60.

Triebal, L.A.: *Fisher's Ghost and Other Essays* (Melbourne: Cheshire, 1950).

Ch.19: New Light on Old Crimes

Collins, John Churton: 'The Merstham Tunnel Mystery and Its Lessons', *National Review* (London), no. 274, December 1905, pp. 656–671.

——————————— 'The Merstham and Crick Tunnel Mysteries: a Comparative Study', *National Review* (London), no. 277, March 1906, pp. 145–158.

Curtis, J.: *The Murder of Maria Marten* (The Famous Trials Series) (London: Geoffrey Bles, 1930).

Doyle, A. Conan: 'New Light on Old Crimes', *The Strand* (London), January 1920.

——————————— *The Wanderings of a Spiritualist* (London: Hodder & Stoughton, 1921).

——————————— 'Clairvoyants as Detectives', Daily Express (London), 21 October 1921.

——————————— *Memories and Adventures* (London: Hodder & Stoughton, 1924).

———————— *History of Spiritualism* (London: Cassell, 1926).

———————— *On the Edge of the Unknown* (London: John Murray, 1930).

Gibbs, Dorothy: *The True Story of Maria Marten* (Ipswich, England: East Anglian Magazine, 1949).

Gillen, Mollie: *The Assassination of the Prime Minister* (London: Sidgwick & Jackson, 1972).

Eyles F.A.H.: 'Crime and the Crystal. Has Crystal-Gazing a Scientific Basis?' *The Strand* (London), Vol. 37, February 1909, p. 170.

Gibson, John Michael & Green, Richard Lancelyn: *Letters to the Press* (London: Secker & Warburg, 1986.

McCormick, Donald: *The Red Barn Mystery* (London: John Long, 1967).

Maskell, William: 'The Mystery of Owen Parfitt', in *Odds and Ends* (London, 1872).

The Times (London) 'Inquest [on Percy Lintott Foxwell]', 6 February 1901, p. 4.

———————— 'Missing Rugby Boy. Lost at Liverpool Station', 21 September 1921, p. 7.

———————— 'Missing Rugby Boy Found. Enlistment in Royal Corps of Signals', 17 October 1921, p. 10.

Ch.20: Conan Doyle and the Motor-Bandit

Though the American novelist the late Irving Wallace confirmed his conversation with Dr Locard in a personal letter to the author, some ambiguity still surrounds the meeting of Locard and Conan Doyle. I am also grateful to my friend the late Dr Bernard Heuvelmans for his assiduous research into the mystery in the Paris libraries.

Asbury, Herbert: *The Gangs of New York* (New York and London: Alfred A. Knopf, 1918).

Ashton-Wolfe, Harry: *The Underworld* (London, 1926), pp. 163–202.

———————— *Outlaws of Modern Days* (London, 1927) With a photo of Bonnot.

———————— *The Invisible Web: Strange Tales form the French sûreté. From documents supplied by Edmond Locard of the sûreté. at Lyons, France* (London: 1929).

Bercher, Jean-Henri: *Étude médico-legale de l'oeuvre de Conan Doyle et La Police Scientifique au XXme Siècle* (Lyons: A Storck & Cie, 1906).

Chomarat, Michel: *Documents anarchistes: revue de documents historiques sur le Mouvement anarchiste français pour la région Rhone-Alpes* (1967–68).

*h>———————— *Les Amants tragiques: histoire du bandit Jules Bonnot et de sa maîtresse Judith Thollon* (Lyon: Edico, 1978).

Crauser, Jean-Pierre: 'L'affaire Doyle-Locard-Bonnot' (http:/www.sshf.com/index.php3dir=articles&file=a_crauser2).

Davidson, Albert [Renée Reauveu]: *Elémentaire, mon cher Holmes* (Paris: Denoël, 1982). A novel.

Lacassin, Francis: *Mythologie du roman policier* (Paris: 10/18, 1974), vol. I, p. 116.

Locard, Edmond: 'La méthode policière de Sherlock Holmes', in *Policiers de roman et de laboratoire* (Paris: Payot, 1924). This appeared originally in *La revue hebdomadaire*, anne 31, tome 2, Fevrier 1922.

——————————: *Les Grands criminals lyonnais* (Lyon: Album du crocodile, 1938).

Thomas, Bernard: *La Bande à Bonnot* (Paris: Tchou, 1968), pp. 20–22.

Wallace, Irving: 'The French Sherlock Holmes', in *The Sunday Gentleman* (London, 1966), pp. 334–336.

——————————— personal communication (12 January 1985).

Winslow, Forbes: *The Insanity of Passion and Crime* (London: John Ousely, 1913).

Ch.21: The Strange Death of the General's Wife

John Winnifrith, the patron of the parish, provided me with an extract from the Ightham Parish Tithe book concerning the Luard case and cuttings relating to the case from the local paper.

Adam, H. L.: 'The Summer House Mystery: The Luard Case,' in *Fifty Most Amazing Crimes of the Last 100 Years* (London, 1936), pp. 339–57.

Berrett, Ex-Chief Inspector: 'The Fish Ponds Woods Mystery' in *Great Unsolved Crimes* (London: Hutchinson, [1935]).

Doyle, A.C.: 'The Problem of Thor Bridge', *The Strand* (London), February and March 1921.

Gribble, Leonard: 'Who Murdered Mrs Luard? Kent Mystery of the Summer House', *True Detective*, October 1984.

Gross, Hans: *Criminal Investigation; a practical handbook for magistrates, police officers, and lawyers*, translated and adapted from the *System der kriminalistik* of Dr. Hans Gross by John Adam and J. Collyer Adam (London: The Specialist Press, Ltd., 1907); (London, 1934 ed.), pp. 428–29.

Hastings, Macdonald: *The Other Mr Churchill* (London: George G. Harrap, 1963).

Higham, Charles: *The Adventures of Arthur Conan Doyle* (London: Hamish Hamilton, 1976), p. 309.

Jepson, Edgar: 'The Luard Mystery,' in *Great Stories of Real Life* (London: Newnes, 1924), pp. 260–269.

——————————— *Great Crimes of Recent Times* (London: Newnes, 1929), pp. 434–474.

Knight, Stephen and Taylor, Bernard: *Perfect Murder* (London: Souvenir Press, 1987).

Symons, Julian: 'An Edwardian Tragedy,' in *A Reasonable Doubt* (London: Cresset Press, 1960).

Villiers, Elizabeth: *Riddles of Crime* (London: T. Werner Laurie, 1928).

Wilson, Colin and Pitman, Patricia: *Encyclopedia of Murder* (London: Arthur Barker, 1961), pp. 561–64. C.H. Norman on Dickman and the Luard Case.

Ch.22: Death Beside the Sea

Ralph Blumenfeld's letter was in Lot 92 in The Conan Doyle Collection; it was unsold and is still the property of the heirs of Anna Doyle.

Blumenfeld, Ralph D.: *R.D.B.'s Procession* (London: Ivor Nicholson & Watson, 1935), pp. 185–92.

The Great Bournemouth Mystery. The Spirit of Irene Speaks (Bournemouth: William Tylar, 1923).

Woodhall, Edwin T.: *Crime and the Supernatural* (London: John Long, 1935), 111-114.

Woodland, W. Lloyd: *The Trial of Thomas Henry Allaway* (*Famous Trials Series*) (London: Geoffrey Bles, 1929).

Ch.23: The Crowborough Chicken Farm Murder

Kathleen Bennett, then of St Mary's, South Australia, shared her personal recollections of Norman Thorne with me (letter 29 June 1985).

Bennett, Kathleen.: 'Partnering a murderer,' *Sussex Life*, June 1985, p. 17.

Browne, Douglas G. and Tullett, E.V.: *Bernard Spilsbury: His Life and Cases* (London: George G. Harrap, 1951).

Gribble, Leonard: *Famous Judges and Their Trials* (London: John Long, 1957).

Higham, Charles: *The Adventures of Arthur Conan Doyle* (London: Hamish Hamilton, 1977), pp. 303.

Lustgarten, Edgar: *Verdict in Dispute* (London: Allan Wingate, 1949).

————————— *The Murder and the Trial* (London: Odhams, 1960).

Morning Post (London): 'Sir A. Conan Doyle and the Thorne Case,' 21 April 1925, p. 9.

Normanton, Helena ed.: *The Trial of Norman Thorne* (*Famous Trials Series*) (London; Geoffrey Bles, 1929).

————————— 'The Crowborough Murder' in *Great Unsolved Crimes* (London: Hutchinson, [1935]).

Wensley, Frederick Porter: *Detective Days* (London: Cassell, 1931), pp. 276–80.

Wilson, Colin and Pitman, Patricia: *Encyclopedia of Murder* (London: Arthur Barker, 1961).

Ch.24: The Case of the Missing Lady

Atticus: 'The Curious Affair at Newlands Corner,' *Sunday Times* (London), 18 January 1976.

Barnard, Robert: *A Talent to Deceive: an appreciation of Agatha Christie* (London: Collins, 1980).

Brabazon, James: *Dorothy L. Sayers* (London: Gollancz, 1981), p. 158.

Calder, Ritchie: 'Agatha and I,' *New Statesman*, 30 January 1976, p. 128.

Cade, Jared: *Agatha Christie and Missing Eleven Days* (London: Peter Owen, 1998).

Evening Chronicle (Manchester), 20 December 1926 [article and editorial on Conan Doyle's role in Christie search] 20 December 1926.

Doyle, A.C.: 'Sir A. Conan Doyle and Christie Case. Psychometry and Detective Work,' *Morning Post* (London), 20 December 1926, p. 4; *Letters to the Press*, p. 322.

Christie, Agatha: 'Mrs Agatha Christie: Her Own Story of Her Disappearance,' *Daily Mail* (London) 16 February 1928.

Gill, Gillian: *Agatha Christie: The Woman and Her Mysteries* (London: Robson Books, 1991).

Higham, Charles: *The Adventures of Arthur Conan Doyle* (London: Hamish Hamilton, 1976).

Hiscock, Eric: *Last Boat to Folly Bridge* (London: Cassell, 1970).

————————— 'Personally Speaking', *The Bookseller*, 19 April 1980, p. 1752.

Keating, H. R. F. ed.: *Agatha Christie: First Lady of Crime* (London: Weidenfeld and Nicholson, 1977).

Leaf, Horace: 'I am a psychic detective', *Liberty* (New York), March and April 1939. Bound tear sheets in the Harry Price Library, University College London, London.

————————— *Death Cannot Kill* (London: Max Parrish, 1959), pp. 122–29.

Lloyd's Sunday News (London), [reply to Edgar Wallace describing Conan Doyle's use of psychometry in Christie case] 1 September 1929.

Morgan, Janet: *Agatha Christie* (London: Collins, 1984).

Osborne, Charles: *The Life and Crimes of Agatha Christie* (London: Collins, 1982).

Rivière, François: *Agatha Christie - Duchesse de la Mort* (Paris: Éditions du Masque, 2001).

Robyns, Gwen: *Agatha Christie* (New York: Doubleday, 1978). This book was never published in Britain for legal reasons.

Stashower, Daniel: *Teller of Tales: The Life of Arthur Conan Doyle* (London: Allen Lane, 2000).

Tynan, Kathleen: *Agatha* (London and New York). A novel based on the treatment for the film of the same name, which Agatha Christie's heirs tried to injunct. It bears no relation to historical or biographical truth.

White, Patrick: *Flaws in the Glass* (London: Jonathan Cape, 1981).
Woodhall, Edwin T.: *Crime and the Supernatural* (London: John Long, 1929), pp. 33–34.

Ch.25: The Zoo Park Murder

I am grateful to Cecilia Zeiss for her help in collating and translating the Afrikaans material on which this chapter is partly based and for her assistance with other sources in South Africa. Information about Stephen Black came from the distinguished writer and academic Prof. Stephen Gray.

Baneshik, Percy: [on Stephen Black], *The Star* (Johannesburg), 14 September 1981.
Bennett, Benjamin: *The Clues Condemn* (Cape Town: H.B. Timmins, 1949).
Doyle, A.C.: *Our African Winter* (London: Hodder & Stoughton, 1929), pp. 182–84.
Howcroft, P. 'Stephen Black 1880-1931' in *The South African Encyclopedia: Prehistory to the year 2000* (in preparation).
The Sjambok (Johannesburg): 'Did the Port Elizabeth Sex Fiend Kill Miss Kanthack?', 30 August 1929.

Ch.26: A Peculiar Death at Umtali

The Umtali Park murder was reported in the *Rhodesia Herald* on 8 November 1928; the inquest was reported on 19, 21, 22, 24, 30 November; the arrest and hearing of the preliminary of the case against Winter on 30 November, 4, 5, 6 December; and the refusal to prosecute on 27 December. The writer Graham Lord, at some inconvenience to himself, put me in touch with a relative who once lived in Umtali.

Doyle, A.C.: *Our African Winter* (London: Hodder & Stoughton, 1929), pp. 176–82.
The Times (London); 'Obituary: Sir Robert McIlwaine', 27 Oct 1943, p. 7.

Ch.27: The Cobbler and the Fish-Pedlar

The Anarchists, edited with an introduction by Irving L. Horowitz (New York: Laurel Edition, Dell Publishing, 1964).

Doyle, A.C.: *Our African Winter* (London: Hodder & Stoughton, 1929), pp. 228–29.

Ehrmann, Herbert B.: *The Untried Case: The Sacco-Vanzetti Case and the Morelli Gang* (New York, 1933; 2nd ed. New York: Vanguard Press, 1960).

Ehrmann, Herbert B.: *The Case That Will Not Die. Commonwealth vs. Sacco and Vanzetti* (London: Little, Brown, 1969).

Jackson, Brian: *The Black Flag* (Boston and London: Routledge and Keegan Paul 1981).

Russell, Francis: *Tragedy at Dedham* (New York: McGraw-Hill, 1962; London: Longmans, 1963).

The Letters of Sacco and Vanzetti, ed. Denman Frankfurter and Gardiner Jackson (New York: The Viking Press, 1955).

Sinclair, Upton: *Boston* (New York: A. & C. Boni; Pasadena, Calif. and Long Beach, Calif.: Published by the author, 1928; London: Werner Laurie, 1929).

——————— 'The Fish Pedlar and the Shoemaker', *New York Institute of Social Studies Bulletin,* vol.2, no.2, Summer 1953.

——————— *My Life in Letters* (Columbia: University of Missouri Press, 1960), pp. 63-70. Letters from Conan Doyle.

Tuchman, Barbara W.: *The Proud Tower* (New York: The Macmillan Co., 1966). See chapter 2: 'The Idea and the Deed: The Anarchists 1890-1914'.

Yellen, Samuel: *American Labor Struggles* (New York: Harcourt Brace, 1936).

Epilogue

Following complaints by the Doyle family, Hamish Hamilton issued a legal corrective for insertion into the copyright deposit copies of Charles Higham's book *The Adventures of Conan Doyle*, concerning the circumstances of Conan Doyle's reburial in 1955, which I have seen in Trinity College Library, Dublin.

Cawte, Godrey: 'Sir Arthur Conan Doyle: the Minstead connection', *Hampshire Magazine*, July 1986, pp. 49-50.

Doyle, Arthur Conan: 'A Tragedy' poem xxv in *Songs of Action* (London: Smith, Elder & Co., 1898).

Charles Higham: *The Adventures of Conan Doyle* (London: Hamish Hamilton, 1976).

Sifakis, Carl: *The Catalogue of Crime* (New York: New American Library, 1979), p. 79.

Starrett, Vincent: *The Private Life of Sherlock Holmes* (New York: Macmillan, 1934; new ed. London: Allen & Unwin, 1961).